Tony Marsh, The Great All-Rounder In and Out of Motorsport

Tony Marsh, The Great All-Rounder In and Out of Motorsport

Tony Marsh

Parley Books

First published in Great Britain in 2007 by Parley Books

A CIP catalogue record for this book is available from the British
Library

ISBN   978 0 9554826 0 1

Tony Marsh is most grateful to the following photographers:

Harold Barker, Daily Sketch, Charles Dunn, Steve Havelock, John
Hayward, W K (Bill) Henderson, Derek Hibbert, Manx Photos,
Walter Manz, T C March, Roger McDonald ABIPP, J H Miller,
Motor Racing, P-3 Motorsport Photos, Hamo Thornycroft Marine
Photography, Worcester News.

Printed and bound in Great Britain by J. H. Haynes & Co. Ltd., Sparkford

Parley Books
18 Heathlands Avenue
Ferndown
Dorset BH22 8RP

Contents

Foreword

People like Tony Marsh don't exist in motor sport today, more's the pity. A Formula 1 driver will just do his eighteen Formula 1 races a year, filling the rest of his time with testing, fitness training and PR work for his sponsors. A rally driver will only do rallying, an F3 racer will stick with his F3. If you race touring cars, that's what you do. A British club driver will rarely venture abroad to take in European events. Even a hill climber will tend to concentrate exclusively on his own discipline. We live in an age of specialisation, not versatility.

But versatility of a quite remarkable kind is what emerges from the life story of Tony Marsh. Not for nothing does the title of this book refer to him as The Great All-Rounder. This is a man who has set about half a century of motor sport with tremendous energy. He competed in Formula 1 races, witnessing from the cockpit the famous race at the Nürburgring when Fangio scored his final, and greatest, victory. He was third in the Brussels Grand Prix behind the works Coopers of Jack Brabham and Bruce McLaren. He did sports car and GT racing, and on his first visit to the Le Mans 24 Hours, in a Lotus Elite, he won the Index of Thermal Efficiency. He packed in a relentless programme of British racing, sometimes at two different venues in one weekend, and also found time to campaign with success in trials and driving tests.

And then of course there was, and is, his hill climbing. This is a unique motor sporting discipline which has attracted its own supporters, and its own specialists, down the years. Tony Marsh stands alone in having earned the title of British Hill Climb Champion three years running, in 1955, 1956 and 1957 – and then achieving the same extraordinary record all over again, in 1965, 1966 and 1967. What is even more extraordinary is that he achieved the second hat-trick in a car he designed and built himself, helped in 1967 by ingenious four-wheel-drive technology that also came out of the fertile Marsh brain, and went on to be much copied by others.

Most remarkable of all, for much of his career Tony Marsh was taking part, and winning, in several of these disciplines in the same season. There has surely never been another driver, with the possible exception of Sir Stirling Moss, who has so completely explored, and succeeded in, such different areas of motor sport.

Tony Marsh is a quiet, modest man. Until I read this book, I wasn't aware of the other sports in which he has excelled, notably sailing, shooting and ski-bobbing – he was the long-time chairman of the Skibob Association of Great Britain. I knew he was a busy farmer, but I was unaware of his additional business interests. Nor did I know that he was an accomplished pilot. It's all in this book, although I still find it hard to work out how Tony seemed to be able to do so many things at once, and do all of them successfully.

His return to hillclimbing after 18 years away is also explained, and this book takes the story up to 2001. Happily, though, Tony is still very much part of today's hillclimbing scene, at an evergreen 76 years of age. He continues to compete at a high level, and remains a familiar sight in the hillclimb paddocks with his delightful wife Liza and his immaculately prepared Gould single-seater.

Tony has been around motor sport for more than 55 years. In that time, while doing what he loves to do, he has met and competed against countless numbers of people. Some of them have been very famous; some of them, like me, have just been minor amateurs enjoying themselves at a far lower level. To all of them Tony has been friendly, good-humoured, and always happy to help with any problem – but always fiercely competitive. His involvement in so many different areas of motor sport has enhanced them all. I feel fortunate to have known him for 40 of those 55 years, and to have been able to learn from watching him in action. I hope that he and Liza will continue to be part of the sport for a very long time to come.

Simon Taylor

Chapter One

Life began for me, Anthony Ernest Marsh, on 20 July 1931. I wouldn't say I was born with a silver spoon in my mouth (or a silver spanner in my hand), but I would have to admit that perhaps one wasn't very far away. We weren't exactly members of the aristocracy but we did have connections, so I'd better start with a bit of family background.

My father was Edward Ernest Marsh, part of the Marsh family which ran Marsh & Baxter the ham and bacon curers, and my mother was Phyllis, née Ceney. I'm not quite sure how they met, but the Ceneys came from Kingswinford and mother's family was in the coal industry. Grandfather Ceney had a small coal mine, one of a great many in the West Midlands. One of my delights in the school holidays was a regular Wednesday lunch with my grandparents, when I used to go down the mine with my grandfather. It was a shallow mine, one you walked down rather than one with a big shaft and a lift, and quite primitive – the miners each had a candle which they stuck to the coal face with a bit of clay before starting work. You might say, I suppose, that the Ceneys were successful business people although a layer or two below the Marshes on the social scale.

Marsh & Baxter, on the other hand, was a very big company. To give some comparison, Grandfather Ceney employed up to two dozen men whereas Marsh & Baxter employed virtually the whole population of Brierley Hill, South Staffordshire, which numbered in the hundreds. They had a Royal Warrant and supplied one of the big shipping lines, P&O or Cunard I think, as well. They also acquired Harris's of Calne, the well-known sausage makers who had a number of factories including one at Eastleigh, in Hampshire.

If anything Marsh & Baxter was, so to speak, rather too full of Marshes. Nearly all the employees worked not just for the company but for the family. It was that sort of company, with a great deal of loyalty on both sides. One of father's more important Christmas jobs was allocating turkeys to his employees: 'Now although this man has a large family', he would say, 'he's only got a small oven'. Details like this were all taken into consideration.

Originally there were several different family lines of Marsh. One ended up running the Midland Gun Company, one was in textiles and several died in the First World War. My grandfather, Ernest Marsh, was patriarch of the meat business started in Brierley Hill by my great grandfather, Alfred Ernest, in 1887.

Now grandfather Ernest often found himself bidding for meat at Smithfield against a man called Baxter. After about five years of this, grandfather took Mr Baxter aside for a drink, pointing out that it was ridiculous for them to keep bidding against each other. Grandfather eventually left the pub having bought Mr Baxter's factory in Birmingham's Dale End, and thus was formed Marsh & Baxter. The Baxter name was retained even though his two sons weren't interested in the business and never took any part in it.

The company was very big and more or less self-sufficient, having its own railway siding for bringing in animals from all over the country. It had its own abattoir, its own chain of shops and its own transport section. It printed its own letterheads, cardboard boxes and assorted packaging, ran a laundry for employees' white jackets and made its own barrels for packing the hams. It even had its own power station, from which the National Grid fed at night when the factory wasn't working.

It was this all-encompassing concept which led grandfather to get involved in farming. He was a great one for buying up land, eventually buying up the whole district and letting the land or the farms back to the business. There were also a lot of trials, both in feeding and breeding, of pigs. Grandfather had a saying: 'It's no good farming unless what you grow walks off the premises'. Everything we grew had to be fed to the animals and buying land with different crops may well have had started off the trials. I remember going round the farms on a Friday afternoon with my father when he paid the wages. On Sundays, we both rode round with grandfather, so I think that's where my love of the outdoors started.

When I was born, my parents were living at The Croft in Wollaston, where we stayed until I was about 19. Then grandmother Marsh died and the family moved into her home, Dunsley Hall. My sister Judith had been born when I was three years old. Sadly, she had a heart defect and was a somewhat weak child, which meant we didn't really play together in the accepted sense. She might run across the lawn and suddenly turn blue so, for me, she wasn't much of a playmate. However I was always very fond of her, and still am. Judith was also a very picky eater with a tiny appetite. I remember as a boy peeling grapes and trying to entice her to eat them. If she ate one, or sometimes even half of one, that was a great success. Later, Judith derived much pleasure from breeding miniature poodles and then, after she married, from breeding and showing Dartmoor ponies.

I wouldn't exactly say that I had a happy childhood, although it wasn't unhappy. That might sound a bit negative, but apart from Judith there were no other children to play with as we lived in a big, solitary house. Eventually I got to know local kids like the gardener's sons, but I was a little backward as a child and it was rather a long time before anyone other than my mother could understand me. I'm told there was one occasion when I caused a bit of a rumpus. It happened when my mother had the local ladies in to tea. They were all chatting away, the cakes were laid out and my seed cake was there on a plate of its own. Of course I wanted one of the other cakes and made quite a fuss, but no one could understand me. Eventually I got so frustrated that I threw a plate of cream cakes against the wall...

While I may have been a little backward in speaking I've always had a slightly impish, offbeat sense of humour. We had, as you may have guessed, a nanny and the odd maid or two in our lives and once one of the maids was helping me look for newts in the garden pond. Suddenly it seemed obvious to me that she would see them much better if she was actually in the water with them. 'In you go, Mary!' I thought, as I pushed her in.

I also had a pony, which appeared in the early spring of one year. Dudley had its own theatre, the Hippodrome, which put on an annual pantomime to which all the local children, myself included, were taken. This particular year it was Cinderella, complete with her golden carriage and Shetland ponies to pull it. I don't know where the ponies came from, but after the pantomime had finished one of them turned up in the little field at the back of our house. I was plonked onto a felt saddle with a grab handle and led round and round. I quite enjoyed the riding and used to join in pony club activities, but I never became much more than an adequate rider and gave it up when I developed an allergy to horses.

Riding was almost a family pastime. Grandfather Marsh led a

weekly Sunday ride round the farm rather like a cavalcade. He would lead the way and all the lesser Marshes, cousins and nephews, would follow on horseback. Occasionally my mother joined in but she wasn't nearly as keen a rider as my father. I sometimes went on the Sunday rides and on rare occasions I went on a hunt, under the strict supervision of a groom. I wasn't really interested in riding though, unlike my cousins. Father's sister Valerie had two girls, Jill and Dawn Palethorpe, who both become very well-known show jumpers and represented Great Britain a number of times.

Riding was a particular passion of my father, who rode in point to point races as a young man and was for many years joint Master of the Heythrop Hunt with Captain Ronnie Wallace. Originally he'd had a pack of Beagles, but soon got tired of running after them so they turned them into a pack of drag hounds with specially prepared fences. Just after the war, father also bought a farm west of Dublin. An old farm manager, who had supported him in the point to point riding, went to manage it for him. The farm raised beef animals, but also looked out for good horses to send over for father, who had taken up three day eventing and even competed at Badminton on various occasions. One year he lent a horse, together with several others for practising on, to the British Olympic Team. The horse, Wild Venture, eventually travelled to Rome as part of the gold medal winning team. Father also entered horses in National Hunt races but he didn't enjoy that so much, it was all rather professional and he preferred the more amateur stuff.

With riding a major part of his life, father did have the odd mishap. Once, out hunting, a horse came down with him Fortunately he was able to hack back to his car, which was an automatic, and drive himself to hospital. He was most insistent that they carefully cut the stitches on the seams of his riding boots so they could be sewn back up again later and called in, the following morning, to the blacksmiths to get measured up for a large stirrup to fit his plaster cast. Father wouldn't let a little thing like a broken leg stop him from riding.

Naturally, school was something that took up a large part of my childhood. I first went, at quite an early age, to the Misses Moberly; two sisters who took in a small number of children from well-to-do families to a schoolroom in their house in Stourbridge. There we learnt to write our names on the blackboard and so on; it was all very basic and old-fashioned. From there I went to Birchfield School, a day prep school at Tettenhall on the outskirts of Wolverhampton. I went to Birchfield because my cousin John was already a pupil there and I could be chauffeured in and out each day with him. Two of the other pupils were from the Guy Motor family and we used to get very envious when an armoured scout car would turn up to collect them. I did find it very difficult to fit in at Birchfield because I suffered from what is now recognized as dyslexia. I was always the one who sat at the back trying to keep out of sight so that I wouldn't be asked to do anything. I made very heavy weather of the educational side of school, preferring the social side of it.

When I was about six or seven we went to watch part of the construction of Dudley Zoo. It was being created by Grandfather Marsh, together with the Earl of Dudley, and was quite advanced for its time. The centre feature was a castle on a hilltop, into which many of the big animal pens were built. You could look down on the animals roaming around their shelters from a viewing platform. I remember when the Polar Bears were delivered and let down into their cages. It was quite exciting.

My godfather, Trevor Guest, who had been married to my Aunt Val, was building the miniature steam railway that went round the zoo. I used to watch him in his workshop, in the wood just below our garden, building the railway engines which pulled carriages to give kids rides round the zoo.

By the time I was eight the war had started and everything changed. When a bomb fell just outside Birchfield School, burst the water main and shattered all the windows, it was decided that I should go to a boarding school. The Lickey Hills School was chosen, but due to its proximity to the Austin Motor Works in south west Birmingham, the pupils had been evacuated to an old manor house in the little Shropshire village of Brampton Bryan.

I won't say I hated boarding school, but I certainly didn't like going back after the holidays. In wartime it was difficult to get leave-outs, though father and mother did come over one Sunday to take me to lunch. With petrol rationing in force they came on a motorbike, it rained the whole day, we didn't have much to say to each other and the whole thing wasn't a great success. I did start to enjoy school as I moved up the scale a little and eventually became very privileged in as much as a boy named March and I were entrusted to exercise the Headmaster's children's ponies. It was quite fun to go off round the country lanes on our own, although I doubt if such a thing would be permitted today.

By the time I was in the top year the Lickey Hills School returned to its base in Rednal. I recall taking my rabbit traps back with me after the holidays and being encouraged to curtail the rabbits' favourite activity of digging up the cricket pitches. This activity also made a contribution to the school catering department, something which never went amiss with wartime food rationing still in place.

Although the war didn't affect us much at school, you couldn't get away from it in the holidays. Big cars were put up on blocks and people came out in little cars like Austin 8s, with visors on their headlights. Father did have an 8-litre Bentley, but he mainly used a fairly modest Austin 16 or 18 as he didn't want the employees to think we were squandering their efforts by running a big car. Mother, too, had a big car, an 8-cylinder Buick, but during the war she went shopping in a horse and trap. We had an old cob called The Cat who used to pull a governess cart, in which the groom drove us around.

Our house had quite large lawns and because petrol for mowers was non-existent, we acquired three goats, two billies and one nanny. In the holidays I started milking the nanny as my 'daily contribution' and made the milk into butter and cream cheese, but I was always grumbled at because the smell from the billies got into my clothing. We also kept pigs and poultry at home during the war. You were allowed to keep a pig provided, when it was slaughtered, that you gave half to the Ministry of Food.

I also went out with the forester or one of the gamekeepers during the holidays. I used to enjoy learning about the woodlands as well as rough shooting and ferreting and this turned out to be the start of a life-long interest in shooting in general.

During the war many of the family joined the services though Father stayed at home running the business. He also spent a lot of time at the Ministry of Food, firstly in London and then at Llandudno, advising on food rations. Sometimes he'd come in just in time to say good-night and be gone again in the morning so I didn't see much of him. He was a Lieutenant Colonel in the South Staffordshire Regiment of the Home Guard, the 38th Battalion of which comprised almost entirely Marsh & Baxter employees. I became quite keen on going with him on some of his duties and he had the local tailor make me a little Private's uniform that I wore on one of the Home Guard Church Parades. I was very proud to lead the procession through Brierley Hill and on to the Marsh & Baxter sportsground. With everyone drawn up, the drums were stacked to form an altar with the battalion banners propped up against it – but it was a bit of a breezy day and all the banners and drums blew over.

Father also had a permanent weekend camp set up in one of the woods, where battalions went for a weekend's training under canvas. There was even an Officer's Mess, complete with an orderly or two outside ready to escort slightly worse for wear officers back to their tents.

One weekend an army Brigadier came to visit. To show off the battalion's latest anti-aircraft technology, a Lewis gun had been mounted in the centre of a pit, surrounded by sandbags. The Brigadier went to inspect it, asking the Home Guard soldier on duty what his role was. 'Well sir, my job's to keep the cows off', replied the soldier. In actual fact no-one really knew how it worked but a Brigadier's questions must be answered.

I remember standing with father and some other bigwigs watching a mock 'battle' when a runner came puffing up. 'Sir, we've caught the enemy, busloads of them'. It turned out that it wasn't our enemy they'd caught but someone else's, en route to their own battle.

On another occasion they set up a firing range for an anti-tank missile launcher. Very modern stuff. It had a framework that you assembled on the ground made of big tubes, with a shield and a pivot supporting the barrel. About a quarter of a mile away a mock tank was set up to act as a target. On the morning we arrived the normal gun location was occupied by a huge puddle of water, so the launcher was moved back a bit. The resulting shot wasn't far short of the target but there was great consternation as it clipped one of the overhead power lines. You can imagine the fun if they'd brought that down.

Before leaving wartime events I must tell another little story. Part of the family land was used for dispersing sewage from the local towns. As we weren't very far from Birmingham, there was a constant threat of bombing. There was a big steelworks nearby and as Brierley Hill had been mentioned by Nazi radio propagandist Lord Haw Haw, we felt rather vulnerable. So the Ministry built dummy factory units on the sewage farms; wooden structures covered in creosoted hessian. When an air raid was imminent they would light these up because the habit in those days was to drop an incendiary bomb to mark the target. On this occasion they set the sewage farm alight and it did indeed get bombed. When everything exploded everybody thought there was a gas attack and rushed around for their gas masks.

Apart from going out with the keeper or forester, one of my main interests as a boy was making model boats for sailing on boating ponds and model aeroplanes. There were none of today's plastic kits of course, but for about two and sixpence – or maybe even one and six – you could buy small wooden kits. Some used hardwood which was quite difficult to shape and you had paint and transfers to finish it all off.

Back at Prep School after we were evacuated, quite an important thing in my life was that I got involved with the local church organ, which our music mistress used to play on a Sunday. Not an organist by trade, she was a pianist but she liked to experiment with the organ stops. The problem was that the instrument was powered by an old fashioned blacksmith-type bellows and she needed someone – me – to keep her supplied with wind. Because of this I got interested in music though I'm not musically minded. I started taking piano lessons and used to enjoy playing little pieces from memory but, like many things in life, it didn't last that long. After two terms the music mistress left. Her successor had a totally different attitude and, as I really wasn't musical, no interest in me. However, this episode engendered an interest in organs and organ music which reappeared when I later went to Uppingham School. I still attend recitals today.

Although I didn't enjoy Prep School very much, by the time I went to Uppingham I was learning to work the system and benefit from the facilities. At Prep School we had all been under the aegis of the Headmaster, Mr Healey, but at Uppingham we lived in separate houses around the town and went into school for classes. My Housemaster was Sam Kendal, who eventually became my form master when I took my exams. He had his own way of teaching and we joined his form to learn physics, maths, algebra and chemistry. The chemistry was rather limited, as Sam had a habit of blowing things up and this restricted us somewhat. It was in Sam's form that we started doing homework, which he had his own particular way of organizing. He would tell us which book we were going to be working from and then tell us to make sure we got a book with all the answers in it. In the morning he would collect up the finished work and put it on the scales to see, by weighing it, whether we had done enough. He also once proved to us that two and two made three… He was a great character, a bachelor, with a funny little housekeeper called Mrs Hind.

In addition to the boys in my own house I had two particular friends at Uppingham, Tony Nixon and Tony Hawley. Tony Hawley was in my house but very junior, two or three years younger and it wasn't seen as correct to associate with 'those little boys down there'. Tony Nixon, unfortunately, lived in another house on the other side of town. We only saw each other at school and Sunday afternoons, when we all took a compulsory walk in the local countryside. It just wasn't done to see other people in their houses unless on official business.

I did see both Tonys in the holidays. The Hawley family had a holiday home in the same Anglesey village that housed the Marsh family's holiday home and Tony Nixon used to come and holiday with us for a couple of weeks in the summer. We used to have great times boating and exploring the coastline.

One year Tony and I borrowed one of father's boats, a motor cruiser complete with its skipper, and we went off to the Isle of Man. We had a schoolmate there, more a friend of Tony's than mine although I knew him well enough. It was quite an adventure. When the skipper came on board his only luggage was a small attaché case. He opened it up, revealing various bits of charts. 'They're a bit old,' he said, 'but they don't move the rocks very often'. Anyway we found the Isle of Man and got back safely, even though the weather on the way back wasn't so good. One interesting thing about that boat was that it was confiscated by the Ministry during the war and used as the local patrol boat. It had a Lewis gun mounted on the front and part of the guard system round Holyhead before Father eventually got it back.

Nearly all my childhood summers involved a trip to Anglesey with members of the family including, sometimes, Granny and Grandfather Ceney. Of course during the war we travelled there by train, complete with lobster pots and shrimp nets, but once petrol rationing was lifted we could go by car.

Although he still spent a lot of time running the business, Father did take holidays with us on Anglesey. He couldn't settle down each day until he'd made a phone call to the office. Just before he finished he'd say 'Oh yes, we need some more sausages, more bacon and another ham'. Whatever he asked for would be packed up, rushed to the station and put on a train for us to collect the next morning.

Back at school, I was always more of a loner than a team player although I did get involved in team sports. Sport came in two parcels really: there were school sports and house sports and I was actually very keen on rugger. My keenness was blunted rather because I wasn't allowed to play in the position I wanted to. I fancied myself on the wing but wasn't deemed to have the right athletic figure for running down the line with the ball under my arm. So I was put in the middle of the scrum, supported by great big hefty chaps all trying to kick the ball out. I didn't enjoy this much, it was something we did because we had to but suddenly, and quite by accident, I got interested in running. Part of our regime at Uppingham was to take exercise every day. Sunday was just a walk in the countryside. You could go where you wanted and with whom you liked as long as you were out of the house for a certain time. On other days there was swimming or a run on the short, triangular cross-country course and it was there I discovered I could run. Across the field, up and down the dales and hills it was great fun. Eventually I made the second running eight, which meant visiting other schools.

Organ music cropped up again at school through another pal, John Steward. One day I came across John making little wooden organ pipes out of cigar boxes, experimenting with the theory of sound that he was learning in class. I asked him what he was going to do with them but he didn't know so I suggested we made a little organ. And that's just what we did. It was very up to date and blown by my grandmother's vacuum cleaner. Built into a wooden fruitbox, its range was an octave and a half and it stood about two and a half feet wide. John was the pipe expert and I did the base on which the pipes were mounted. It looked very smart as I'd purloined my sister's toy grand piano for the keyboard, but as we wanted it to look like an organ we thought we'd better have some display pipes on the front. Grandfather Ceney was never short of a contact or two and knew of someone up the lane who made pipes. I spent many a happy hour watching this chap make them - I even helped a bit - and I finally bought a set for the façade of our organ. It even had stops on it, a small pedal keyboard and carried our name plate: 'Marsh and Steward, Organ Builders, Uppingham'.

Every summer the school had an exhibition of biology experiments, paintings, photos, etc. and our organ was also on display. The Director of Music - who, incidentally, went on to become a cathedral organist following the circuit of Salisbury, Worcester and London - composed some music for it, which I still have. When John and I left school we gave it to one of the biology masters who could often be found playing the big organ in the hall, a monstrous, wheezing contraption with a three-second time lag between pressing the key and hearing anything. He was leaving school to do biology research up in Sheffield.

Eventually it was time to leave school and while I have to admit that I was never the best of scholars, I did manage quite a few passes and credits in my School Certificate exams. As an inducement to do better (I got quite a lot of 'could try harder' comments on my reports) father promised me a sailing boat of my own in Anglesey if I passed my exams. I got the sailing boat and, for my 18th birthday, was also given a lovely little BSA .22 rifle by my grandmother. She had a little chat with me, as grandmothers used to do in those days, saying 'Always remember, life is what you make it'. That's so true, and over the years I've thought about the opportunities which so many have had but failed to grasp with both hands. I was very fortunate in my upbringing but, unlike my father, making money wasn't, for me, the most important thing. I like to manage on what I've got and do as much as possible with it. This is why I've always been more of a do-it-yourself person, rather than one who has it done for them and still not been satisfied.

So now I was eighteen and much, I suspect, to my father's dismay, I had written to him from school to say that I didn't want to join Marsh & Baxter. There was some discussion at home as to what I did want to do (I remember boat building was suggested), but I said I'd like to go into farming. Father decided that having seen our extensive family farms it was time I saw farming from the bottom and so he advertised my services in *Farmer and Stockbreeder* as a working student.

Eventually, I was taken to meet a farmer somewhere between Wolverhampton and Stafford. Realising that I would be more of a liability than a help to start with, Father agreed to pay him £20 a week on the understanding I was given the opportunity to do everything, including driving the tractor.

I have very fond memories of that farm. The owners were a lovely couple with a young daughter living in a very old farmhouse built from hand made bricks. There was no electric light and no running water except for what was pumped into a header tank from a little petrol driven pump. There was a cold tap but the hot water came from a big copper which had to be heated daily in the farm kitchen. We needed a lot of hot water to wash the dairy utensils every day and when I was asked if I would like a bath on the first Saturday I said 'Yes please' in double quick time. Everyone else retired into the front room and I was left with a hip bath in front of the fire on the kitchen floor. It was lovely, that bath, but once it got cold and I got out, I was left with having to ladle out a bath full of tepid water.

I only spent a short time at that farm. It was quite small – about twenty five cows, six pigs, a few poultry and a couple of calves. The farmer grew potatoes and stored them for sale in a potato bury in the field. That's the way it was in those days; a big pile of the potatoes was covered with straw and a trench dug round the outside. The soil was used to cover the straw (hence potato bury) and if done properly, this kept the frost out.

Before being sold the potatoes had to be riddled and graded

and the stones taken out. Luckily we were mechanized with a potato riddling and sorting machine operated by the farmer, his permanent young worker and myself. The young man forked the potatoes from the bury (or clamp as it's sometimes known) on to the elevator. They travelled up the elevator, over the reciprocating riddle and then up another elevator, where the boss man bagged and weighed them before putting them on the trailer. Not only was I picking out the stones and the bad potatoes but I was also the motive power turning the handle.

So after a while I felt I'd learnt all that there was to know on this particular farm. OK, I hadn't done a whole year to observe crop rotation, but then there weren't many crops. Alongside the potatoes and a field of mangols there was silage, hay and that was it. So I asked father if I could work on the family farms where there was a greater variety of things going on. And by kind permission of the other family members in the business, it was agreed that I should be taken on as a labourer, which gave me my qualifying period to go to college.

I enjoyed my time on the family farm, which was mixed farming. We had proper rotation of crops and it was all aimed at producing livestock, which you then sold off the farm – there was a great variety. We even had a herd of Jerseys, which was a hobby of my uncle Walter (cousin John's father). On two other farms we had Ayrshires (that's where my lifelong love of the breed came from) and, of course, it was all a very, very big enterprise. I even did a stint at relief milking.

Because Marsh & Baxter were interested in carrying out feed and housing experiments to demonstrate to other farmers what they could do in their particular situation, there was a wide variety of crops. We grew wheat, barley, oats, maize and cut green fodder at the end of the summer when grass got a bit short. We also grew mangols, kale and swedes for the sheep. We grew the swedes in blocks of about four rows each and then put up temporary fencing (we didn't have electric fencing in those days) to strip graze them. We also did a little bit of market gardening – cabbages, leeks, carrots, peas and so on. There was quite a cross-section. The farms also employed a man to mix the food for all the animals, grinding it and incorporating various additives. As a general labourer I had a go at most things including driving the tractor and I used to particularly enjoy ploughing. We had a combine harvester, which I co-drove. This was long before combines had air-conditioned cabs, we just went along in a big cloud of dust. It was before the days of tanker combines too and to start with I was chief bagger-upper. Eventually I got to drive the combine and also had a go on the caterpillar tractor which was yet another experience.

All this qualified me to go to college and father decided that if I was to go into farming properly, I should go to the Royal Agricultural College at Cirencester. He duly enrolled me on the two-year course on the assumption that it would be twice as good as a one-year course. I stuck it out for a year, but the whole thing bored me to tears. I wanted to be a farmer, not to be able to survey a field or identify grass seeds. If you buy a bag of grass seed from the agricultural merchant you're not going to empty it out and check it, you assume it contains what it says on the bag.

I suppose it was the mechanical side of farming that really interested me most, although I do like the animals. Except sheep, which I have no time for and while I liked the pigs, I didn't have much to do with them apart from trying to move them from one field to another. Incidentally, pigs have very good memories – one lot wouldn't go through a gateway where previously there had been electric fencing. I can't say I blamed them.

By this time I was 18 and driving a little Series E Morris 8 horsepower which my parents acquired for me. I passed my test as soon as I could but I'd already been driving for some while on the farm, as most farmers' sons do. Although I'd got this little car I had always hankered after a motorbike so I saved up and bought a little 350 Triumph Twin. My parents weren't particularly happy about this, but it was *fait accompli*. I had a whole series of motor bikes (most of which I should have been killed on) but I did have a thing about Triumphs. I particularly remember my 650 Triumph Thunderbird that had a beautifully shaped headpiece with all the bits and pieces and a sprung back wheel – oh, the comfort! Unfortunately I wore that bike out very quickly; after about 15 or 20,000 miles it needed a rebore. I just levelled it all the time. I had a target time for my regular journeys such as up to Anglesey and then down to Cirencester on a Sunday night. Something like 63 miles in 65 minutes. Both the big rubber buffer on the end of the pedal and my motorcycle boots had flats on them. But I do think motorcycling had something to do with my learning to read the road - choosing a line, anticipation, judgement, etc.

I did have one big fright. I was on my way from Cirencester to the motorcycle shop in Stroud and passed through a farm on a lovely sweeping bend with the farm buildings on one side and the house and fields on the other. Right on my line was evidence that a cow had recently passed by. First the front wheel slid then the back wheel did the same in sympathy. Somehow I managed to stay on, but it was a very near miss.

I had also wanted a Vincent. My first choice was a big 1000cc Vincent V Twin but it was completely out of my price bracket so I bought a Vincent 500 single instead. That was a big disappointment, so I didn't keep it very long and went back to Triumphs. It was while I was out one day with my old school pal, Tony Hawley, on our motorbikes that we discovered motorsport. There we were, beating up the countryside (as you could do in those far off, traffic free days), when we came across a group of Dellows competing in a trial.

And the rest, as they say, is history.

Chapter Two

I'd been driving for about three years by the time we discovered the Dellows. Having been taught to drive round the farm by my father I'd taken my test as soon as I was able to do so. I'd sailed through it and taken a couple of tractor tests as well. In those days you couldn't drive a small agricultural tractor on a car licence and you also needed to take yet another test if you wanted to drive a caterpillar tractor. Mind you, they weren't like the driving tests of today. If you could start the thing up and drive it round a few corners, you passed!

So there we were, Tony Hawley and I, watching these Dellows. I was really taken with them. There were some specials on the trial as well, but it was the Dellows that interested me. Having acquired a competitive spirit from racing my sailing boat, I thought I'd like to have a go too.

I asked a few questions and discovered there was a Dellow for sale in a local showroom. Until then I'd driven one of the family's two Austins or my old Morris. I started with a Morris 8 sidevalve and upgraded to a Morris Minor. It was this car that was eventually exchanged for the Dellow once I'd persuaded father that a Dellow would be much more suitable for me! 'Let me see it,' he said and clambered in (it didn't have a door) with his long leather riding boots as he was just about to go hunting. 'Is this really what you want?' he asked. I assured him it was, the salesman told him the price and father said 'Right, we'll take that one, have it delivered'. And that was how the Dellow came into my life.

When the car first arrived I was only allowed to drive it in the paddock at the back of the house. It was December, and not allowed on the road until a tax disc had been bought for it in January. Those few days hung about a bit, although my mother became quite interested in the car as she had done a little motorsport herself.

Shortly after the Dellow was acquired my uncle, Jack Palethorpe, got to hear of it and mentioned it in passing to Ron Lowe, who used to get his Christmas tree every year from Uncle Jack. 'Tell your young man to come round and see me,' said Ron who, as I learned, was in fact the 'low' of Dellow, 'I could talk to him usefully' - and that was how my association with Ron Lowe started.

Although I joined Hagley and District Light Car Club to find out details of forthcoming events, it was Ron who became my guiding light in those early days of motorsport. He immediately started giving me tips; car preparation, how to enter events, the importance of a clean car at the start and all that sort of thing. There were a lot of young lads in the district who had Dellows and who went to see Ron. If their car wasn't clean he'd send them away to clean it before he even thought about working on it. It was Ron, too, who instilled in me the need to drive back from an event as well as drive there.

I mentioned that my mother had an earlier association with motorsport and so, in fact, had my father. It all happened before I was around. My mother had owned a little Brooklands Riley, the latest thing in roadgoing sports cars and father drove it at Brooklands. He subsequently drove a supercharged front-wheel-drive Alvis at Shelsley Walsh and in a couple of circuit races as well. In those days there was very little motorsport in England, maybe two Shelsley meetings and a race or two at Brooklands or Donington, certainly not the number of events we're blessed with today. There were also other members of the family, too, who were interested in motors and motorsport. Father's brother, uncle Ron, had several cars including a Railton and an Invicta which he drove at Shelsley in the early thirties. Father's cousin had a Lagonda, although that was a saloon car, and his sister, my aunt Val Palethorpe, drove a 1496cc Frazer Nash single seater at Prescott and Shelsley. She held the Ladies' hill record at Prescott from 3 July 1938 until Sheila Darbishire took it on 22 September 1946, in a 2-litre Bugatti. The Frazer Nash belonged to some local people, the Goodwins, and I recall as a very small boy being taken to an outbuilding, probably at the Palethorpes', seeing this dark coloured racing car and being allowed to sit in it.

While I don't remember my father or my aunt competing I do remember, again as a very small boy, being taken to Shelsley and standing near the finish, watching Austin Sevens with my head through the fencing. In the paddock, I was curious to see that several of the smaller cars had their steering wheels taken off to enable the driver to get in and out, so removable steering wheels for competition cars have been around for quite a number of years.

Now I needed to find an event to run the Dellow, a Mark I

model, registration number WRF 81 and my very first event was a fairly major trial organised by the Hagley club. It started at Bridgnorth and at the end of it I felt very smug, because Ron Lowe went home with a dent in his rear mudguard and I got away without a scratch. OK, he'd be much further up the results list, but at least I didn't have any repairs to fix.

The event was a typical trial of those days with generously laid out sections. There was always the odd tree to get tangled up with, but the main challenge was working out the best way to negotiate each section. I'm afraid I can't remember who 'bounced' for me, but there were quite a few young fellows working on the farm willing to act as passenger in those early years. One lad passed his driving test in my Dellow, becoming a driver in Hong Kong when he went off do to his National Service. The fact that he could already drive a car probably helped. I didn't do National Service myself as I suffered from what the doctors called an allergic asthma, which made me unfit for service. The asthma developed from an allergy to horses when I was a boy and while I quite enjoyed riding, I wasn't as passionate about horses as my father was.

After seeing me drive that first event, Ron Lowe said that if he'd known me before I bought the Dellow he would have recommended a Mark II instead of the Mark I. He was quite keen for me to do well, in fact I found out later from my brother-in-law, Duncan Hollingworth, that Ron had said to him 'This young man is worth watching'.

Based on Ron's opinion of my driving, Dellow Cars were prepared to build me a lightweight Mark II and so LWP 757 arrived. It was this car that really launched me into motorsport, and in fact I own the car today, although it had various owners in between my two custodianships of it.

To widen the scope of available competition I joined other clubs as well as Hagley. As they can today, club members could take part in their own events but needed a licence to be invited to take part in those run by another club. SUNBAC (Sutton Coldfield and North Birmingham Automobile Club) was one such club, which I joined as they regularly issued invitations to their events. However I didn't take much part in the social scene. I'd go home after a club night and wonder just what I'd had to show for the last two or three hours. Working on the family farms I didn't have much time for socialising as we worked to at least 5pm every day while in the summer we would be haymaking or harvesting until dark. But being family, I was in receipt of the odd perk or two. We worked Saturday morning as a matter of course, but I would be excused this duty if I'd put in enough unpaid overtime during the week. Initially, this was so that I could go and race my Menai Straits One Design sailing boat, but the practice continued when I became interested in motorsport.

To acquire the Mark II Dellow, though, I had to consolidate things a bit. I'd still got my motorbike and my sailing boat, but I'd already discovered that motorsport was a year-round sport whereas sailing occupied just a few summer months. So the 'bike and the boat had to go.

My second competitive event was a trial in February 1952, organised by a small Hereford based motor club. I had a double interest in the event as Hagley was an invited club and our family woodsman came from Hereford. By good fortune I won my class. Not that it meant very much as there were a number of classes, including several for specialised cars like Dellows, but I still have the class winner's trophy in my cabinet.

There were other trials too. SUNBAC used to organise a big one which I competed in, albeit very much with L-plates! During the summer we had autotests, or driving tests as they were called then, and inter-club competitions where Hagley used to compete with SUNBAC and Shenstone and District Car Club. The clubs took turns to organize these annual events and one year the Club Trophy (as opposed to the individual trophies) was a firkin of beer. Now while I'm not a great drinking man, there were some members who took this club competition very seriously indeed! I was content with another first class award. Hagley also organised their Ludlow Rally, a very small event but great fun, where I managed second in class.

Then along came something organised by the Hants and Berks Motor Club – a versatility trial. This consisted of trial sections, driving tests and a lot else besides and I received another first class award. The awards were generous as, quite often, besides the overall winner and the runner-up's prizes, the next 10% would get a pint tankard and the following 10% a half pint tankard.

As that first summer wore on Hagley ran a speed trial, which *Autosport* reminds me was at Westwood Park, near Droitwich. That was a much bigger event, with single seater racing cars as well as sports and saloon cars. I managed second in class there, just ahead of Ron Lowe's wife Mary.

With events being organised by the Hereford club, Shenstone, SUNBAC and Hagley I picked up a few more class awards so at the end of that first season there were several prize presentations to attend with various awards to collect. All this helped fuel my newly found enthusiasm, as it's nice to have some recognition of your efforts. I tried various types of events that year; if there was a competition for the car I'd have a go. I have a photo of the Mark I Dellow taking part in a race at Silverstone, although it really wasn't suited to racing. I tried rallies but with many of them run at night, as I'm rather fond of my sleep they didn't feature very highly. But I did win one rally, an evening event with strict time controls. I found it easier to look at the map for a while and then drive the bit I'd memorised rather than listen to my navigator. Perhaps he just wasn't very good at it.

It was all rather interesting and exciting and I did quite well in that first year, albeit on a very lowly level but I was getting results. My mother in particular was quite keen on the little bits of silverware I was acquiring and a small table was put aside for their display. It was quite hard to know what father felt, but if Hagley were running an event on the family land a figure would suddenly appear on horseback, watch for a while and then disappear. I suppose he could simply have been making sure we weren't doing too much damage or disturbing the pheasants, but I think he felt a bit of enthusiasm as Hagley were allowed to continue using the family land for some time.

I still have copies of *Autosport* reports from 1952, and in one I seem to have impressed Francis Penn as he wrote: 'This young man will be to the fore, with a little more experience, as he drove consistently well all day'. Prophetic words.

Ron Lowe, to whom I owe so much, continued as my guiding light and we used to spend hours in the evenings talking motorsport. He would keep me on track with car preparation and when it came to looking for a bit more performance, he'd help me with work on the engine. Mind you, we weren't talking about a lot of horsepower – around 35bhp was your lot!

The Dellow was both my competition and road car, but it eventually got to the point where Ron said that he had a rather special engine I could use for speed events. As a family man with commitments, he felt that I'd make more use of the engine than he could. I used this engine for hill climbs and sprinting, but as I didn't want to wear it out going into town or round the farm, I developed a routine whereby on Friday nights after work the ordinary engine came out and the motorsport engine went in. Then on Monday mornings I had to get up early and swap engines again. They were both Ford E93A sidevalves, but Ron's competition engine just happened to be a very good one.

My only ambition at that time was to do as much motorsport as possible. On the weekends when there wasn't any I was left twiddling my thumbs and tinkering with the car. I liked collecting the silverware, but really enjoyed the fun of competing for it. There were no thoughts of becoming a racing driver, let alone competing in the top echelons of the sport. There were big meetings at Silverstone with International names such as Farina and Ascari racing in what were still effectively pre-war cars but I didn't (and still don't) go to meetings to spectate. It was all about taking part as far as I was concerned.

By the end of 1952 I was starting to work my way up the ladder. I'd been to the inter-club Prescott as part of the Hagley team and wanted to go more often. Some of those early events would actually have been equivalent to today's Nationals, and that would have been another stepping stone had I realised it at the time. My thoughts were always focussed on the next event.

1953 followed much the same pattern except that I was much more aware of the different types of motorsport available. *Autosport* reports a SUNBAC trial on 21 March where I beat both Bill Bodenham and Ron Lowe in one section and 1953 was the first time I met Ken Rawlings, who used to drive a Standard Vanguard Special. Ken was a great character, given to recounting his experiences in WW2 when he was one of the first pilots to be shot down in a Wellington bomber. Fèted around Paris, he eventually went to the prisoner of war camp that staged the famous 'wooden horse' escape. He sometimes took his trombone and bowler hat to events and did a turn at the social afterwards. His friend Jackie Waldron often accompanied him and they were a bit like a double act. Once, at a hotel in Bognor during a Goodwood race weekend, three old ladies were playing 'tearoom music' in the foyer when Ken decided to join in on his trombone – we had a bit of trouble in that hotel! Ken's car, painted yellow and called Buttercup, was a Triumph Mayflower with a Standard Vanguard engine. A bit heavy for trials Buttercup was more suited to sprints, hill climbs and driving tests.

Meanwhile Lydstep hill climb in Pembrokeshire on Easter Saturday netted second in class behind A P Rhodes' Ford Ten engined Rhodes Special. It was a great weekend and Hagley used to take over a local hotel so lots of jollity and celebrating went on.

Perhaps at this stage I ought to mention a car that I would really prefer to forget. Even in those early days I was looking at ways to improve my competition cars and this was an early attempt to shape one of my own. The Dellow had certain limitations and I thought that something with a bigger engine might prove itself in events like hill climbs, sprints and even racing. I'd seen, in the Dellow basement, some independent front suspension units bought for a special project that never got off the ground. I eventually got them to make up a special chassis for me, incorporating those parts and which would take an Austin A70 engine. Despite the A90 being a bigger unit which found its way into early Austin Healeys, I preferred the A70. I used an Austin gearbox designed for a steering column gear change but which I adapted for a conventional right hand lever, which was easier for the linkage. The car had an Austin back axle and bodywork along the lines of a Dellow. I had the help of a panel beater, but it was a ghastly looking thing and not very good either. I wasn't proud of it. I think the Dellow register keep in contact with the car and I have seen a photo of it with a different body, which looked much better.

Then I came first in class at Cheltenham MC's sprint at Staverton airfield in May. The event wasn't much of a challenge in the Dellow whereas in a racing car it would have been much more interesting. It was just a drive to the finish on very wide runways marked with straw bales.

Me aged about 1

The first car, me with mother, Aunty Val and cousin Jill

Grandfather Marsh

Father

Aunty Val at Shelsley

Mary Lowe driving mother at a driving test

Me with Roy Lee as passenger in Dellow

Father supervising at Westwood Park

He won 'em, he can clean 'em

1955: with Paul Emery's Emeryson

1955: championship winning car at Shelsley

1955: Cooper Jaguar at Goodwood during last 9 hour race held there

1957 With George Wicken

The cooper Bobtail was often taken to the same meeting

1956: driving Peter Bell's ERA (left) with John Cooper in the F2 Cooper
Prototype

1958: Max Trimble's Lotus at Goodwood

Next came the Bugatti Owners' Club hill climb at Prescott in June and another class win. There was one Bugatti I always wanted to drive, Peter Stubberfield's twin rear wheeled, ex-George Eyston 35B. Peter went to a lot of events so I had plenty of chance to see it in action. When it wasn't being driven by Peter, his pet Boxer dog was usually to be seen sitting in the driving seat. Another car I remember from those days was Pat Reynolds' Dellow, which he'd bodied in Tufnol panels (a material made by his own company) and given motorcycle type mudguards.

I was third in class at the inter-club July Prescott, beaten by a certain A F Rivers-Fletcher. Tony Rivers-Fletcher was PR man for the BRM team and definitely someone to beat. Pat Reynolds and Frank Wall were in our team and Peter Stubberfield – also quite a force to be reckoned with – took BTD.

As a bit of a diversion, most motor clubs organised summer gymkhanas, rather like a horse or pony equivalent, which were great fun. At one of these was an archway you had to drive through with a little platform supporting a bucket of water. A circular disc hung down on a pole, which your passenger had to hit with their hand. You had to drive reasonably quickly to avoid the shower-bath but slowly enough to make sure your passenger hit the disk. There was also a test where your rear bumper was tied to a stake with a 20 foot long piece of string with a weight in the middle of it. You had to drive round this stake several times without the weight touching the ground. That one was quite difficult. While the tests were fun they did make you think about your driving and how to approach each challenge using precise positioning and car control. Hagley used to organise a gymkhana at Bentley Manor, a delightful old house with a courtyard. On one of these we had to drive into the yard, into a garage and back out, before driving round the laurel bush in the driveway. The yard and garage weren't too forgiving but the laurel bush was tremendous fun as the driveway was gravel and encouraged opposite-lock power slides at all of 20 mph.

Now came a significant step. A move to a single seater racing car. This came about through a friend of the family, Eddie Marsland. Eddie had been a motorcycle competitor himself and used to take my mother to watch me compete when my father was out on his horses.

Eddie felt sure I could do justice to something better than the Dellow. Father was keen for me to do better in hillclimbs, like beating reigning champion Ken Wharton (father's ambitions were always greater than mine). 'Would a V16 BRM be the thing to have?' he asked. This rather caught me on the hop and I said I'd like to think about it. I'd already had one engine disaster with the Dellow when four pistons had to be replaced, so the thought of 16 of them…

My first course of action had to be to see Ron Lowe, to whom I owed so much. 'I know just the car,' said Ron. 'It's not far away, just down in Kidderminster.' This car was being sold by a young man named Peter Collins, who I hadn't heard of at that time. So off Ron went and negotiated the purchase of this car, a Mark IV Cooper which had rather a unusual engine. Most of the V-twin JAP engines were 1100cc but this had been enlarged to 1260, which put it up a class. It also had a motorcycle gearbox, either a Burman or an Albion, a proprietary gearbox that a lot of manufacturers used. Ron towed it over behind his Dellow on a fixed towbar and we put it in one of the garages. When father arrived home, I peeped out of the window to see him making a beeline for my new acquisition, the first racing car to live at Dunsley Hall.

It was as the result of owning a racing car, as opposed to a sports car, that I really got into racing. It opened up a whole new area of competition for me. If there was nothing on at the weekend other than a race meeting, I felt I ought to go and race the car. I'd done the Silverstone race at in the Dellow as part of the reliability trial, but the car wasn't suited to it and I didn't find it exciting enough. Somewhere, there's a picture of me in that Mark IV Cooper in a Formula Libre race at Castle Combe, but I quickly discovered that this particular car and engine wasn't suited to the longer type of event.

Of course, now that I owned a racing car I had the problem of transporting it to events. Here the Marsh & Baxter garage department came to the rescue. During the war the company had its own private fire brigade, by now disbanded, and I was able to borrow the redundant fire pump trailer. I had the pump taken off and the trailer extended just enough to get the car on. It was an enormous, heavy trailer and father lent me his Land Rover to tow it.

My debut in the Cooper came in August at a wet Shelsley

International, where I ran second in class to Michael Christie's V-twin. Ken Wharton was there in the V16 BRM, running 37.97sec in practice, but rain marred later performances. Ken's BRM was another car I would love to have driven, particularly at Shelsley. Besides Wharton and Christie all the top hill climbing people were there – Bill Sleeman, Bertie Bradnack, Austen May, George Abecassis and so on. Christie beat me by just half a second so I must have come home from that meeting relatively satisfied.

When I arrived home, father asked if I'd beaten Ken Wharton. When I told him I hadn't, he decided to come along to the sprint at Westwood Park the following day to find out why I hadn't done better. As I took BTD and set a new course record, this must have convinced him that I was learning to drive the Cooper and he didn't see the need to attend again for a while. The record at Westwood Park was a particular bonus, as Peter Collins had set the previous record in the same car and I was beating names like Ivor Bueb and Austen May along the way. And as one could drive more than one car at an event, I also took a third in class in the home-built car for good measure.

October saw me at Lydstep again for another first in class before moving into the trials season, where SUNBAC's Vesey Trial netted a second class award. But on the Herefordshire Autumn Trial that year, I retired with a seized blower drive. There was a brass oil feed to the supercharger shaft controlled by a little knob, which you had to turn to give so many drops per minute. Maybe I hadn't turned it enough, but I did manage to sort the problem out in time to drive home again.

At the Chase Trophy Trial in November I picked up the Rugeley Bowl for the second best performance of the day. Then came Leicestershire CC's annual Sporting Trial at Slawston, where I was one of four competitors out of an entry of 25 to clear four sections.

In early December, the London Motor Club's 35th Gloucester Trial went well too, and I picked up the Committee Cup. That was particularly gratifying because if you did enough championship events and scored enough points, you were invited to take part in the RAC Trials Championship. I think I was the last Dellow driver ever to do this.

But motorsport being what it is, not long before Christmas

I came down to earth with a broken axle in one of the tests on the Hagley Trial and Rally. I tied on the hills with Frank Lewis, who had failed the first driving test. The club couldn't find an aggregate to settle the tie, eventually deciding the event on the first driving test. I was awarded the win after Frank's fail, but he can't have held this against me as he still sends a Christmas card every year! This event also saw my cousin, John Marsh, competing. John did just a few events, in a Riley. His father didn't approve of him doing more than one sport and told John that he had to decide between shooting or hunting as he couldn't mess about with both. John settled on hunting and his guns were put in store with a gunsmith in Birmingham. Later, John entered Hagley's Welsh Rally, a 12-hour night event and one of the few rallies of note that I took part in. Winding down a twisty hillside, I rounded a corner and came upon a big kerfuffle. John's car was upside down in the road and he was in a big panic because his lady navigator was covered in a red liquid. But the problem evaporated when we realised that it was tomato soup from their broken Thermos flask! We tipped the car back up on its wheels and John drove the car home, probably to a roasting from his father - at any rate that was his last event.

So the 1953 season came to an end, but before we could get started on 1954 there were club dinners and prizegivings to attend. An *Autosport* report from 12 March 1954 reads: 'Last Friday, the Hagley and DLCC held its Annual Dinner Dance and Prizegiving......Tony Marsh collected an impressive number of awards, so many that his father, in a short speech, remarked that "as he'd won 'em, he'd clean 'em!"'

All in all, not a bad second season in motorsport.

Chapter Three

1954 was a much busier year for me. Hill climbs seemed more abundant, or perhaps I was just finding out about them better and with a racing car, as well as the Dellow, there were more options open to me.

It was about this time that mother bought a Dellow and ventured into motorsport herself. The *Autosport* report of the 1954 Clee Hill Trial says that we '...probably made history by being the only mother and son ever to drive in an event of this type.' This was also the first time I had my picture published in *Autosport*, which was quite exciting.

Trials, with or without mother, took up the early part of the season with the Clee followed by the Kitching. A couple of more well known names competed too, Nancy Mitchell, who went on to become a successful rally driver and Raymond Baxter, the TV broadcaster and former Spitfire pilot, who sometimes used to drive Reg Phillips' car. Driving back to the finish after one trial we came upon this rather odd looking sight. It was Reg, with wife Peggy sitting on the bonnet and steering one front wheel by hand. They were proceeding very cautiously, but you wouldn't get away with that today.

About this time I was given a test drive in Peter Bell's ERA, R11B, round Oulton Park, which I must have passed because I was to drive it at a later date. Perhaps fortuitously, crash helmets were also gaining in popularity. Ken Wharton wore one and I bought one too, for speed events. An *Autosport* news item in February 1954 described the Eagle Safety Helmet which was available 'in specially designed form for car work.' It was made of Cobex, which was a type of plastic, and had been tested in excess of the regular standards of the day, but how good those standards were is anybody's guess. Still, it was a start and the makers had asked the Cooper Car Company 'to advise at all stages of development.' Sold by Coopers, it cost 59s 6d.

The racing season started at Easter with a meeting at Castle Combe and my first race in a single seater. Roy Salvadori was there in his left-hand drive Maserati sports car and so was Les Leston, who was well known as a 500cc Formula 3 driver and hill climber. Easter also meant Lydstep again, and while three of us broke my old course record I managed to take BTD with a 31.60, beating CAN (Austen) May who was one of the top hill climb drivers. Austen's mechanic was Fred Fletcher, chief mechanic for Dellow and in later years, course manager at the Hagley Club's Loton Park hill climb. Fred had a double transporter to take Peter Collins' and Austen May's cars to meetings. Nowadays, the British Hill Climb Championship is run by Fred's son, Tony.

But back to 1954, a class win ahead of Les Leston at the Gosport Speed Trials shows I was venturing further afield in pursuit of motorsport. Gosport always seemed such an unlikely place to have a speed trial. It was a straight line sprint which finished on a bridge over the local railway line. It used to get a good entry with some interesting cars - single seaters such as Connaughts and Lady Mary Grosvenor's Alta.

The early May Prescott hill climb saw Michael Christie run within five hundredths of a second of Ken Wharton's 43.70 hill record. Although I couldn't get near that in the Cooper I was still ahead of Tony Rivers-Fletcher, Ivor Bueb and the Hon Edward Greenall, all well known hill climbers and racers in the early fifties. I still took the Dellow to events and at this one took two of them, my supercharged car and the lightweight special. That was a nice little car, very light and updated with a four-speed Morris gearbox instead of the normal three-speed one. Sadly it never got the results we'd hoped for as other manufacturers were really forging ahead with their developments. It could have been quite a problem getting three cars to an event but Ron and Mary Lowe used to help out, particularly once Ron had given up competitive motorsport himself.

Westbrook Hay produced a BTD over Michael Christie's blown Cooper on my first visit to this almost suburban hill climb, near Hemel Hempstead in Hertfordshire. Once again I took the Dellow along too. In those days I used to drain the gearbox oil and replace it with RedEx in an effort to find that extra fraction of a horsepower. I also had a tiny battery on the car just for ignition and the SU fuel pump. We must have push-started the car as we certainly didn't have a starting battery on board. If you're investing in better performance, the cheapest way has to be to 'add lightness' – adding horsepower is very expensive.

Driving the Cooper, I didn't appear in the results of the next meeting, a race at Silverstone, but I did take a third place in the Dellow. The Dellow also took the award for Best Performance in the car section of SUNBACs Double Sporting Half-day.

The Bugatti Owners' Club members' meeting at Prescott was always good fun and although the rain poured down that year, it didn't dampen spirits and I managed third fastest overall, beating the man *Autosport* described as the 'potential hill climb champion', Michael Christie. I also took the class win in the blown Dellow, so it was a good day out.

Then it was off to Shelsley and *Autosport* for 25 June tells me I stalled the Cooper on the line. Well, it may have been a stall or it may have been a split gearbox case. The gearbox in those Coopers was fine for the 500cc cars but not really man enough for the 1100 V-twins. As it wasn't a big job there was plenty of time to change it for the second runs and a 37.71. This was good enough for third BTD behind Ken Wharton in the famous ex-Mays ERA R4D and Michael Christie, driving Peter Bell's ERA.

At the International meeting at Bo'ness, on the banks of the Firth of Forth, I was third BTD again but this time it was behind a busy Ken Wharton who took second in his Cooper and won in his ERA. While it was great fun, if a little hectic, competing in two or even three cars in one meeting, I do think today's system of one car per driver does tend to concentrate the mind somewhat.

Driving up to Scotland took quite some time in those days, but Bo'ness tied in with an event at Rest and Be Thankful the following weekend so I took my tent and camped. Either one of the young lads from the farm came along to help, or possibly a trainee mechanic from Marsh & Baxter's garage.

We then sped from the far north to the far south, to the Channel Islands and Bouley Bay. I had an incident at Radio Corner but I remember more about other aspects of the trip. We went over with British Rail, the cars having to be craned on to the boat and dropped down into the hold, where navvies pushed them into their parking spaces. When we got to St Helier there were fierce arguments among the local club members deciding who was going to tow Tony Marsh, or Ken Wharton, and so on. Sitting on the end of a tow rope through those narrow Jersey roads with big banks either side was a hair-raising experience as the local lads were determined to show us mainland speed boys how to drive!

There was also an incident when we got back to Southampton. Doc Taylor had a little car called the Caesar Special, which customs officials wanted to charge purchase tax on, or impound it or some such nonsense. Apparently he'd managed to get the car to Jersey without going through the proper exit procedure so they had no record of his car being in England prior to going to Jersey. He got into a whole load of trouble but they did eventually sort it out.

I was still competing in small, and not so small, club events and there is a record of a Midland AC Hill Climb and Gymkhana at Shelsley where I won Best Aggregate as part of the winning Hagley Team. I couldn't quite manage best on the hill in the Dellow, an Allard won that in 41.2, but I did take a class win in 52.4.

At Great Auclum I managed two second class awards. In fact the Dellow was more suited than the Cooper to the hill, which was not one I enjoyed driving. It was alright in those early Coopers but when the multi-cylinder engines and the big V8s came along the venue wasn't really suitable and didn't, to my mind, warrant being kept on as a championship venue. It's a bit like Monaco – it would never get a track licence now if it applied for the first time, but it's an institution so they can't actually drop it. The track at Great Auclum was a bit like Gurston Down is today in that you rushed off downhill. But then you negotiated a steeply banked corner, had two or three twiddles through the trees and that was it. Quite a short track, only 440 yards. Father knew the man who owned it, Neil Gardner, who was something big in the Huntley and Palmer biscuit company. He was a Brooklands enthusiast, hence the banked corner. Whereas Rivers-Fletcher delighted in driving round the top of the banking, most of us took a much lower line.

By the time of the August Shelsley meeting, a year after my first outing in the ex-Peter Collins car, I'd acquired a second V-twin Cooper. I acquired it because the old one, while quick at the smaller meetings, always seemed to have problems at the bigger ones. Father and I had talked things over. 'You'd better order a new one then,' he said. I duly went down to Surbiton with the trailer to collect it only to find there was no engine in it. 'The chaps are just fetching it,' said John Cooper, who always had an answer for everything. I eventually took the engine home in the back of the Land Rover. However, it wasn't a straightforward visit to Coopers – I found out later that they very rarely were – as the car didn't fit properly on the trailer. The handbrake lever on the front of the trailer fouled the Cooper's long nose, so John got out his hacksaw and cut the lever off. Unfortunately he wasn't watching what he was doing and cut the end off his tie as well. This visit started a long association with Coopers and I always enjoyed going down there.

About this time I bought another engine – a JAP - because I was interested in a particular race at Silverstone. In fact there were two events, the first a short race for JAP engined cars, because they were deemed inferior to the Norton engined cars. The second race was the main attraction of the meeting and was a 100 mile race for 500cc cars with a special prize for the first JAP engined car to finish. It was this second race that was the object of my exercise. The only problem being, I hadn't got a 500 JAP engine. The manager of the Marsh & Baxter Transport Department came to the rescue. He had a young friend, Ronnie Mountford, who was a local speedway star, and he used to build frames for Ronnie in his garden shed. Ronnie said he'd build an engine for me. He had nearly enough bits and what he hadn't got, he could get hold of. Sure enough he built the engine, which I received the day before the event and still had to make up an exhaust pipe for it. But despite the fact that it was a real old 'cobble job', that engine went like stink. Ronnie was an excellent engine builder and later taught me how to build V-twins.

Anyway we made it to Silverstone, the race was going very nicely, when suddenly there was a loud bang and the con-rod appeared. The engine was nearly written off, although Ronnie and I did repair it as it was really rather quick.

I started with a JAP engine because I felt they ran in slightly more low-key events than those for the Norton people such as Stirling Moss. Later I did buy a Norton, not a top tuner but it gave me some good experience. One bank holiday weekend I entered three races, Snetterton with the Norton, Brands Hatch with the V-twin and Crystal Palace with the JAP single. Maximising my opportunities, you might say, although it was a bit of rush getting to the next venue and changing the engine as well.

The new Cooper had problems initially, because it didn't scavenge the oil out of the engine properly. There were clouds of smoke and oily plugs and we decided the engine had to go back to JAP. However I did find out straight away that the two cars were totally different to drive. The old one felt very vintage and quite frightening after the new one, which was a Mark VIII, the long chassis version designed to take the V-twin JAP 1100. The oil problem was solved after JAP told me I had to restrict the oil supply to the engine and once we got that sorted out it went like a dream. The following year I did more racing with it and because it wasn't as highly stressed as the 1260, it would last a 20-25 mile Formula Libre race, which was rather fun - but I'm getting ahead of myself.

The International meeting at Prescott in September 1954 saw a third in class with the faithful Dellow and my 49.89 was the first time a Dellow had climbed in under 50 seconds. The new Cooper wasn't on song yet and the old one had been sold, but I enjoyed the event which saw the notable American, Masten Gregory, competing in a 4.5 litre Ferrari. I found it very interesting to watch the modern sports cars against the older single seaters.

Now we were into the trials season and at SUNBAC's Vesey Trial, I gained a first class award and my future brother-in-law, Duncan Hollingworth, gained second best performance of the day and took home the Watson Glynne Bowl. Duncan very much enjoyed driving in trials. He had a little car called the Oliver (built by Lou Oliver) and was also a friend of Ken Wharton. In fact Duncan often used to drive Ken to events and said it was amazing how Ken would be sleeping but know exactly where they were. They'd stop at a junction and before Duncan had time to look at the signpost, Ken would wake up and tell him which way to turn.

Ken was, of course, a very good driver in many different cars and at many types of events. But when we took part in the North versus Midlands challenge match at Blackpool in the early winter of that year, he thought he'd been given an inferior car and that I was trying to beat him by the back door. We were both in the same Midlands team, I was driving my faithful supercharged Dellow and Ken was driving my mother's Dellow, which I think he thought I'd spiked. It was all good fun and Ken Rawlings and his sidekick, Jack Waldron, were there too. Now Jack had a very nice cavalry type helmet with a point on the top, which he wore when he and Ken were fooling around. Unbeknown to him I'd acquired a fireman's helmet for the event. I didn't wear it myself, but wrapped it up and got the Mayor to present it to Jack for the Best Fireman of the Day award. Jack went up to collect this thing, then unwrapped it in front of us all amid much amusement. We used to have a lot of fun at prizegivings in those days.

After another couple of trials, the Cotswold Classic and the Chase Trophy, then it was on to what became the highlight of the winter for me, racing at Brands Hatch on Boxing Day. It was the first time anyone had organised a race meeting in the depths of winter, but with nearly 90 entries it was obviously quite a popular idea.

I took the Mk VIII Cooper to Brands and had a superb race with Don Beauman in his A-Type Connaught. Les Leston led for a while in his Cooper Twin and we all had a great tussle. In the end Don got across the line first, followed by me two seconds later with Horace Gould third in his Cooper Bristol. I think Les got on the grass at some point because he only managed sixth in that race. It was also the day when Stirling 'Santa' Moss demonstrated the new Mercedes 300SL for the first time in Britain. All in all a lovely end to a most enjoyable year.

Before we finally leave 1954 I should point out that I ended fourth overall in the RAC British Hill Climb Championship. Compared with today's two or three dozen rounds we only had six championship events, with the best four scores to count, but I was already being marked as one of the 'men of the hills'. I was 19 points behind Ken Wharton with Les Leston and Michael Christie ahead of me and all three had managed to get in a full season of racing as well. However, I was ahead of the Hon Edward Greenall and Bill Sleeman. Pretty good when you consider that this was only my third year in any form of motorsport.

1955 started with more trials, some of them in rather snowy conditions like the Kitching Trial where, according to *Autosport*, I did 'apparently impossible things' with my supercharged Dellow. The varying conditions of trials driving do, of course, teach marvellous car control and I think this greatly helped in my hill climbing and racing.

Easter marked the start of my racing season, this time at Goodwood. It was a very prestigious event with the likes of Stirling Moss, Edward Greenall, Ron Flockhart, Jack Brabham, Roy Salvadori, Ken Tyrrell and Mike Hawthorn among the entry. Salvadori had a good day with three wins but I didn't fare so well and in the Earl of March Trophy race I didn't even appear in the first six in my Formula Three Cooper. I still had an awful lot to learn about racing and the next opportunity was only a few weeks later at Silverstone in the 500cc race, but I was still learning my trade.

After the national championship event at Prescott, *Autosport* published a picture of hill climb personalities chatting with comedian Norman Wisdom in the paddock. Norman was very keen on motorsport and lived very near to the Rivers-Fletchers at that time. I remember him sitting in my car at one of the Westbrook Hay meetings with his cap on back to front – I think he (or maybe Phillipe Etancelin) must have started this trend, which seems popular with some of the baseball-cap wearing fraternity these days. Back at Prescott, I came second in class (and took third best time of day) in the 1100cc Cooper to Rivers-Fletcher who, according to *Autosport* '… realised a long-standing ambition by beating both Michael Christie and Tony Marsh …'

Next came Westbrook Hay on 21 May where I took BTD, as I had done the previous year. 'This year the Cooper was running unblown,' said *Autosport*, 'and it is interesting to note that his time was only half a second slower.'

Back again to racing, this time at Snetterton, where I had a tussle with Don Iszatt in his Cooper. He eventually went on to win the race but unfortunately I didn't finish. I did manage fastest lap, but that may have been the race when my engine gave up the ghost from being pressed too hard. This was the weekend when I did three different race meetings with three different engines. After the Brands Hatch Formula Libre race, *Autosport* reported that 'Tony Marsh in the 1100 Cooper Twin made a very impressive showing and thoroughly deserved his eventual fourth place among much weightier machines, after working up through the field from the back row of the grid.' The third meeting that weekend was Crystal Palace where I had another tussle with that man Iszatt and this time he shunted me off!

At Gosport Speed Trials on the Flight Test Road at Brockhurst, I took BTD in 13.74sec. None of the usual hill climb names were there but to me it was another event to add to the list. I still couldn't get enough motorsport and driving from the West Midlands to Gosport for an event seemed the thing to do. Venues for speed trials or sprints were, of course, much easier to find than venues for hill climbs. Really, any bit of straightish, private road would do as long as you could get permission from the owners.

June saw the national hill climb round at Shelsley Walsh where I managed BTD in the wet. I didn't like driving in those conditions, but I didn't dislike it as much as some other people. Being a trials driver I usually made pretty reasonable starts in the wet, much the same as Roy Lane in later years – and he was another trials driver. Said *Autosport*: '…onlookers were treated to a demonstration of how to use a lot of brake horses sensibly in the wet'.

I took another BTD at Prescott with 44.42 in the Mk 8 Cooper and Tommy Sopwith (of aeroplane manufacturing fame), who was a pretty good driver, set a new sports car record in his 1100 Cooper-Climax, but none of us could get near Ken Wharton's 43.70 hill record.

In early July we were off to Scotland again for a visit to Rest-and-be-Thankful. It was here that Bertie Bradnack had asked me to have a drive in his supercharged Cooper. He couldn't go there himself, but the car was entered and he knew I would be able to take it as my transporter took two vehicles. Bertie was a Midlands industrialist whose Cooper was similar to mine. It had twin rear wheels, which was most unusual for a small, modern car. This was obviously to provide more grip, but why he wanted more grip when he weighed about 18 stone I'm not sure. I had to be very careful with my gear changing too. On my car the changes were one forward and three back whereas his was one back and three forward. I had to think about that, so much so that I was becoming flummoxed with my own car, so intent was I on getting it right in his.

At Rest-and-be-Thankful the previous year Michael Christie had managed to achieve the three best times of the day – a remarkable feat. This year I managed the two best, with 56.12 in Bertie's car and 56.90 in mine, leaving Michael to take third BTD with 57.01. It was unfortunate that Ken Wharton, still recovering from burns following his accident in the Vanwall at the May Silverstone, couldn't be there. I'm sure we would have had a battle royal. In the week following Rest-and-be-Thankful, as well as a cover photo of my own Cooper leaving the line at The Rest there was an advert in *Autosport* for Bertie's 'championship round-winning twin-wheeled Cooper-JAP'.

Now came the highlight of my motorsport career to date – the 10th RAC British Grand Prix at Aintree on 16 July. I was entered in the Formula 3 event, one of the supporting races for the Grand Prix itself, but the excitement of competing at the same meeting as the legendary Juan Manuel Fangio in his Mercedes W196 cannot be adequately described.

I make no apology for listing the lineup for the first British Grand Prix to be held at Aintree, on the circuit that interwove with the famous Grand National course. Leading the German challenge, in four straight-eight Mercedes W196 cars were Fangio, Stirling Moss, Karl Kling and Piero Taruffi. Italian opposition came from the 4-cylinder Ferrari 625s driven by Mike Hawthorn, Eugenio Castellotti and Maurice Trintignant, with a mixture of works and privately entered 6-cylinder Maserati 250Fs in the hands of Jean Behra, Luigi Musso, Roberto Mières, Andre Simon, Roy Salvadori, Horace Gould, Peter Collins and Lance Macklin. Robert Manzon, Mike Sparken and Nano da Silva Ramos were in 6-cylinder French Gordinis, while Ken McAlpine's Connaught team consisted of Jack Fairman, McAlpine himself, Leslie Marr and Tony Rolt. Tony Vandervell's Vanwall chassis, designed by Owen Maddock at Cooper Cars, were in the hands of Ken Wharton, now recovered from his Silverstone accident, and Harry Schell. Jack Brabham drove the 'Bobtail' Cooper-Bristol.

My own race fielded a number of well known F3 drivers amongst its 34 entries including, Ken Tyrrell, Les Leston, Jim Russell, Cliff Allison, Ivor Bueb, Stuart Lewis-Evans and David Boshier-Jones. All these were in Coopers, other makes such as Revis, Staride and Martin having a much smaller representation. The other three supporting races were all for sports cars and unlike today, several Grand Prix drivers were taking part in these too. Peter Collins and Roy Salvadori were driving DB3S Aston Martins, Mike Hawthorn drove a Jaguar D-Type and Ken McAlpine a Connaught alongside George Abecassis' HWM, Archie Scott-Brown's Lister-Bristol, Ivor Bueb and Tommy Sopwith in Coopers, Les Leston's Connaught and Colin Chapman in his Mk9 Lotus.

The Grand Prix was, of course, the main attraction and to the delight of everyone it was narrowly won by Stirling Moss from team-mate Fangio in a slightly controversial finish. *Autosport*'s Editor Gregor Grant reported: 'It has been said – and reiterated by Moss himself – that Juan Manuel Fangio could have won, but preferred to give his young team-mate the chance to score his first major GP success. This may well be true, but in my opinion Stirling Moss *had* to drive all he knew to secure his victory. The slightest falling off would have seen the Champion of the World in front.'

Of the twenty-five starters, only eleven finished the 90 lap, 270 mile race. Apart from Moss, the other British finishers were Mike Hawthorn, Lance Macklin and Ken Wharton, who managed 72 laps. Obviously Ken's strength of character had overcome his injuries.

My race of just 17 laps was won by Jim Russell and while I didn't finish too well up in my faithful Cooper I had a good battle with Edward Greenall. Mind you, the Cooper had lost its V-twin and acquired a single cylinder engine for the day. I enjoyed the race, even if I did feel a bit out of place in such exalted company. It was a particularly interesting experience as, after being so long in hill climbing, this level of circuit racing was something I'd only read about and it was good to mix with the professionals. You could also get around the paddock too and see all the top Grand Prix cars, which you can't today. Mercedes Benz had an impressive, professional set up even in those early days. They had some beautiful transporters including the famous elongated 300SL converted to a flat-bed pickup to carry a single seater. The Liverpool Police got a bit miffed when the Italian mechanics drove the racers to the circuit on the road, but as the cars didn't carry any numbers, the Police couldn't take any down!

I was quite busy that day because I was also driving a Connaught sports car owned by Peter Bell. Peter was quite a well known entrant and provided cars for both Ken Wharton and Michael Christie. The car had a pre-selector gear box with a push-pull gearshift on the floor, and you changed gear by pressing the clutch. You then select the next gear, but nothing happens until you jab the clutch. I also drove Peter's ERA, which had a similar arrangement but with a bit of a dodge. You selected first on the startline and held it there, not quite on the clutch but almost. With your foot coming back part way on the clutch you can select second gear, so you complete your getaway in first gear with second gear already selected, just waiting for the jab on the clutch to engage it. You would already be in second gear, fighting the thing like mad, and you didn't have to take your hands off the wheel. It was quite handy on occasions.

The Grand Prix was also the event where John Cooper sent people over to me for welding repairs. I often took welding equipment to races in those days and at Aintree I had to weld up at least one oil tank. The tanks used to sit on rubber blocks held in place by a rubber band and the vibration used to crack them – as it did chassis tubes around wishbone pickups. The oil tanks were aluminium and while a number of people could weld or braze steel, aluminium was a different matter altogether.

I don't think I ever thought that, for myself, this level of racing would become the norm. To me it was merely the next event and it just happened to be the British Grand Prix meeting. You certainly wouldn't be able to race at that level today with such limited experience.

After the excitement of Aintree it was back to hill climbing, this time in the Channel Islands at Bouley Bay. Sadly, this was the event at which Bill Sleeman died when he crashed his supercharged Cooper Twin before Les Platons Corner. Ken Wharton took BTD, in a time of 53 seconds, for an incredible sixth year running. I was second in class to Ken and third in class with the Dellow, which I still took to events whenever I could as my main object in life at the time was to pack in as much motorsport as possible. Local man Frank Le Gallais came third in his Jaguar-engined LGS and Michael Christie tied for fourth with Ken in the ERA. I felt rather sorry for Michael. He had always been the runner-up to Ken and now he was becoming the runner-up to me. He had his moments of glory, but his career was rather like Stirling Moss and the World Championship. When Fangio retired, Stirling must have thought it was his turn. But as it turned out, it wasn't. He was certainly a good enough driver but, to mix a metaphor, he was riding the wrong horse. He had a lot of mechanical troubles through asking more of the car than it had to give. One of Moss's problems was that he was driving for a private owner, Rob Walker, and written into their contracts of both Cooper and Lotus works drivers was that Moss wouldn't be sold a current car. So he'd always got out of date machinery and, I felt, he didn't seem to have the confidence in himself to blow the opposition away. I don't think that it helped when Rob and his mechanic, Alf Francis, decided they would run a specially made 5-speed Colotti gearbox. Coopers were still using 4-speed boxes and while the new box should theoretically have given Moss an advantage, it gave him a lot of trouble instead. Of course it was only a matter of time before Coopers built their own 5-speed box.

The Bouley Bay result gave me the lead in the RAC Hill Climb Championship, with 19 points over Ken's 14, although he wasn't able to do all the championship events because of his racing commitments. In fact he'd flown over to Bouley from France, where he was racing that weekend.

Then we were off to Brands Hatch for the Rochester Cup. This was a Formula Libre race which was decided on aggregate after two 15 lap races. I enjoyed this sort of race as you had two chances to get a decent start and put up a good showing. In the first part I finished fifth just behind Roy Salvadori in his 250F Maserati, which was good going and in the second I enjoyed a good ding-dong with Cliff Davis. I just pipped him for fourth place in my old Cooper, which gave me an aggregate finish of fifth overall. I quite enjoyed Brands Hatch, but always had to take a deep breath coming up to Paddock Hill Bend. Sitting low down in the Cooper-JAP, you couldn't see over the top of this steep, downhill right-hander and I used to find that particularly daunting, especially in the early days.

Back into hill climb mode, it was off to Great Auclum where my first run broke the hill record and put me in the mood to do even better on the second. This was not to be as I sheared a gearbox mainshaft on the starting line, travelling all of about six feet. I still took BTD, being lucky that no-one else managed to better my first run. I also took a class win in Henry Taylor's Cooper 500. Henry and I swapped cars on a number of occasions, so we could both get an extra go at an event. Henry sprang to prominence circuit racing a 500 in which he did very well at a very wet Silverstone. He enjoyed a flourishing career in International racing in sports cars, and in single seaters from Formula Junior to Grand Prix racing, later becoming Ford's Competition Manager. He eventually retired to Monaco and still sells boats there today.

Next it was Goodwood for the Nine Hours race on 20 August. This was by far the longest race I'd ever taken part in, starting at 3 pm and finishing at midnight. I was co-driving with Bertie Bradnack alongside a typically large field that included Aston Martins, D-Type Jaguars and Ferraris. It would be a great experience for me as a 24 year-old.

Bertie had sold his championship round-winning Cooper Twin with the twin rear wheels and bought himself a Cooper-Jaguar, a car far more in keeping with the size of its driver. It had very low cockpit sides, so you had to be careful that you didn't fall out. When I accepted his invitation to drive with him at Goodwood I didn't realise that this was going to be his swansong, his big ambition being to join the British Racing Drivers' Club. Then as now, you had to qualify to be able to join BRDC and one of the ways to do this was to finish in an international race of a certain length, and the Goodwood Nine Hours qualified. So somehow, we had to finish.

We practised both in the daylight and at night, which proved quite difficult at Goodwood as there were no real track boundaries to shine your headlights on. There were markers round the track at the apex of each bend, but they seemed little more than sticks with a little reflective flag and most were inevitably knocked over as the race wore on. In fact my fastest lap was actually at night. A car came storming past me and I thought 'This chap knows where he's going, I'd better follow him'. I found out later that it was Mike Hawthorn in a Ferrari.

After practice Bertie said 'You're an agile young chap, you'd better do the Le Mans start''. Well I didn't mind having a go, although it was always a bit of a free-for-all and in fact the number plate light got knocked off somewhere during the start. Another slight problem was the big difference in size between the two drivers, so I had an aluminium frame seat made that fitted inside Bertie's own seat.

The nine hours of racing got under way and I eventually came in to hand over to Bertie. But it wasn't long before he was back in the pits complaining that 'the brakes are no good at all!' The mechanics started to rip out all the panel work round the gearbox to discover that a shaft had broken on the mechanical brake servo. 'Let me have a toot round and see how bad it is,' I said. 'I'll see if I can manage without the servo.' I thought maybe we could alter our style of driving a bit and get by through using the gears more. I found that in fact I could maintain quite a respectable speed but the point was that we had to finish, so I circulated for a while and brought the car back in for Bertie. He sent me off for a rest and took the car out again but before long he was back in saying the handling had gone and he didn't know why. So out I went again. He was quite right, the car seemed to have a life of its own when it came to corners. But I carried on and heard later that Bertie's consumption of cheroots rocketed during that last hour and a half. He was so nearly in the BRDC, but not quite.

I eventually finished the race and we all went off to bed, parking the Cooper Jag next to my transporter which I had brought as living accommodation. The next morning we had a look at the car and found that one rear wheel bearing was turning in the magnesium upright casting. It would have been practically steering itself, which would certainly have accounted for the handling difficulties.

After all that we ended up in eighteenth place out of 20 finishers. With 35 starters it might look as if we didn't do too well, but we did manage to finish, and Bertie was able to join the BRDC after all. This meant that I, too, had qualified to join and by the same token so had my young mechanic, who was eligible to join the mechanics section. It was also rather nice for me, around 50 years later, to see the car again at one of the Goodwood Revival meetings.

At that particular Goodwood Nine Hours, Aston Martin had a big fire in the pits on one of their refuelling stops. That caused a bit of consternation! They also had great difficulty in timing their pit stops because they ran three cars. As nine hours breaks down into three hour stints, it was a question of servicing all three cars at about the three hour mark. Goodwood, although it was smooth, has a very abrasive surface and the Aston tyres would just about last the three hours, so the chap who came in last would have been driving on canvas.

I've always said that what ever else Italians can do, at least they're very good at making ice cream. Well, we certainly had quite a bit of entertainment from the Ferrari mechanics at Goodwood. They brought a lorry with a scaffolding framework to carry one car up and one down and this also towed a big four-wheel trailer. Not like your conventional four-wheel trailer, but with two wheels at the front and two at the back. There may have been an upper deck as well; at any rate the cars were all out in the open. The people at Goodwood had very thoughtfully built an unloading ramp, which had a double purpose. As well as being able to put a car up on horizontal ramps to inspect it, you could also back a lorry up and unload your car on it. The only problem was that the 'ice cream makers' hadn't come prepared and they'd no way of getting the cars off the top deck of their lorry. They had to back up to this ramp, then with several hefty Italians supporting planks on their shoulders, another mechanic would carefully drive the car off the top deck so that the hefty men could lower it down.

This was also the meeting where Jim Russell and Ivor Bueb were driving one of the first 1500cc Cooper cars. It had a works Climax engine and those early Coopers used to have trouble getting all the air out of the cooling system. Ivor was miserably working away with the car on stands when a reporter came up looking for a story. 'Mr Bueb, we notice there's a case of Ribena on the edge of your pit. Would you like to tell us about it?' 'It's quite simple,' said Ivor, 'I'm having a few overheating problems and we put it in the radiator to aid the cooling.' Now Ivor used to appear regularly in an advert for Ribena in *Autosport*, which was why he had a case with him. But at that time the staff in Chichester hospital used to watch Goodwood on the television for possible customers due in following an accident. However on this occasion they were not amused, as at the time they couldn't get Ribena for their patients and they were not at all pleased to hear that Ivor was pouring it into his radiator.

The third memorable event for me in 1955, the Midland Automobile Club's Golden Jubilee International Hill Climb on 12

August to celebrate 50 years of hill climbing at Shelsley Walsh.

There was a motorcycle v car challenge at this half-centenary event which featured a team each of four motorbikes and four cars, with Ken Wharton, Michael Christie, Dick Henderson and myself in the car team. Sadly, I can't remember who won but we certainly all enjoyed ourselves. Now until quite recently, Shelsley also used to run a team competition for cars. On one occasion Ken entered the Wharton Team comprising Messrs Wharton, Wharton and Wharton in three different cars, which you could do in those days. Leslie Wilson, the Shelsley secretary, got very uptight about this but there was nothing in the rules to say Ken couldn't do it. By the next meeting they'd changed the rules…

That 50th anniversary event was also memorable for me because it was the first time at Shelsley that I managed to beat Ken. I beat his ERA R4D, by seven tenths, to take BTD in 36.08 in my Cooper-JAP. The engine was supercharged for the first run, but after that I took the blower off as I felt it was holding us back.

Pathe News turned up to record the event for posterity and later we all trooped down to the local picture house to watch it on the big screen. I still have the little 16mm piece of film that they very kindly sent me.

However I wasn't the only Marsh at the meeting. Father's brother, Uncle Ron (A R Marsh), took his 300 SL Mercedes-Benz up the hill. His time was a careful 46.24 with *Autosport* reporting: 'But who wouldn't be careful of a 300 SL on Shelsley?' This was the uncle who had gone to Le Mans one year with a Singer co-driven by my godfather. I know Uncle Ron kindly lent me his Mercedes one weekend and later, when he decided to sell it, he asked if I was interested. I tried it out and I could have had it for about £1,500, but decided that it really wasn't a very practical proposition to drive it as an everyday farmer's car.

The next event, at Silverstone, saw the first appearance of my Bobtail Cooper sports car. While I really enjoyed driving the V-twin it was better at relatively short races, say 20 or 25 miles. After that it got a bit tired, but the Bobtail was something different again. It had a four cylinder Coventry Climax FWA, based on the company's fire pump engine, and the Coopers, Charles and John, thought it would be a very good car for me to use both for circuit racing and on the hills. In fact the handling was very similar to the Cooper Twin. At hill climbs I'd practise first in the sports car and then in the single seater and as often as not I'd have the fastest racing car and the fastest sports car awards.

Before the Silverstone meeting I'd been rushing up and down to the Cooper works in Surbiton helping to stick the car together. In those very early days my everyday transport was a modified Ford Thames van that had close ratio gears and a re-worked head and exhaust manifold. Going downhill into Henley I always knew when I was going quickly, because the wing mirrors would fold back. On one return trip I was stopped by a chap in a Jaguar who enquired what I'd got under the bonnet, because he'd had some difficulty in keeping up. It was only a Ford 100E sidevalve – just that it was not quite standard.

Back at Prescott and another international event, driving the Bobtail I managed second in class to Peter Hughes' Tojeiro in the wet even though I was still learning how to drive the car on the hills. With an open wheeled car, you can place it very precisely on the track whereas the Bobtail was all bodywork. Or at least that's how it felt. When you've got bodywork hanging out over the wheels you've got to re-think how you drive the corners. I got nowhere with the Cooper Twin and this left me on equal points with Ken Wharton in the hill climb championship. This gave the RAC something to think about, as it was the last championship event of the year. In the end *Autosport* announced that: 'The RAC has awarded the 1955 Hill Climb Championship to A E (Tony) Marsh, 24 year-old driver from Stourbridge, Worcs. After the final event, the Championship hill climb at Prescott on Sunday, Marsh and the current holder, Ken Wharton, were tying with 29 points each, and the rules required that the RAC should designate the winner on the basis of meritorious performance. In making his points for the Championship, Marsh used only one type of car, while Wharton used a choice of machines.'

So that was that, the championship was mine and I've often been asked if I thought that the decision was right. I can only say that had it been another driver tying with Ken in the same circumstances, I think the driver using just one type of car should have the win.

I went to the rather imposing RAC Club in Pall Mall for the presentation and very nearly didn't get past the doorman because I wasn't wearing a tie. Fortunately after I'd told them, several times, why I was there they did eventually let me in.

Now it was time to put the racing cars away and start the trials season once more. The TV cameras came to a specially organised event at Wendover Woods in Buckinghamshire where on one test I disappeared in a cloud of smoke with a blown head gasket. This wasn't an uncommon occurrence and I replaced it in about 12 minutes, which caused one of the locals to be very disgruntled with his local garage who'd taken more like a couple of weeks! Sadly the Midlands team of Bill Boddenham, Frank Lewis and myself couldn't manage to beat teams from the South or the North, but we enjoyed trying and seeing ourselves on television afterwards. Raymond Baxter, who would later present Tomorrow's World TV programme, was the BBC's chief motorsport commentator at the time and presided over the event at Wendover. He was a keen motoring man, an international rally driver as well as a triallist and hillclimber, the latter often with Reg Phillips.

Next we were off to North Wales and the final sprint of 1955 at Rhydymwyn. I took the Cooper Twin and the Bobtail and did rather well in both. I set BTD with the Twin in 1m15s, breaking Austen May's record by 2.2sec, and broke the Peter Hughes' Tojeiro sports car record by 1.4sec in the Bobtail.

Rhydymwyn was a delightful little place, a little bit like Curborough. You could do two laps there too and they ran pursuit races, setting off the cars at intervals which gave you the incentive to try and catch the car in front. The Bobtail was just starting to get run in nicely, whereas it had been very stiff at Prescott on its first hill climb. Rhydymwyn was one of my very happy hunting grounds.

Back to trialling, where I won the Shenstone and District MC's Chase Trophy Trial in the Dellow after a consistent drive, but now I felt that the car was starting to become a bit outclassed by the cars such as the new lightweight Cannons. The win preceded rather a bad time in my trialling when I had a succession of crown wheel and pinion breakages. It was only after the third that I really gave it some thought. One breakage was acceptable, fair wear and tear for trials, but three in a row was abnormal. The cause proved to be a distorted axle casing, which meant the gears weren't meshing properly.

The first one broke on the John Bull Trial, which started near my old school at Uppingham. The second breakage came at the London MC's Gloucester Trial where I was the only driver eligible for a Gloucester Goblet, awarded if you'd been first in class at three successive events at the venue. I never did get one. I also took part in the Shropshire Trial and Rally, which Hagley organised in the December that year. Ken Wharton won the rally and the Marsh Trophy, in an Austin Westminster. I took a first class award in the trial, having worked the night before replacing the crown wheel and pinion after the Gloucester Trial. It didn't take that long if you were geared up to do it. The Shropshire Trial took place on some of father's land. A working party used to come beforehand to cut down the undergrowth on some of the hills and make sure the tracks on the old gravel pit were suitable, but I was never invited to help so I didn't really have any advantage.

But by winning the Chase Trophy, I qualified to take part in the 1955 RAC Trials Championship, which was the last year a Dellow took part. Still basically a road car, the Dellow was getting a bit big and outdated for that sort of thing, which became my main reason for building the TMS – the Tony Marsh Special.

The final event of the year was another Boxing Day Brands Hatch meeting, an event which was proving popular with drivers and which had a fair sprinkling of 'names' in the entry list. Ken Tyrrell was there in a 500cc Cooper and Archie Scott-Brown in Tony Brooks' 2.5-litre Syracuse GP winning Connaught. In the wet Lex Trophy race for 1200cc sports cars, Ivor Bueb was now driving a works Cooper Bobtail and I came third behind him in my own version, Colin Chapman in his Mk9 Lotus-Climax took the win. The meeting's traditional festive celebrations were completed by well known sports car driver Duncan Hamilton, who arrived by helicopter dressed as Father Christmas.

Although it doesn't appear in the results I would probably have taken the Cooper Twin along as well, as by this time I had a transporter with a platform which could carry two cars with ease, one upstairs and one down. The weather at Brands that day could have been drier but it didn't dampen our spirits for racing, although

I did wonder whether some people had sampled the spirits of the day before a bit too liberally! But once again, it was a good end to a memorable year of motorsport 'firsts' for me.

For 1956 I'd built my own trials special, the TMS. While the Dellows had been built from high quality, large diameter tubing bought as a job lot from Ackles and Pollock, the TMS was a spaceframe car built from small diameter tubes. I used all the familiar Ford bits and pieces such as engine, gearbox and axles, but in a very much lighter and compact car with which I competed in a great many trials.

The Leicester Car Club's sporting trial for the Silver Starting Handle was our first event. I dropped a lot of marks early on and never quite made them up, but it was a good starting point for the TMS.

Then it was straight back into racing with the British Empire Trophy meeting at Oulton Park in April. All the names of the day were there for the main race; Colin Chapman and Mike Hawthorn with the latest Lotus sports car, the Eleven, a host of Cooper Bobtails in the hands of Roy Salvadori, Stirling Moss, Jim Russell and Henry Taylor. Tony Brooks was also there in a Connaught. In amongst that lot in heat one, I finished eleventh in my own Cooper Bobtail. Reg Parnell won heat two, for the bigger machines, in his Aston Martin DB3S ahead of Archie Scott-Brown's Lister-Maserati. Swiss motorcycle champion Benoist Musy, who was very quick in a car too, set a new Oulton Park sports car record lap in his Maserati 300S on the way to winning heat three. His 1m 56s lap was an average speed of 85.68 mph.

With such illustrious names from international circuit racing it wasn't surprising that I didn't make the final, which was won by Moss from Chapman and Salvadori. But I was keen to get in as much practice with the Bobtail as possible and drove in a sports car race at Goodwood. I finished just behind Mike MacDowel's works car (Mike would later twice win the British Hill Climb Championship in the early 70s). Colin Chapman won the race from Mike Hawthorn, Jack Brabham and Cliff Allison, with Mike MacDowel fifth and myself sixth - all very respectable company.

Next came a 2-litre sports car race at Aintree amid more

illustrious names where Chapman was the star of the show once again. Despite starting from the back of the grid after taking over Allison's Lotus, Colin drove superbly to win the race.

At Prescott's Twelfth International hill climb meeting, despite my best efforts Michael Christie took BTD and a new hill record with his 1100 Cooper-JAP in 43.65. I climbed a tenth slower in my own Cooper-JAP and took second in the 1500 sports cars class behind Tommy Sopwith but ahead of Mike MacDowel, all three of us in Bobtails.

The Daily Express International Trophy meeting at Silverstone was next on the calendar. I'd originally entered the 1500cc class in the sports car race but was moved into the 1100s, where I managed third place behind Peter Gammon and MacDowel which left me eleventh overall. There was a team award, and the three of us won it for the Cooper team, so it was a good day's motorsport all round.

Goodwood's Whit-Monday meeting and I finished sixth in the 1500 sports car race. It was a 26 lap affair and ideally suited to the Climax engined Bobtail. Behind a finishing lineup of Chapman, Hawthorn, Brabham, Allison and MacDowel, I really wouldn't have expected to come any higher. But for me, it was all about getting out there and having fun. I just love competing in motorsport, which is why I still compete today.

Everything just seemed to go right on our next outing, to Prescott, as I managed to get the Bobtail to the top in 46.49, a new sports car record. I also took Michael Christie's outright hill record in 43.32 with the single seater. This was another milestone for me – the first time anyone had held the outright and sports car records at the same time.

At a particularly soggy Shelsley I led the 1500 sports car class with a 43.59 in the Bobtail and was half a second quicker in the Cooper-JAP, but it was Wharton's ERA and Christie's Cooper-JAP that set the best two times on the day.

Aintree, the following weekend, was rather disappointing with only nine cars in the main Formula One race, the Aintree 100. Tony Brooks and the 4-cylinder BRM turned up very late, straight from testing at Silverstone, and only stayed a very short while before stretching a valve. Horace Gould won the somewhat dull F1 race in his privately entered Maserati 250F, while I finished fourth in the 1100cc sportscar race behind MacDowel's Cooper and the Lotuses of Keith Hall and Cliff Allison.

After another BTD at a Shelsley club event at the end of June came the long drive back up to Scotland's Rest-and-be-Thankful hill climb at Glen Croe. Happily, my record breaking streak stayed with me and I took half a second off Wharton's 4 year-old hill record. Ken was there with both the Cooper and R4D, but he broke the gearbox on the Cooper and had to settle for third BTD in the ERA behind Michael Christie. It was becoming clear that with his time being divided between hill climbing and circuit racing, hill climbing was beginning to take a rather poor second place. He was driving for both Vanwall and Ferrari at that time, which was quite serious stuff.

The next meeting was a bit of a landmark for motor racing with the first ever Formula 2 race. Theoretically at least, because the formula didn't officially come into being until 1957 and we were allowed to compete in our old, non F2, cars. It took place at the British Grand Prix meeting at Silverstone where Fangio won the main race in a Lancia-Ferrari. Significantly, it would be his only GP win in this country. However our Formula 2 race was, in a way, a bit of a farce as there was only one proper Formula 2 car in it. The rest of us were in Climax engined Cooper or Lotus sports cars. As it wasn't a sports car race, we took out things like headlights, dynamos and passenger seats. Roy Salvadori was driving the sole Formula 2 car, the newly finished Cooper with a single cam FWB Climax engine. It was a good debut for the car as he won the race. I qualified in tenth position on the third row of the 4-3-4 grid, alongside Jack Brabham and Graham Hill, and finished tenth, funnily enough just behind the same two men.

Formula 2 racing looked to be very much the thing to be in. As a very successful private owner of both a single seater Cooper and a Bobtail, in which I was usually just behind the works drivers, I was always in the back of the minds of John and Charles Cooper. John had already said to me 'We're bringing out this Formula 2 car, you ought to have one.' They were being designed to use an enlarged version of the Climax FWA fire pump based engine that I ran in my own car. In fact the following year I would take charge of the first privately owned Formula 2 Cooper – but more of that later.

The first national status championship event to be held at Westbrook Hay was another good event for me, with BTD and another hill record in the Cooper, I also broke the outright sports car record by eight seconds. Weather conditions were ideal and six out of eight class records were broken that day. But the course wasn't very long, really it was just one great big 'S' bend. It became a British Championship venue in 1959, but only for four years.

The next event was also a hill climb, when we tooted over to Jersey and the Bouley Bay event. We went by Silver City Airlines Bristol Freighter and because I'd taken both cars, my young mechanic drove the Bobtail and towed me, in the Cooper, across the island to Bouley. It became a bit embarrassing at one point, when we had to make a difficult start over an uphill crossroads. This was a bit severe on the sports car clutch, and much to my horror I spotted a car coming down the main road before I'd vacated the junction. I don't know whether the locals had been warned about people like us, but this one managed to avoid hitting us.

The event produced another record and BTD for Ken Wharton, this time driving his Cooper-JAP with myself and Michael Christie tied in the runner-up position. This result put Ken ahead of us both in the championship.

Still with hill climbing and a little bit more off the Great Auclum outright hill record when I took the 1100 Cooper-JAP up in 20.60. This was around a second faster than my class win in the 1300 sports car class with the Bobtail, which did sterling work with Henry Taylor sharing the car and finishing second in class. It was a reciprocal arrangement and I took a third in the 500cc Racing class in Henry's Cooper-Norton, when he finished second to Austen May's record-breaking Cooper-JAP. It was great fun in those days; you could enter more than one car, even if it was a little busy at times. It was always good to win at Great Auclum as they had a very nice gold plated trophy for BTD.

A couple of days later, on August Bank Holiday Monday, it was back to racing at Mallory Park. When Len Bramley's leading Lotus went off the track I inherited the lead in the 1200cc sports car race, which I kept to the end. The Formula Libre race was held in heavy rain and no less than twelve competitors retired, leaving Brian Naylor (who only the previous weekend had won the Leinster Trophy in Ireland with his Maserati powered Lotus 11) and myself to complete the one/two. Then I finished third in the 1500cc sports car race, and with the big sports car race opened up to the smaller cars due to a lack of entries, I finished third in that too. I always entered the obvious class for my car, then looked at all the other races to see if there was something else I could do as well.

Next was the Nottingham SCC meeting at Silverstone and a very full day. First came a great ding-dong in the 1200 sports car race, which *Autosport*'s Gregor Grant described as: 'like the Brighton Road on a holiday Sunday'! At the flag, I'd managed to break away from the second of two groups of battling cars to finish fourth behind Alan Stacey's Lotus 11, Chris Summers' Cooper and Edward Greenall's Lotus. The Formula Libre race was closely fought too with Michael Head (father of Williams F1 Technical Director Patrick Head) in his Cooper-Jaguar almost dead-heating with Summers for first and second places with the C-Type Jaguar of Max Trimble and my Cooper Bobtail almost dead heating for the next two places. When all the excitement had died down I still had one more race to go, a ten lap 1500cc race. This time I managed to get in the lead and stay there, finishing ten seconds clear of Peter Ashdown's Mk9 Lotus.

Back in the Cooper Twin at Shelsley's International meeting I took BTD with 36.02. I took the Bobtail along too and collared the 1500 sports car class on 39.34. But then came the rain and poor old Henry Taylor, who was double driving the Bobtail with me again, could only manage 46.89. Now Henry was very good in the wet, which just shows how much the conditions affected the times. When we both took wet runs, Henry was only just over a second behind me.

After all this hill climbing and racing, we finally got the chance to drive in a straight line along Madeira Drive at the world famous Brighton Speed Trials in September. On a breezy day at the seaside, Ken Wharton broke his own record with 23.34sec over the kilometre course in R4D, the ex-Mays supercharged 2-litre ERA not much altered from when it was built in 1938, which shows what a remarkable vehicle it was for its time. I was driving Peter Bell's R11B ERA again and Rob Walker beat me into second place in his Grand Prix Connaught, by half a second.

Rob was a very wealthy man and ran cars for top grand Prix drivers such as Stirling Moss. I think he would have liked to have driven more himself but the family (Rob was part of the Johnny Walker whisky empire) weren't very keen for him to go circuit racing. He obviously persuaded them that driving in a straight line was a lot safer and he took full advantage of it, driving the works Formula 2 Cooper at Brighton as his own version wasn't quite ready. This was clearly to be a day of seconds for me. As well as second in class with the ERA (which was also 3rd BTD), I was runner-up in both the 1100 sports car class with the Bobtail. This was behind record breaker Peter Gammons' similar car. My other second coming with the Cooper Twin in the 1100 racing class, which was won by Rupert Instone's legendary Djinn.

The International meeting at Prescott was next on the agenda. Michael Christie and myself were the only two drivers to get into the 44sec, leaving my June record (43.32) totally unscathed. It was a good day as I took a class win in the Bobtail and a class second and second BTD, both behind Michael, with the single seater. It was a significant day for me too, as the overall result gave me my second British Hill Climb Championship title. I also double drove Henry Taylor's 500cc Cooper-Norton but didn't get the best out of it, only managing fifth in class. Incidentally, a driver who would go on to make quite a name for himself on the International circuit racing scene was competing at this meeting in a Lotus 11. His name was Graham Hill.

More second places followed firstly at Mallory Park, behind Edward Greenall's Lotus 11 and then at the Peterborough MC's Silverstone meeting where I followed Chris Summers home in one race and then Brian Naylor in another. The first race was quite exciting when I managed to climb from fifth to second place, all on the last lap. The second race was hotly contested too. Several of us were dicing for places until I managed to break away from Chris and just pip him on the line behind Brian's hybrid Lotus-Maserati.

But at Hagley's sprint meeting at Staverton aerodrome, near Cheltenham, Ken Wharton broke my old course record twice in R4D. The course, being a perimeter track with wide open spaces and longer distances, was ideally suited to Ken's ERA but at least I took a racing and sports car win, 29.32 in the Bobtail, which gave me the Best

Sports Car award to take home.

A trial or two took us up to the middle of November and another trip to the RAC Club's Pall Mall Headquarters for the championship presentation. About the same time I had the honour of being the subject (No.58) of *Autosport*'s Portrait Gallery. The magazine used to run a story on a different driver each week, with a picture by Patrick Benjafield. I was quite pleased to be asked and remember I had to look a bit smart even though I didn't put a tie on!

I mentioned earlier that I'd taken ownership of one of the first privately owned Formula 2 Coopers and that I had got into the habit of going down to Surbiton and building my own car on the premises. I used to do that because it saved having to take it to pieces and put it back together again as soon as I got it home. I remember once somebody being sent off in the Cooper van to pick up an engine. The trouble being that John Cooper had promised it to umpteen people and there was a bit of an embarrassing moment when one of them actually turned up. Somebody else was sent out to waylay the returning van and tell the driver to take it round the block until the customer had left the works. Then there was the time when another customer came in to look at his chassis being built and stamped his name on it with a centre punch, to make sure it didn't go to somebody else! It was useful building my own car alongside the Cooper mechanics and it worked both ways – sometimes they'd crib some of my detail while they were building the works cars.

I always used to get good service and quite a quick turn-round from Coopers. One reason was the good results I was getting with the cars, but another was my family connection with Marsh & Baxter. 'Don't forget to bring a ham with you,' Charlie Cooper would say when I rang to tell them I was coming over. As soon as I arrived he'd come to collect it, but I'd say 'I'm living off it while I'm here – you can have what's left when I go'. That always ensured a quick turn-round.

In January 1957 we heard the very sad news that Ken Wharton had been killed in New Zealand, while racing a Ferrari Monza sports car at Ardmore. Ken was a good friend and a great competitor. He had done so well in so many different disciplines of motorsport and was very much missed within the motor sporting fraternity.

Now this was around the time of the Suez crisis with its subsequent fuel rationing and in the middle of the trials season to boot. The London Motor Club decided to move their Gloucester Trial to Buckinghamshire this year due to the petrol shortages.

Trials were followed by a class win at a Brands Hatch sprint in the Bobtail and a new course record at Rhydymwyn. Then we had the British Empire Trophy meeting at Oulton Park in April. There were a number of well known names competing including my old friend Henry Taylor driving a D-Type Jaguar for the Murkett brothers. The Murkett brothers were Jaguar agents in Cambridge and Henry lived near to them.

Unfortunately I missed the Easter Goodwood meeting as the Formula 2 Cooper wasn't quite ready, which was annoying for me as I liked to be out competing at every possible opportunity. The car was also absent from the May Prescott meeting, a round of the British Championship, but I was really on song in the Cooper-JAP and took a whole second off my previous hill record. Conditions were ideal and five class records fell that day, including my old 1100 sports car record which went to C M J Andrew's Climax engined Lotus 6. There was, however, a blight on the day when Lord Ebury's ex-Ecurie Ecosse C-type Jaguar struck the bank and overturned at the Esses. A great enthusiast of hill climbing and motor racing, Lord Ebury was sadly killed instantly in the first fatal accident at Prescott since the hill opened in 1938.

At the May Brands Hatch meeting my new Formula 2 Cooper, with its Climax FPF twin-cam engine, finally appeared. Despite *Autosport* reporter Maxwell Boyd, wondering if my car was 'perhaps too new', I managed fourth place in the first race and third in the second one, so I was quite pleased with the result, as I was with a win in the F2 race on the Silverstone Club circuit the following day. This 15 lap race had only two genuine Formula 2 cars in it, but it was nice to win at an average speed of 72.7 mph. These two meetings were among the first to be held after petrol rationing was lifted after the Suez crisis had ended.

Brands and Silverstone were the precursors to a handicap race at Oulton Park, where Brian Naylor and I had a terrific scrap but

Di handing me my goggles

Following Cliff Allison at Pau

With mechanic Mike Walton after winning at Zeltweg

1958: Di and I chatting to Mike Hawthorn in the TR2 at the Ken Wharton Memorial Trials

1957/58 Oulton Park in Bobtail Cooper following Peter Bell's Connaught driven by Tony Brooks

1958: German GP won by Tony Brooks. Note the racing overalls!

British Speed hill climb champion 1957. Standing by me (left to right) are the Manager of the Regent Petrol Depot, Stourport; Ron Lowe and Stan Peckham (Stan, Stan the Redex Man)

With Peter Boshier-Jones

Silverstone, July 1960 – in the Cooper Monaco

Silverstone, 1961 – in the Cooper Maserati

Lotus Elite at Le Mans overtaking a Birdcage Maserati at Dunlop Curve

Ex-works BRM, 2.5 litre engine

Brussels GP podium (left to right) Bruce McLaren; Jack Brabham (winner), me, Lucien Bianchi (on ground)

The Marsh BRM

The Marsh BRM had a problem at Rest and Be Thankful!

with neither of us featuring in the awards. Obviously we were out of favour with the handicappers that day.

Then came my first racing trip abroad, when I took the F2 Cooper to the Prix de Paris race at the combined banked and road circuit at Montlhéry, on 16 June. Unfortunately I got a puncture out in the countryside where someone had gone off previously and left a lot of debris on the track. I picked up something with a front tyre, which went straight into the centre of my rear tyre, leaving a hole I could put my thumb through. Some Frenchmen appeared from nowhere and were interested to see that the Cooper had a Citroen gearbox. What particularly fascinated them was that the road cars they knew had a three speed box whereas mine had been adapted by Coopers to take four gears. Considering I don't speak any French we got on remarkably well aided by my drawing diagrams on the dusty ground. A strange end to my first race on the continent.

Back home, I went to Mallory Park a couple of times. At the first meeting Paul Emery in his front-engined F1 Emeryson and I had tremendous battles in no less than three Formula Libre races. In two of them I ended up at the front when we crossed the line and in the other Paul took the honours. My Cooper was nimbler and had better braking but Paul's 2.5-litre Alta-engined Emeryson had more torque out of the corners. As an indication of how close we were, we both broke Bob Gerard's lap record at the identical speed of 85.86 mph.

At the second meeting a few weeks later I won two more races at Mallory. *Autosport* reporter Francis Penn said of the first one '(Marsh) was far too fast for the rest of the entry and giving a perfect exhibition of driving, won by exactly a minute'. And of the second race he said: 'Again this was all Marsh. Even the ERA, well driven as it undoubtedly was by Bill Moss, could make no impression on the flying Cooper, Marsh romping home by nine seconds.'

But then it was back to the hills and a trip to Rest-and-be-Thankful where I quite liked the course. A modern by-pass had been built and the event took place on the old road, which was very narrow, very cambered and very rough with a wall on one side and a cliff face on the other. A place full of character. This year, despite intermittent rain, I managed BTD in the 1100 JAP-engined Cooper. I'd also taken the 1475cc Climax engined car and took a class win ahead of Tommy Dryver's 6.5-litre aero-engined De Havilland ATN. Dryver wasn't Tommy's real surname but his wife wasn't happy about him competing so he used a pseudonym to throw her off the track. Michael Christie took second BTD, which reminds me I was a bit naughty to Michael at times. We'd all be lining up for our class and I'd go and sit on his wheel – no seat belts to confine you to your car in those days. Suddenly I'd apparently notice something that didn't look quite right, just to get poor old Michael wondering what was wrong with his car.

Back at Mallory again for the BRSCC's National meeting and a two heat race with the best aggregate score winning £100, quite a lot of money in 1957. I got ahead at the beginning of Heat 1 and managed to stay there, winning by 13 seconds. George Wicken, with whom I had many a good tussle around this time, maintained second place throughout although Les Leston, who was third for a while, had to concede the place to Bill Whitehouse. In Heat 2 Wicken got to the front and, although I stuck to his rear bumper all the way round, George stayed there. Mind you, with my 13 second lead from Heat 1 I was in quite a strong position and eventually bagged the £100 prize.

More racing abroad, and this time at Reims where, very sadly, Bill Whitehouse and Herbert Mackay 'Mac' Fraser lost their lives in separate incidents in the F2 race. The race was led turn and turn about by Roy Salvadori's Cooper, Maurice Trintignant's Ferrari and Jack Brabham's Cooper but on the 24th of 37 laps Jack Brabham succumbed to a dropped valve. This was a constant source of worry to Climax owners at that time and, on his last lap, Roy Salvadori stopped with the same problem. Ever mindful of results, Roy waited until Trintignant had crossed the line before pushing his own car over. But he didn't make the line until after Jean Lucas and myself had finished second and third, albeit a lap behind. Although third place was good, it wasn't as satisfactory as it might have been. Reims is a very fast circuit and very wide, so you don't get much sense of speed. All through the latter stages I was right on the tail of Lucas in Alan Brown's Cooper and swapping places with him. I would slipstream him and nip past on the long straight to Thillois Hairpin, then he'd pull out and pass as we went past the pits. When it came to the last lap I slip streamed him as usual, whereas I should have held back and slipstreamed him on the run to the finish. A lack of big race experience showing there, I think. Actually, I was really enjoying the battle and when an opportunity to overtake came I just couldn't resist it.

Following Reims we went abroad again, well at least to the Channel Islands and the national hill climb championship round at Bouley Bay, where I managed BTD in the Cooper JAP in 53.30 and third BTD in the F2 car. Local driver Frank Le Gallais did me a favour by beating Michael Christie, which increased my championship lead.

Another BTD came at the Inter-Club Team event at Prescott, although this event didn't count towards the championship. Then it was off to the continent again and the German Grand Prix at the Nurburgring to which I'd been invited as a result of my third place at Reims. I'd only intended to do one race abroad that year as getting entries was a problem, so having been invited to Germany I jumped at the chance.

Nurburgring was the first time I'd been in a combined F1 and F2 race and, while I wasn't surprised to be on the back row of the grid, it was quite satisfying not to have been the slowest qualifier. On the front row of the 4/3/4 grid they ran in those days was Fangio's 250F Maserati alongside Mike Hawthorn's Lancia Ferrari V8, Jean Behra's 250F and Hawthorn's great friend and Ferrari team mate Peter Collins. At the back of the 24-car grid were three of the nine F2 cars in the race: myself in the T43 Cooper, Australian Paul England in his T41 and Dick Gibson's T43.

The 1957 German Grand Prix was, of course, the scene of the epic battle between Fangio, Hawthorn and Collins. Fangio won after the race of his life when, after a prolonged pit stop for fuel and new rear tyres, he caught and passed the two Englishmen who had raced straight through. This caused enormous excitement in the final stages, but my own race was a little different.

When I went to Reims I had put in a 'longer' crown wheel and pinion to suit the fast circuit, but for the Nurburgring I'd put the standard one back in. In doing so I had noticed that two of the crownwheel bolts had quarter inch pegs on the end. I thought it was strange, but reassembled them without thinking too much about it. Until, during practice, the car ground to a halt and I freewheeled into the side of the road. One of these bolts had come out and furthermore, I'd lost all the oil in the gearbox. There were very few marshals at the Nurburgring and no communications system at all, so I hopped over the fence down to a little access road and thumbed a lift back to the pits from a passing car. We retrieved the car, found a hole in the gearbox casing made by the errant bolt and with the help of one of the support tradesmen welded it up, filed it flat and put the car back together again.

During the race itself I knew I was going to have to make a pit stop for fuel as the F2 cars simply didn't have the capacity for a Grand Prix length race. Shortly after this fuel stop the car started feeling most peculiar in the road-holding department. With no full harness seat belts to worry about I managed to wriggle myself up in the seat and saw a back wheel pounding up and down. I pulled into the pits and found a rear wishbone broken at the damper mounting, probably as a result of the Nurburgring bumps. Now I don't usually carry many spares but my mechanic, Mike Walton, noticing a number of retired Coopers in the dead car park, suggested we borrowed a wishbone. Various unemployed pit crews descended on Roy Salvadori's car and cannibalized a wishbone. In such a long race (22 laps and just over 300 miles) I knew I might still be in the running for fourth place in the Formula Two category. This had prize money attached to it, a bit of an incentive to get going again.

I rejoined the race, hanging on as Hawthorn, Collins and Fangio swept past, and was going through the bends down to the stone parapet of Adenau Bridge when the car suddenly understeered like mad. Perhaps the gearbox repairs hadn't been entirely satisfactory and the differential was going a bit stiff. I took it fairly steadily round the bends on the last lap as when I backed off after the finish line a front wheel started to wobble furiously. A steering arm had cracked, which explained the understeer as the wheel was having to make its own arrangements. But I got to the finish and did indeed take fourth place in the F2 category along with its associated prize money. My time for the race was 3 hours and 43 minutes during which I managed 17 laps. Fangio's 22 laps took just 3 hours 38 minutes...

Back to Britain, back to the hills and back to Shelsley where Staffordshire publican Dick Henderson made the 'best run of his life' according to *Autosport*'s Francis Penn. Dick took BTD in his twin rear-wheeled, supercharged Cooper-JAP, which is driven on the hills today by Roger Willoughby, with myself taking second and third overall in my normally aspirated version and the Climax engined F2 car respectively.

On our annual pilgrimage to Brighton, Eunice Griffin shared my Cooper F2. Eunice worked as a 'girl Friday' for David Porter, a Council member of the Bugatti Owners' Club, and driving my car at Brighton all came about because of George Wicken's daughter.

Mike Walton and I were having a weekend break at the family holiday home on Anglesey when we read, probably in the *News of the World*, that Miss Wicken was going to do all sorts of marvellous things at the Brighton Speed Trials. With the piece was a picture of this rather glamorous girl - all eyebrows and so on. 'We can't have this,' said Mike, 'we'd better make sure she has some opposition.' So Eunice agreed to have a go and after a first run she'd rather forget about (she forgot to put the car in gear on the line) she really did the business. 'She rocketed up Madeira Drive in 26.55sec,' reported *Autosport*'s Martyn Watkins, 'nearly a couple of seconds better than Tony Marsh's fastest run!' Perhaps I was having an off day...

Memories of Miss Wicken's progress are rather hazy, but Eunice led home renowned lady drivers Patsy Burt and Jean Bloxham that day. She passengered for me on a number of trials after that, before doing Brighton again the following year. We were fairly serious for a while, but then she went off to University and we rather drifted apart, although we still exchange Christmas cards.

The following day was Prescott, or so I'd hoped, but as I'd been at Brighton the day before and not practised at the Gloucestershire hill, I fell foul of a new RAC requirement which said that you must have driven the hill during the previous month. I wasn't allowed to run in the competition although, as current hill climb champion, I did do a demonstration run. Dick Henderson took yet another BTD but wasn't quite quick enough, fortunately, to break my hill record. However, by that time I knew I'd done enough to take the British Hill Climb title for the third year running, ahead of Michael Christie and Dick Henderson, having won every championship event that I'd competed in.

In mid-September, Silverstone's Daily Express International

Trophy was running later than its usual May date because of the fuel crisis. It was also run, unusually, in two heats and a final, in which I managed to put myself on the third row of the grid ahead of some very well known drivers including Ivor Bueb, Innes Ireland and Graham Hill. Considering the calibre of the other drivers, I was pleased to finish second in a race which produced a memorable one/two/three for the BRMs of Jean Behra, Harry Schell and Ron Flockhart.

But the 1957 season wasn't over yet by any means. We still had a sprint at Rhydymwyn where I took BTD and the 1500 racing class win with the F2 Cooper-Climax, plus third in the same class with the JAP engined 1100. The Wirral 100 Club also ran two pursuit races at the meeting. I drove one in each car, winning both, and interestingly the 1100 Cooper was almost a second faster than the F2 car.

After Rhydymwyn we had the first ever hill climb at Chateau Impney, Droitwich, where the 550 yard course started beside a lake and the surroundings were lovely. Hagley and DLCC had been trying to get permission to run an event there for years and had finally succeeded. David Good took BTD in his Cooper-JAP, beating me by a couple of tenths. My future brother-in-law, Duncan Hollingworth, was there in the late Ken Wharton's Cooper and Eunice Griffin had borrowed an XK Jaguar coupe, but sadly she had a bit of trouble negotiating a bridge and rearranged one or two front teeth.

My final circuit outing of the season offered a £1000 first prize and a real gold cup to the winner of the Oulton Park's International Gold Cup F2 race. Again there were some top names in the race so Cliff Allison and myself were delighted with an incredible joint fastest practice time, lining up on the front row with Jack Brabham and Tony Brooks. Graham Hill took the award for the fastest lap with a new record of 87.81 mph but only finished eleventh. Jack took the win with Cliff second and myself third, although a lap behind. Sadly my old sparring partner, George Wicken, was taken to hospital with a broken leg and other injuries following an accident when his Cooper rolled and hit a brick building at Clay Hill. At least he had the winter to recover, which I'm sure he appreciated.

Back on the trials scene I collected a special award at the High Peak, had a good day's sport at a wet Chase Trophy and a win in the Specials class at North Midland MC's Autumn Sporting Trial.

These were followed by sixth best overall in the John Bull Trophy Trial in TMS 1 (Duncan Hollingworth drove TMS 2) and being in the winning team for the BBC TV Trophy Trial at Aston Hill near Wendover when Eunice came and bounced for me. Although part of the winning Midlands team, I blew a head gasket at the event which I had to replace before continuing. My engine was supercharged to quite a high pressure, so did give trouble from time to time.

After all this excitement I narrowly missed winning the national Trials Championship in 1957. I ended up in third place, one point adrift after getting a bit mixed up with a marker post. At this time the championship was still awarded on the result of one event, in this case Shenstone and District's trial near Draycott-in-the-Clay. Eunice was passengering for me and I remember I made up a little shield with a griffin on it to put on the front of the car whenever she was with me.

I did collect another award that year, the Autocar F2 Championship. *Autocar* magazine sponsored a series of races and while not definitely targeting them, I did as many as would fit in with my season and had tremendous fun along the way. This championship was for British drivers only and with points awarded according to race length and status, national or international, it also included races at foreign circuits. The works Coopers and Lotuses were so busy racing each other and blowing up as a result that my being just a little more sedate paid off in the end. After all I was paying for any repairs out of my own pocket.

If I hadn't missed that important point in the Trials championship this would certainly have been a vintage year. As it was, I was pleased to win two prestigious national awards.

It was at about this time, late in 1957, that I met Diana, my wife to be. I was racing the Bobtail at Oulton Park when I noticed a young lady in the pits and was moved to make a few enquiries. I found out that she came from Kidderminster, quite close to where I lived, and used to attend some of the Hagley social meetings; the weekly 'Noggin and Natters' that most motor clubs have. I went along to one of these sessions to investigate and somehow got chatting. At that time I had a little racing boat, a hydroplane, which she was tempted to come and view. I suppose it made a change from etchings!

After that, if I went to an event and she was there we'd spend time together. However it took a bit of time to gain her parents' approval – they weren't terribly impressed by someone coming to take their daughter out in a Ford Thames van! We became engaged a year later, on 5 November 1958.

Chapter Four

In January 1958, about a year after he had died, Hagley ran the first Ken Wharton Memorial event. This was an inter-regional team driving test and was won, appropriately, by the Midlands team (Ken, of course, had been a very active Midlands member in previous team events). The best individual performances were by myself and Duncan Hollingworth, as we finished first and second. Driving tests were very much like the modern autotests and a jolly good way to have fun and learn car control.

Trials are also a very good way to learn both car control and how to read a track. I think my grounding in trials and driving tests has stood me in good stead in all my motorsport. Notable trials in that first part of 1958 were Hagley's Clee Hill Trial, which I won and which, for the first time since the war, was held in the Kinver area on Marsh family land. Mike Walton, my young mechanic, accompanied me in the TMS and was delighted to win the Bouncers Trophy. I also took second overall in the Kitching and went on to win the Wilshire with my future wife, Di, in the passenger seat.

Then I had a good start to the speed event season as I won my first sprint of the year at one of my favourite venues, Rhydymwyn, by seven seconds. This was the first time I drove Max Trimble's Lotus 11. Max is a great character who started his competition career in 1954 in a Jowett Jupiter. In 1955 he raced and hill climbed an Austin Healey 100M and a Kieft and the following year bought an ex-Ecurie Ecosse C Type Jaguar, becoming quite prominent on the racing scene. In 1957 he moved onto a D Type, also from Ecurie Ecosse, but had a big accident at Spa when the car went sideways into a telegraph pole, which resulted in him losing a leg.

I was approached by Max's mother and asked if I would like to drive his Climax engined Lotus 11 in the hope this would maintain his interest in motorsport. I completely rebuilt the car at Kinver and drove it several times during the 1958 season. Happily, Max returned to active motorsport in 1959. He finally retired from competition in 1976 and is frequently seen – and heard – at Shelsley Walsh as a commentator.

Easter, of course, meant Goodwood and the International

meeting. My first race was the 15 lap Formula 2 event, which was also the first race for the new British Racing Partnership. BRP was formed by Ken Gregory and Stirling's father, Alfred Moss, and their entry, a pale green Cooper, was driven by Stuart Lewis-Evans. *Autosport* reported they had a radio fitted in the car '...for the reception of pit instructions, but the system did not seem to be in use in the race itself.' Was this an early sign of things to come. Other drivers included Graham Hill, Cliff Allison and Dennis Taylor in Lotuses with Jack Brabham in the works Cooper and Roy Salvadori in C T 'Tommy' Atkins' Cooper. Tommy was a regular entrant and usually had a prominent driver in his car from whatever country he happened to be racing in.

Soon after the start the cars split into two groups with Brabham, two of the Lotuses and Lewis-Evans' BRP Cooper in the first group. I hadn't made a particularly good start but worked my way up to the front of the second group and there I stayed, eventually finishing fifth.

My second race was in the Formula 2 category of the main race, the Goodwood International 100 for the Glover Trophy over 42 laps. Cliff Allison won the F2 category with fourth overall, but I managed to finish as the second F2 contender, ahead of Ian Burgess's Cooper. *Autosport* ran a picture of our battle, with Ian leading at the time. They reported that we had '... both driven well, if unspectacularly.' Ian was a sort of spare driver for Cooper Cars and quite a good driver, but he had an enormous accident at the high speed Avus track in Germany from which, fortunately, he escaped unscathed.

Jean Behra did his BRM a bit of a mischief at that Goodwood meeting when he ran out of brakes and drove into the chicane, taking the front corner off the car. In those days the chicane was made of proper bricks, not the polystyrene of today's circuit.

I took Max's Lotus to Oulton Park for the British Empire Trophy meeting. and was in the second of three heats for the main race, which was for smaller engined cars. A chap called John Horridge in a Lister Bristol was so keen to overtake me that he outdrove himself and ended up down an escape road, leaving me to finish fifth. The final was, of course, made up of front runners in the heats and so the smaller engined cars didn't stand much of a chance against the

Aston Martin DBR2s of Tony Brooks and the winner, Stirling Moss, but it was fun to be there.

Then it was Prescott and the first round of the national championship where David Boshier-Jones took BTD and broke my hill record. This was a busy day for me with Max's Lotus 11 and my two Coopers. A good day's competition, too, as I managed second in class with the Lotus, took the racing car class with the F2 Cooper and ran second overall to Boshier-Jones in the Cooper JAP. This was the event where Ken Wharton's father officially opened the memorial to his son in the form of a new timing hut, which meant Ken's name was still at the heart of hill climbing.

A mixed Silverstone meeting saw a win in Max's Lotus but engine problems with the twin ohc engine. This meant I was the only one with a single ohc in my subsequent race at Brands so didn't do terribly well. However it was back to normal for Shelsley where I had better luck and redressed the balance after Prescott. I took BTD over David Boshier-Jones by over half a second on a damp track, although *Autosport* commented that I'd need to do well in the five championship events I was scheduled to drive in if I was to retain the championship. I'd already made a poor start at Prescott and was going to miss Rest-and-be-Thankful due to racing at Rheims. However, the JAP engined Cooper did the business at Shelsley, even if we did clip a bank on our first run. It was a shame about the rain, as this was the last meeting to be organized by MAC Secretary Leslie Wilson, who had run events at Shelsley since WW1.

Fortunately the weather was better the next day for the BOC Members' meeting at Prescott. In fact my 41.87 on my first run in the 1100 Cooper was the first time the 42 second barrier had been broken. I also had the Climax engined Cooper there and, on a really clean run, beat Michael Christie in his Lotus-Climax. On the second runs, Boshier-Jones also stopped the clock under 42 seconds. I was sitting on the line when his time was announced but knew I had BTD with my earlier time and pipped him by just five hundredths. Looking back I find it interesting that two of us were able to break the 42 second barrier three times between us, whereas hill records seem to stand for a lot longer these days.

Another record, which I may or may not have broken, was

at my next meeting at Silverstone. I only took the Formula 2 car this time and was entered in the Formula Libre race alongside a couple of privately entered F1 Connaughts, Bill Moss in ERA Remus, Peter Mould's Cooper Jaguar and a couple of Lotuses as well. The car was on song and my practice time was good. I shot into the lead at the start and, while there was some good racing going on, kept ahead of Geoff Richardson's Connaught until the finish ten laps later, averaging 84.12 mph on the club circuit. No one seemed to know if it was a new lap record or not (although it was almost off the speed table in the programme!) and we never did find out. Max Trimble's Lotus 11 was also at this meeting, now being driven by David Shale who took over the drive from me. David raced his own Austin Healey and Max had asked him to drive the Lotus when other commitments, such as racing abroad, prevented me from doing so.

In fact my very next meeting was the French Grand Prix at Rheims in early July and by now some of the Formula 1 drivers were starting to muscle in on Formula 2. If there was a separate F2 race, some of the F1 drivers took part as they found it a good way of earning an extra bit of cash. Of course if they had an accident and injured themselves before the main race they weren't too popular with their teams, but several of them tried it. Can you imagine today's Formula 1 drivers being allowed to take part in a 30 lap supporting race either before or after a Grand Prix?

At this meeting on the fast Rheims road circuit our race was after the 12 hour sports car race which finished at noon. Following the traditional local ceremony of introducing the drivers, we lined up for the F2 'Coupe de Vitesse'. With such illustrious names as Behra, Collins and Moss on the front row, I was on row six alongside Brian Naylor. It wasn't a race I particularly remember, although engine problems on lap 25 sidelined the Cooper so perhaps I didn't want to. *Autosport* said that my engine 'chucked a rod through the side', although I think this was an assumption because of the oil smoke as it was only faulty oil pipes and unions. You have to remember that although the Coopers were rear engined, the oil tank was sitting on the chassis behind the radiator. This meant very long oil and water pipes running from the front of the car, through the cockpit and into the engine. Oil temperatures were something like 120 degrees and water about 80 degrees, so it was quite a Turkish bath in the cockpit at times. In fact when I went back in 1959, I put several melons in a bucket of water in the shade of the transporter for consumption after the race. But in 1958, although I'd dropped out when in eighth position I was officially classified fourteenth, with Graham Hill thirteenth having dropped out with three laps to go.

I was back in France again at the end of July for the inaugural meeting at Clermont Ferrand. This new public road course was in the Auvergne region and was a true mountain circuit, its only straight in about 8 kilometres being barely 600 yards long. The first race was a three hour event for Grand Touring cars and this was followed by the 20 lap Formula 2 race. With Innes Ireland's Lotus winning, Maurice Trintignant finished second in the three hour race driving a 250GT Ferrari and had about half an hour before taking part in the Formula 2 race in Rob Walker's Alf Francis prepared Cooper. I'm not sure that would be allowed these days. Away we went and several good tussles ensued. Perhaps because he'd just finished a three hour race on the circuit, Trintignant took the win ahead of Ivor Bueb's Lotus, Stuart Lewis-Evans' Cooper and my Cooper, all of us in the 1 hour 21 minutes bracket and with our nearest rivals over two minutes behind us. For Trintignant that meant nearly four and a half hours of high speed driving with only a half-hour break, some achievement on a brand new circuit. Of course Maurice was the reigning French Champion and a very highly regarded driver, on a personal level he was a lovely little man and very polite. He always shook me by the hand and said 'ca va' – whatever that meant!

The start of that F2 race was a story on its own. Toto Roche was a senior man in French motorsport and renowned for his ability – or inability – to start a motor race with a flag, as was the custom in those days. He was quite a chubby man and once actually stood in front of Moss's car and dropped the flag so that Moss couldn't go until he'd stepped back. At Clermont he dropped the flag before most of the drivers were ready, but we did get our own back on him. They had given us a loo in the paddock quite close to the edge of the mountain and when Toto was inside we went and gave this slender wooden structure a good shake, prompting a big shout from within! There was also a big advertising balloon anchored at the track and some drivers (no names, of course!) went back at dusk and undid the odd securing rope or two in the hope that it might break free in the wind during the night.

This meeting was full of little incidents like that. I remember slipping into Race Control, finding the chequered flag and carefully removing the flag from the pole. I almost severed the pole halfway down before replacing the flag. The idea was that as soon as Toto started to wave it, the flag would collapse. Just before the race started I spotted frenzied activity in race control. Unfortunately someone had already broken it so they were frantically looking for a replacement. I also remember Ivor Bueb's Volkswagen pickup transporter which had a little flatbed at the back over the engine. His race car sat on that, but it was a couple of feet too long and stuck out the back on a couple of planks. Imagine top drivers turning up with something like that today…

While I returned home after each of these continental excursions, which each took the best part of a week, the beginning of August saw me away again for another visit to the Nurburgring and the German Grand Prix.

The weather during practice seemed to cover most known meteorological phenomena apart from snow and the track was very slippery. Phil Hill's Ferrari had caused amusement at the start of one session. A mechanic drove it to the start area and just as it arrived in front of the crowded stands a rear wheel fell off. Someone had forgotten to put on the knock-off wheel nut. As I've said before, the Italians are very good at making ice cream… However, with the wheel nut in place Phil recorded the second best F2 time. Jack Brabham was quickest but having only completed five of the six practice laps he was on the back row of the grid with Graham Hill. Overheating problems with the 'Mini Vanwall' Lotus 16s meant that Graham's engine momentarily seized, causing a spin.

After my first practice session I told my mechanic, Mike Walton, that the car wasn't handling nicely at all. The previous year I'd had transverse leaf spring front suspension and by now I had an updated front end with double wishbones and coil springs. Then Mike told me I was a minute a lap quicker than last year, so I decided I'd try and live with it.

At some of these continental meetings I often had concerns about the relative lack of marshals. At the Nurburgring, which is fourteen miles round, I had a moment in one of the twisty downhill sections during practice and came in for a bit of a breather. I wandered up to the BRM pit, as I used to do in those days, and found they were worried about one of their cars that hadn't come round. No reports had been received so I said I'd go and have a look. I did another lap and couldn't see it anywhere, but by the time I got back to the pits the driver had appeared. Apparently he'd gone off through a beech hedge that had closed up behind him, completely hiding him from view, but there were no marshals about to see this. I think this was when Jean Behra tried out Harry Schell's car and Harry was quite worried about it. Up until the mid 1990s British motor racing marshals were the best trained and the most numerous in the world, and it's only due to regulations laid down by the current Formula 1 authorities that the rest of the world has had to catch up.

At the Nurburgring I'd managed what I thought was a very creditable fourteenth place in qualifying, in 9 minutes 57.5 sec, for the fourth row of the grid. For the early part of the race I tussled with Formula 2 drivers Brabham, Barth and Bueb for position. At one stage Ivor Bueb and I were wheel to wheel, swapping positions like mad. Later I decided to have a break and just followed while Ivor, Edgar Barth and Ian Burgess continued to battle it out. Eventually Ivor stopped at the pits with lack of oil pressure. As he sat there a pipe burst and shot hot oil all over the place to end his race. The fifteen lap race finished with Tony Brooks' Vanwall in first place and, of our little group, Edgar Barth finished sixth in the Porsche, some six and a half minutes adrift. Ian Burgess was a further half minute behind in his Cooper and myself another ten seconds back in eighth place.

Sadly, at the finish we learnt of Peter Collins' 100mph accident. His Ferrari didn't quite make a corner and somersaulted over a hedge, throwing him out. Although Peter was flown to hospital he died without recovering consciousness.

Although we knew about Peter's accident I wasn't aware of its sad outcome in the mad rush to pack everything up, collect the starting and prize monies and get to Ostend for the ferry, as I was due to race at Mallory Park next day, Bank Holiday Monday. I don't think I even got out of my racing overalls between the two venues. While on the boat we went for something to eat in our grimy gear and weren't getting a lot of attention. Not wanting to make a fuss, I simply got out the multi-compartment wallet I used for continental events and started counting out the starting and prize money. It was amazing how the service improved.

Once off the boat it was straight through London and on to what short bit of the M1 we had in those days. Tooting through London the exhaust got sooted up and shot sparks as we blew out the cobwebs on the motorway. And I got booked for speeding in Leicester for exceeding 30 mph. It was only about a year or so later that travelling over 30 mph became legal for larger vehicles, so you can see how difficult it was for us then. No cruising down the motorway at 70 mph in an air conditioned juggernaught in those days!

At Mallory the Formula Libre event was held in two heats with a final for the fastest finishers. I managed fourth in heat one, just behind my old sparring partner Henry Taylor. Whether we'd been conserving our energies or not I can't remember, but in the final Henry led after the first few laps and we went round a couple of yards apart until the end.

The next Shelsley was a memorable day for me as, with 35.60 in the Cooper Twin, I finally beat Ken Wharton's hill record in ERA R4D. Patsy Burt was also in good form as she broke the Ladies' record in her F2 Cooper, becoming the first lady to climb the hill in under 40 seconds. Having already taken the record I must have been trying to achieve a similar result with my own F2 Cooper as I half spun and hit the bank by the VIP enclosure. The car was basically alright even if the tail was a bit crumpled, but I didn't take it out again that weekend.

At Brighton Speed Trials Eunice drove my Formula 2 car again, but she couldn't beat Patsy who set another new Ladies' record and also took second BTD. I managed a class win in the JAP engined hill climb car and another in the Formula 2 – quite a satisfactory weekend's work.

David Boshier-Jones had already won the 1958 hill climb championship by the time we next went to Prescott. In front of a record crowd he broke my outright hill record with a 41.00 but it was good to give him something to think about as I was just eight hundredths behind, which wasn't bad considering I'd been away from the hills for most of the season. I also took a class win in the Formula 2 Cooper – after all I didn't want people thinking I'd forsaken the hills completely.

I'd done fairly well at Montlhery the previous year and went back to France again for another shot in 1958. Montlhery is a banked bowl, but at one end you run off to the side and drive out into the country before coming back into the second part of the bowl. The concrete bowl itself was quite rough; you seemed to thump along from segment to segment, which was pretty awful. Whereas the bowl at Avus was made of brick and had a curved bottom portion and a straight line to the top so, in effect, there was a maximum speed, at Montlhery the sides of the bowl just got steeper and steeper. This meant you didn't have to choose a line, you just let go of the steering wheel and the car found its own height according to its speed.

During the race a Frenchman by the name of Jean-Claud Vidilles shunted Jack Brabham at the start then later somersaulted his car three times out in the country, you could see debris all over the track. I must have run over some of it as I had to retire with a puncture. Rather a shame as I was lying third at the time.

My final race meeting of the season was at Oulton Park. At the time I had a Porsche 356 as a road car. It was really a souped up Volkswagen but it was a pretty little car and I had a good old battle with racing cyclist Reg Harris's TR3 in the saloon car race. Sadly I think he got the better of me in the end as we finished fourth and fifth. The Formula Libre race for the Daily Mirror Trophy was a different matter and I lapped the F2 Cooper at over 80 mph to win by quite a way. In fact we got mixed up with the tail-enders just after halfway, but managed to avoid any trouble.

Just to keep my hand in, so to speak, we rounded off the year with a few trials which were always good for a few laughs. We also staged the second Ken Wharton Memorial Driving Tests, televised this year, in the Marsh & Baxter Transport Department's gigantic indoor garage at Brierley Hill. It was always nice to be driving on home ground, and also to be able to help provide a more unusual venue. Di and I had just announced our engagement and were photographed with the new World Champion, Mike Hawthorn. Ever the enthusiast for grass roots motorsport, Mike turned up at the event in a TR2 to compete in a special match race with expert Ken Rawlings. He won by nearly six seconds...

1959 started, as 1958 had finished, with the odd trial or two on the motorsport front – including a Production Car Trial in my Ford Thames van – and the odd wedding on the social front. I say the odd wedding because Di and I didn't want a lot of fuss. We certainly didn't want a big society wedding and were married in the local registry office which, much to the disgust of Di's mother, was above the local Mac Fisheries. This, combined with the fact that we were married in January having announced our engagement only the previous November, meant that one or two people were looking at us a little sideways.

We had a very small reception before taking my Porsche to the continent for our honeymoon, where we indulged in some winter sports. That's where I discovered ski bobbing – but more of that later.

When Di and I first started going about together she came to some driving tests at Chateau Impney and made me cups of tea. Soon after that came the time when, after a social evening at the local motor club, I took her to see my hydroplane. In addition to motorsport I'd had a season of motorboat racing as well. My hydroplane was about the size of a three-seater settee which you knelt on behind the steering wheel and was like a big saucer with an engine on its back. We used to race them on gravel pits and reservoirs around Birmingham and on the old gravel workings near Reading. As I'd got one of the smaller engines I started first in the handicap races. The big 1000cc machines started last and had to overtake you a couple of times. It was a very wet sport, especially round the corners where you were soaked in the wash from other boats. You got bounced around all over the place and I remember going over the side at least once. I was lucky that in 1958 the hydroplane races slotted in quite well between the motoring events.

After our honeymoon and another couple of trials, the hill climb season started at Lydstep towards the end of March where reigning champion David Boshier-Jones and I opened the hill with him driving me up it in a borrowed TR3. 'Bosh' might have had control in the TR3 but I managed to beat him by half a second in the event, taking BTD in the Cooper Twin in a time some four tenths down on Ken Wharton's record.

It was dry for practice at Oulton Park's British Empire Trophy but poured with rain for the race itself. Jim Russell won after 40 laps in the wet in his F2 Cooper with my own version second, 29 seconds behind. Nearly a minute later, Ivor Bueb came in third with his Borgward engined Cooper and we were the only three to go full distance.

The race at Oulton Park was a good warm-up for the Aintree International 200 a little later in April. On the seventh row of the grid, I was in front of some quite illustrious names including Maurice Trintignant, John Campbell-Jones, George Wicken and Graham Hill. David Piper was in there too with his F2 Lotus, and he still races in historic events these days in a variety of cars from a Ferrari 250 LM to a Porsche 917. David was unfortunate to lose a leg while driving in Steve McQueen's film *Le Mans* in 1970 and now usually carries a spare artificial one in the boot of his car.

At Aintree I had to stop fairly soon after the start to investigate oil problems. In those days I used Notwen Oils. Jack Newton (his name was spelt backwards for the company name) was a local competitor in a very pretty little MG sports car and his company provided an ex-army vehicle which acted as race control, starter's van and time keeper's office for club events. We found that with the Climax engines I was having trouble with oil frothing. There was nothing on the car to remove the air and I'd end up losing a lot of oil. The tank wasn't big enough to hold the oil plus the froth and what did remain in the engine got terribly hot. An additive eventually cured the problem, but at Aintree we just poured in more oil and went out again, finishing ninth in the Formula 2 section and fourteenth overall, not bad with the stop.

The first public appearance of the 'Motus' (Marsh modified Lotus) came at Prescott. This was a Lotus 12 that Colin Chapman had built especially for Michael Christie to run in hill climbs. Michael was very disappointed in the car, so I bought it to see if I could make it work. I moved the 1.1-litre Climax FPF engine back in the chassis, rebodied the car and did several other modifications which evidently worked, as it came up in the results a number of times. At Prescott we came first in class and second behind David Boshier-Jones in the championship run off.

The International Trophy race at Silverstone saw my F2 Cooper on the fifth row of the grid between Bueb and Ian Burgess. Up front, in his 2.5-litre Cooper-Climax, was Jack Brabham who won the race from Roy Salvadori in the new front engined Aston Martin F1 car. I held my own in the race, finishing third behind Russell and Bueb in the Formula 2 category and only a couple of laps down on the leaders. Overall we were in tenth position, which was pretty good out of 24 entrants.

Over in France, for the Formula 2 Pau Grand Prix in the middle of May, I had quite a good race, finishing in fourth position behind Maurice Trintignant, Bruce McLaren and Lucien Bianchi before making another of my increasingly rare visits to the hills. On a newly resurfaced Shelsley, where abnormally hot weather had left pools of molten tar in places, I gave the Motus a little more exercise, finishing second in class behind BTD man David Boshier-Jones' Cooper. In a newly introduced system, British Championship points were now scored in the best of two separate run-offs at the end of the meeting. Bosh won with BTD ahead of David Good's similar 1100 Cooper-JAP, with the Motus a further four hundredths behind.

At Mallory Park, I led the 30 lap Formula 2 race for the first eight laps before being passed by Tim Parnell's Cooper. This was the order in which we finished though I did manage a fastest lap. Again the weather wasn't particularly good although I didn't seem to mind racing in the wet quite as much as some of the other drivers. Perhaps my trials experience helped here.

Over in France again, I was on the fifth row of the grid between Jack Lewis and Harry Schell at the F2 Grand Prix Des Auvergnes at Clermont-Ferrand. Several of us had problems here, mine being a broken fuel pump drive. I ended up in the pits, blowing into the tank in an effort to get the fuel to come up. The pump ran off the end of one of the camshafts with a modified drive, which used to break. It was always frustrating if something broke, particularly so if it was a big occasion or if you'd had a long drive to the event. Stirling Moss won the event – despite this being the race that Toto Roche stood in front of his Cooper-Borgward as he dropped the flag! Sadly, poor Ivor Bueb had a big accident in his own Cooper-Borgward which eventually proved fatal.

Back at Mallory Park I took second place in the first heat of the Formula Libre race and repeated it in the final, sandwiched between Brian Naylor and Henry Taylor, though I did set the fastest lap with 87.73 mph.

By the time of my second visit to Shelsley in 1959, I'd sold the V-Twin Cooper and was using the Motus on the hills just for a bit of fun. David Boshier-Jones again took BTD, beating my old class and hill records into the bargain. In fact he twice broke the hill record and won the championship run off so it was a very good day for him. I finished second in the run-off, prompting *Autosport* to speculate that excess weight was the problem and that I should diet!

I had another quick trip to the continent, this time to Graz in Austria for the first time on an airfield circuit near Zeltweg. It was definitely worth the effort as after an excellent ding-dong with David Piper's Lotus, Lucien Bianchi's Cooper and Ernst Voge's RSK Porsche I won by over twelve seconds.

By now, Coopers had brought out their Monaco sports racing car and as I was already a successful Cooper driver, I was offered one. The Monaco came with either a 1.5-litre or 2-litre, four cylinder, twin OHC Climax FPF so as I already had a 1.5 in the F2 car I chose the 170 bhp 2-litre option. Both engines were externally identical and it was quite a simple job to swap engines over. Also, swapping engines from one car to another was a simple way of both carrying them around and giving me more options of cars to race at any one meeting.

At Mallory Park, where I seemed to be spending quite a bit of time in 1959, the weather was good this time. I had the 2-litre engine in my F2 Cooper and in practice I broke Henry Taylor's existing 55sec track record (unofficially, of course) by 1.6 seconds. After a good start in the first heat of the Formula Libre race I led Brian Naylor before his JBW-Maserati's gearbox blew, won the race and made the record official at 54.40sec. In the final I got another really good start, which stood me in good stead as the car was losing water. Then at about half way the brakes started playing up, requiring five or six good pumps on the pedal at each corner. It took all my efforts to stay in front of sports car race winner Peter Gammon's Lola and avoid falling off the track. Fortunately I managed both.

Fresh from his win at Monza in the Italian Grand Prix, Stirling Moss won the 54 lap Oulton Park Gold Cup at the end of September. I managed the second row of the grid with the 2-litre Cooper behind Stirling, Jack Brabham, Chris Bristow, Graham Hill, Bruce McLaren and Roy Salvadori although to be fair there were a few non starters. BRM didn't appear at all, Horace Gould's private 250F Maserati was driven by Bruce Halford while George Wicken gave up his works Cooper drive to Bruce McLaren. Brian Naylor was still in hospital after a crash in his JBW-Maserati and Henry Taylor had engine problems in practice so the field was somewhat depleted. It was a good race for me; I didn't distinguish myself with any heroics but plodded on to finish sixth and delighted to collect some prize money. For such a prestigious event the total prize money was £3650, with Stirling taking £2000 of that for the win. Still, £100 for sixth place wasn't to be sneezed at in 1959.

After the Gold Cup meeting I returned to Oulton Park for their last race of the season. I took the 2-litre Cooper (which *Autosport* described as 'virtually Formula 1) for the ten lap Formula Libre race, the Daily Mirror Trophy, which I had won in 1958 and I managed to repeat the previous year's performance. Second was Stanley Hart in his Cooper, who *Autosport's* Francis Penn thought very highly of and who shared my fastest lap, and in third place was Chris Summers' Cooper.

With racing over for the year it was back to other forms of motorsport. Trials once again occupied the winter months, while the third Ken Wharton Memorial Driving Tests were held in the courtyard of the huge Vono works at Tipton in Staffordshire. Whereas last year's event was held indoors at Marsh & Baxter's garage, this time it was outdoors – and it rained! But it was another well run Hagley event, televised again, and as usual was great fun. Once again I drove the TMS for the Midlands Team, one of seven teams taking part. This year the Irish Team, captained by Paddy Hopkirk, won.

The 1960 racing season started at the end of March, at Snetterton, where I drove the Cooper Monaco. I found the Monaco fairly easy to drive but was never quite happy with the way it flexed round corners. This didn't seem to have much effect on speed though as we came second in the big sports car race to Mike Taylor's 2-litre Lotus, despite having a certain amount of oil floating around in the cockpit, and took the fastest lap in the 3-litre division. I had the Formula 2 Cooper there too, finishing third in the single seater race behind Keith Greene's Gilby Engineering F1 Cooper-Maserati and John Campbell-Jones' F2 Cooper. And working on my usual principle that you entered as many races as you were eligible for, I also ran the F2 Cooper in the Formula Libre race. This saw a good battle between Greene and Brian Naylor's JBW-Maserati until Keith had to retire with gearbox troubles, which left Steve Ouvaroff and myself battling it out for second place in our F2 Coopers. I just couldn't pull enough out of the car to pass Steve and had to be content with third, but it was a good start to the racing season.

Then came the Grand Prix of Brussels and the only time I remember being disqualified. It happened like this.

The Grand Prix was at a new 4.5 kilometre road circuit near Heysel and was run in two heats. There were only 18 places on the grid and unfortunately I failed to qualify by one place. As cars lined up on the grid I noticed that David Piper, who was seventeenth fastest, had failed to appear so I quietly wheeled my car out to make up the numbers. Sadly, by the time I got there so had David. As I'd made the number up to 19 I was later disqualified for starting without permission. Interestingly though, I was posted as being on the fourth row of the grid for the start of the second heat. Oh well, it was worth a try!

A couple of weeks back home and then it was off to the continent again, this time for the F2 Grand Prix of Pau at Easter where, despite a clash with Goodwood, several notable drivers were present. Pau is a twisty 1.7 mile road circuit in the town and I was pleased to finish ahead of Belgian motoring journalist Paul Frere's Cooper. Paul was a good driver, a Belgian Grand Prix winner and a sports car specialist, particularly at Le Mans. Pau was something of a Cooper whitewash. Jack Brabham won from Maurice Trintignant, Frere's regular sportscar co-driver Olivier Gendebien, Ron Flockhart, myself and Frere all of us in Coopers.

The Aintree 200 always had a good turnout of top names. Having the Cooper Monaco, I was now able to drive in the sports car races at some of these bigger meetings as well as the single seater races. While this could sometimes be a bit tiring, I found it very useful practice as the two cars drove similarly. Roy Salvadori won the sports car race from Mike Taylor while I was third, which set a good feeling to the day. In the 50 lap '200' I started on the fifth row, a couple of rows behind John Surtees who was just starting to race on four wheels and who in fact set fastest lap in his Cooper Climax. Even so I kept ahead of some quite notable drivers, but 50 laps of Aintree is bound to see some failures. Several cars retired, so I was quite pleased with 16th place and 48 laps, particularly as only 18 drivers out of 31 finished the race.

At Silverstone's International Trophy I started from the sixth row in a lineup that was worthy of a Grand Prix with Moss's Rob Walker Cooper, Bonnier and Gurney in rear engined BRMs and Phil Hill's Ferrari on the front row. Really beginning to go well this year, Innes Ireland scored a good win in his Lotus-Climax 18 but once again the 150 miles took their toll, with eight retirements. Fortunately I wasn't among them and finished 15th, second in the Formula 2 section behind New Zealander Denis Hulme. Unfortunately, this was the meeting where popular Franco-American driver Harry Schell met with a fatal accident in practice. I was following him up from Club Corner towards Abbey Curve when he spun and hit the low open wall as I went past. At the time I didn't realise that he had been killed. Mention of Harry reminds me of my first visit to Rheims for the French Grand Prix, where Harry was the talk of the paddock for arriving in a bubble car! Some of the drivers decided it would be cruel to part Harry from his handy little car for too long, manhandled it into his hotel and somehow parked it outside his bedroom door! I was not, on this occasion, one of those drivers…

After a second place at Oulton Park in the Cooper Monaco it was off to the continent again, this time to Chimay on Whit Sunday for their 30th anniversary race. For a few years they had run sports car races but this year they returned to single seaters and my F2 Cooper was on the third row of the grid. This was a road circuit and from the start, you rushed down a hill into a little village. Then came a sharp bend where there were several houses. During practice they put up a chestnut paling fence on the edge of the pavement, to stop people coming out of their front doors and straight on to the racing circuit. It was a problematic race for me, with a long series of pit stops. It was at Chimay that my young mechanic went into town for supplies, returning with the groceries and a very red face. His French, like mine, was very limited so he didn't really understand what the woman in the village shop was offering him until a scantily clad young lady passed behind the door leading into the lounge. I suppose you must expect to have a few adventures when abroad!

The Grand Prix of Spa was, in fact, a 128 mile race for 1600cc Appendix C sports cars. I ran the smaller engine in the Monaco but the weather was against us and I still wasn't over confident about the way the chassis flexed when cornering. Even so I finished sixth, rather good considering the conditions.

One of the most well known of all sports car races is the Le Mans 24 Hours. Up to now my only previous experience of it was on TV, but one thing that struck me was that many of the top drivers didn't seem to like the race. With two drivers per car there weren't really enough top men to go round and some of them felt uncomfortable among the relatively inexperienced competitors, particularly on the high speed Mulsanne straight.

My opportunity to race there came about because of the race at Spa with the Cooper Monaco. The French, as always, had a champagne party a couple of nights before the race where David Buxton, who ran Team Elite, asked me if I'd be interested in driving one of their Lotuses at Le Mans. Naturally I said yes, although I had to put my hand in my pocket to the tune of about £2000, quite a lot of money in those days. In fact I got about £3000 back when we won the Index of Energy award – but I'm getting ahead of myself...

Like many French races Le Mans had fun fairs, stalls, and even offered services such as laundering shirts. There was a big overnight parking area and Di and I took our Borgward estate car with reclining seats, so I could get a bit of sleep between driving stints.

The French scrutineering was quite a laugh. As this was the first year of the Index of Thermal Efficiency, or Index of Energy, award we had to go in with empty tanks so they could fill them up and check the fuel capacity. Running fairly big tanks, the car tended to squat but the next test was a ground clearance check. The car had to pass over a wooden block, so all the mechanics were nonchalantly leaning on the car with their hands discreetly under the mudguards, easing it over the block. Next we had to start the engine and rev it over a patch of dry sand to make sure the exhaust angle wouldn't create too much dust. Finally, as the regulations stated that certain parts of the car couldn't be replaced during the race, a man with a big rubber stamp marked everything within reach. Evidently the people at Lotus knew a thing or two because when he got as far as the starter motor they said 'It's down there under the exhaust, be careful you don't burn yourself'. So he didn't bother to stamp it. Just as well because we had to change it during the race.

We then had to line all the cars up on the track, in order, with the fastest at the front, after which we then had to move them in front of our pit at a 45°angle, ready for the Le Mans start. No longer used these days because of full harness safety belts, this was when drivers ran across the track, jumped in, started up and drove out into the race in a free for all. Typically, the slowest cars nearest the back of the grid had their pits nearest the first corner, so moving them all from the line up to their starting positions was chaotic.

Eventually we got to the start and my co-driver, John Wagstaff, did the running. Di sat on the pit counter the whole time recording times and positions while John and I swapped three hour stints in the car. I can't say it was a terribly exciting race, as most of the time you didn't know where you or anyone else was, you just kept driving. Or in our case you drove at a reasonable speed but not flat out. During the night the car felt a bit like a Christmas tree with all the lights hanging off it. As well as a good pair of headlights the Elite had a pair of 'flame throwers'; extra long distance lights. There were also lights to enable the timekeepers to see your racing number, lights that differentiated you from your team mates and finally coloured lights on the rear, which indicated to cars coming up behind what size engine you had. These all took their toll on the electrical system. We found, too, that we needed extra springs to hold the windscreen wipers on the screen at high speed. This was fine until you needed the wipers at slow speed, when the poor old motors nearly had smoke coming out of them with the effort. The car had no window winders, either, but a little flap arrangement. Unfortunately we found that with the flap open the car was slower down the straights, a great pity as it got very hot in those Elites. I had to lean forward in the seat to try and get a bit of airflow behind my back.

We just drove and drove and filled the car up with fuel, which was an adventure in itself. The new Index of Energy award meant we had lots of officials in attendance. One to break the seal on the petrol tank or the oil filler and seal it up again, a 'plombeur' who inserted the hose and filled you up, plus another to write everything down. Then there was a policeman, I don't really know why, but the police always wanted to get in on the act.

As I mentioned, we had to change the starter motor during the race. John brought the car in to change drivers and when I pressed the button to restart there was just a whirring noise. Due to some sort of frequency problem, the end of the starter spindle used to fall off. The Lotus people had anticipated this and had welded a captive nut on to the gearbox adaptor plate to enable the starter motor to be changed quickly. Fortunately this happened at night, the motor was removed and thrown over the pit counter where there were hammering noises in the background before it was handed back, 'repaired'. None of our officials noticed it wasn't the same one, but I'm sure we weren't the only people to bend the rules a little.

But without changing a wheel or even a brake pad throughout the 24 hours, we finished sixteenth on the road. Our approach of driving a 'softly, softly' race rather than driving to the car's maximum paid off and after a final fill-up after the race had finished we were awarded the Index of Energy prize. That fill-up was interesting too. One of our team had to shout out when the fuel was coming up the filler pipe and I'm sure we could probably have got more fuel in if we'd really tried! But there was one more drama to come, at the Parc Ferme for post event scrutineering.

The press were everywhere taking photos and Colin Chapman's father Stan was in charge of us, bustling around. When he saw the scrutineer coming Stan produced our own personal photographer and got the scrutineer to sit on the car for a photo with the drivers and mechanics. Eventually he asked for the car to be started and once again there was just this whirring noise. It was a very hot engine, we said, and understandably reluctant to start. Amazingly the scrutineer swallowed that one and so we got our award. All in all Le Mans 1960 was a very memorable event, one I'm so glad I had the opportunity to take part in.

Incidentally, the Index of Energy award was eventually brought in because Colin Chapman had won the Index of Performance award in 1956. The little 2-cylinder DB Panhards had tended to monopolize it and Colin had beaten the French at their own game with a 750 cc Lotus Climax, which they didn't like. It must have been a bit much for them to have this new award taken by another Lotus!

After Le Mans it was back home for a rest before a 25 lap race for sports cars at Silverstone. It wasn't the best of races for me because on lap four I had to come into the pits with a water leak.

Then it was back to the continent for the German Grand Prix at the Nurburgring – and what filthy weather we had for it. In all honesty it was barely fit for racing. You would be in trouble if you had today's soft compound grooved racing tyres on but with the rock hard, spindly little tyres we had then it was terrible. We didn't even have slicks and wets in those days, you just raced on what you'd got.

But we did race and there were four works Porsches entered plus Graham Hill's privately entered one – I think the Germans were quite keen to win that race. I was in amongst them on the fourth row of the grid, but it wasn't the weather to stick your neck out. It was a question of trying to stay on the track and out of trouble. However we did manage to finish, in tenth place too, so that was pretty good.

Next came another race for Team Elite, the 25th RAC Tourist Trophy at Goodwood, but it wasn't the best of races for me. Team Elite wasn't a works team but a private enterprise and when I got to Goodwood they were in a state of confusion. After the differential had started to break loose from the back of the chassis during the Le Mans 24 hour race, the car had been back to Lotus to have the mounting repaired. The team had only just got the car back and were reassembling it at the track. Generally Team Elite ran two cars but at this race they had three; John Wagstaff in the Le Mans car, Mike Parkes in Sir Gawaine Baillie's car and myself in the third.

During practice I found the car starting to handle in a rather peculiar manner – the feel was completely different in right-hand corners to what it was in left-handers. Coming down to Woodcote, the double right-hander before the chicane, I had to use the grass in a big way. I managed to keep going and went into the pits where we discovered the reason very quickly. The Elite used a typical Chapman rear suspension design with two very long shock absorber and spring units which came up into the back of the car to two pinnacles moulded into the glassfibre chassis. These 'Chapman struts' were rather like the front suspension on a lot of production cars today. A retaining nut had come off the right-hand strut so that when the car leaned round right-hand corners, it came out of its hole. Round left-hand corners, sometimes it dropped back in and sometimes it didn't. After we'd sorted this out John Wagstaff's car began to suffer from fuel starvation, so as No 1 driver he was swapped into my car.

All this left me rather disillusioned and I didn't drive for Team Elite any more. However I'd quite liked the Elite as a car, they're lovely little things, so I bought one as a road car and took it to Prescott once. It wasn't in race condition; I used it for driving from the Midlands to Finmere, near Silverstone, where Motor Racing Stables held their racing school on the now disused aerodrome. I'd been asked if I would go down and do a demo and a bit of instructing. I went there a number of times and ended up with my picture in *Autosport* a couple of times with pop stars. One was a chap called John Leyton and the other one was Adam Faith.

About this time I sold the Formula 2 Cooper and bought a Lotus 18. It wasn't that I'd fallen out with Coopers, far from it, in fact I remember John Cooper coming over when I was having a snack in the Goodwood paddock. Someone had crashed their car and John wanted to go and look so he collected me, together with a large, creamy jam sponge cake I was enjoying. John and I came back, but the cake didn't. The problem (apart from John Cooper also liking jam sponges) was that I very much enjoyed my continental racing but was finding entries difficult to get because privately entered Coopers were becoming ten a penny. Having something a little different like the Lotus didn't, of course, guarantee you an entry but did improve your chances.

My first race with the Lotus was at Brands Hatch for the Kentish 100. I got a good start and was lying seventh when, according to *Autosport*, I had some adventures at Druids and dropped right back to 17th place. I can't remember what the adventures were; I might have spun or something. But even though there were some top drivers in the race such as Jim Clark, the eventual winner in his works Lotus 18, Dan Gurney and Jo Bonnier, I managed to claw back up to sixth place ahead of Jack Lewis. It was always satisfying to finish ahead of Jackie, he used to give me a lot of trouble one way or another with some great battles along the way.

After Brands came the chance to take the Elite to Prescott, where I won the Grand Touring class. I also took the old hill climb Cooper along and managed a class win in that too. It was good to let the hill climbers know I was still around and could still be up there with them if I chose to. And it was good, too, to see some of the old names at the top such as David Good, Patsy Burt, Phil Scragg and David Boshier-Jones, who took BTD with a new hill record to set the seal on his third consecutive British title.

My penultimate race meeting of the year was at Brands Hatch for the Formula 2 Lewis Evans Trophy. I got a really good start in the Lotus, which took me into the lead and I stayed there for the whole race in front, satisfyingly, of my great rival Jack Lewis. I remember Jack as being a tiny little man, smaller than me, but he always seemed to have a very tall girlfriend.

After the heady excitement of racing, I still found myself in the Midlands team for the Ken Wharton Memorial Driving Tests, alongside Frank and Harry Livingston. I always enjoyed this event as it took me back to my driving roots and this year in particular, very close to home as well. Dunsley Caravans premises at Kinver was just half a mile from home. And for the second year running the Irish team took the trophy, with Paddy Hopkirk, Robert Woodside and Dr Thompson Glass as their drivers.

After fitting in another sprint meeting at Rhydymwyn, with a new sports car record in the Cooper Monaco, it was time for the last race meeting of the year, the Boxing Day Brands event. I entered the Lotus in the Silver City Trophy Formula Libre race and after one or two excursions in practice, the damage from which had to be remedied at lunchtime, I took the lead from the second row of the grid. Despite the best efforts of John Campbell-Jones and Dizzy Addicott I kept the lead. It was a great end to a very good year's motorsport.

There's just one more thing to mention about 1960. *Autosport*'s Boxing Day Brands report said that I was in the process of modifying the F2 Lotus 18 for next year's Formula 1 series (1961 would see the start of the new 1500cc F1) and that it already boasted a Cooper gearbox. Earlier in the year I'd discovered that the driveshafts of the five-speed Chapman 'queerbox' had started to twist. I phoned Colin, who told me that when the splines got one rib out of line I should take the shaft out and put it back on the other side to twist it back again. This idea didn't instill a lot of confidence in me, so I installed a Cooper gearbox and shafts instead. Another thing I didn't like was that the driveshaft, being part of the rear suspension, helped to hold the wheel upright. There was no top wishbone, just a bottom wishbone and the driveshaft, so I'd fitted a top link together with a conventional sliding spline driveshaft. As we were leaving Brands Hatch Colin came running up and asked to look at the car. Then at the first meeting of 1961 he came across again and said 'If you move the inboard link up or down a touch on your rear suspension it'll improve it'. Interestingly, the works Lotus cars were now sporting top links…

The 1961 season started over the Easter weekend at Goodwood. I took Lotus 18 (chassis number 909) for the International 100 race for the Glover Trophy, which was the first full scale race for the new 1500cc Formula 1 in this country. I finished in seventh place, with no great battles for me in the race, but as always I liked to get value for money if I could and I also took along the Lotus Elite for the 10 lap Fordwater Trophy GT race. Mike Parkes won this in a Ferrari 250GT Berlinetta ahead of the Aston Martins of Innes Ireland and Stirling Moss. I only finished eleventh, but that wasn't bad for a car in road trim.

Next stop, Heysel in Belgium for the second Grand Prix of Brussels. Around this time there were any number of non-championship Formula 1 races and this Grand Prix was one of them. One of the problems of running such a meeting was that often the organiser's budget simply didn't stretch to a number of different formulae racing, so they had to make the most of what they could afford. In this instance it meant that the 'Grand Prix' was run in three heats. This, of course, imposed a great strain on the engine and gearbox and if you had a slight problem there was very little time to work on the car between races —all you really had time to do was tweak something and refuel. This sometimes worked to my benefit because being a one car team and on a limited budget myself, I knew the car inside out, had done most of the preparation and might drive the car a little more considerately than some of the works drivers.

If I do say so myself, I drove rather well at Heysel. I was on the third row of the grid behind some of the top F1 drivers of the day, with Bonnier, McLaren and Gurney up front, I was ahead of several more, including Stirling Moss and Innes Ireland.

Heat one was a good race and I finished fifth after a good battle with Roy Salvadori's Cooper. Heat two saw me lying fifth again and I might well have finished there had John Surtees not driven into the back of Jo Bonnier and taken them both out. So it was up to third for me and that's where I stayed. Heat three saw ten of us on the grid – after all it was very much a battle for survival – with Jack Brabham, Bruce McLaren and myself on the front row. A good start, but I couldn't quite hold off Stirling Moss. His Lotus had had engine problems earlier but was now back on four cylinders, so I eventually finished in fourth place for that heat. All this led to me finishing third on aggregate behind Brabham and McLaren, a wonderful podium finish to the day.

That year's Aintree 200 was held in the most atrocious Liverpool weather. Now while I don't mind driving in the rain quite as much as some people seem to, Henry Taylor was quite an expert at wet weather driving. After a few laps I was lying sixth, leading the second batch of protagonists, until Henry decided to draw on his vast experience and pushed me down to seventh, where I finished the race.

After Aintree came Silverstone and my first venture into Inter-Continental racing (the British formula that countered the new 1500cc F1 by still using large capacity engines) which came about through Fred Tuck. Fred's motor racing was done on a broken shoestring, but it was fun to drive for him and on this occasion I

The Marsh Special's first appearance – at the 1963 Debden Speed Trials

On the way to Bouley Bay, Jersey

1967; The Marsh Special with V8 Buick engine, 4WD

1967; The Marsh Special with V8 Buick engine, 4WD

Cessna 182 Skylane in hanger

Twin-engined Piper Apache – parked in the back garden

Ski bobbing (left to right): sons Simon, Peter and Paul

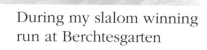

During my slalom winning run at Berchtesgarten

A successful weekend

Judith Yates
with ships
dog, Sacha

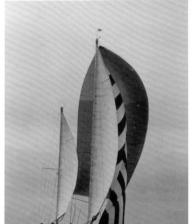

Syanora II
under sail

Syanora III guarded by Boris

Another feather in his cap

Pheasant shoot-
ing party of hill
climbing friends

An early shooting foray with Father in
Norfolk

With Gillian Goldsmith in Top Esses at Shelsley (Bill Chaplin's championship-winning trike)

On the startline at Gurston with Ian Drowne

Rejuvenated 4WD Marsh Special at Prescott – in the early 1990s

Rovercraft at Gurston's Deer Leap

drove the ex-Salvadori Cooper-Maserati, with the engine from a 250F. We started on the fourth row of the grid beside Lorenzo Bandini in another Cooper-Maserati that belonged to the Italian Centro Sud team and was a year younger than the one I was driving. I had a good old ding-dong with Bandini until one of the twin magnetos gave up the ghost, which rather dropped me down on power and eventually I retired. However, I was also driving a Ford engined Lotus 20 at Silverstone for Ted Robbins in the Formula Junior race, which is a story in itself.

Ted took the Lotus to Silverstone in his van and when I arrived he was checking the rear suspension. The car, he said, had been moving about in the back of the van and the rear radius arms had been bent. However they'd been straightened, so we started off the race with a car which had already been damaged. I later heard a story, which I'm not entirely sure if I believe, that Ted had made a hash of changing down into first gear going up the very steep Sunrising Hill and the Lotus had shot out of the back of the van… So we started off with a damaged car and then found that the gear ratios were way out and not at all suitable for Silverstone. Ted went off in search of a high crownwheel and pinion while Di and I started to take the Renault gearbox off the car. We found there were still a few teeth left on first gear, but not many. I was a bit worried about this but there was not much I could do about it. We put the higher crownwheel and pinion in, put it all back together and finally, before we could get on the circuit, we had to overfill the engine with oil as it wasn't a dry sump unit and tended to use a lot of oil.

At 75 miles it was one of the longer Formula Junior races and while we knew the engine would be dry by the end, that extra pint of oil was a bit too much. I eased very gingerly off the start because of the problems with first gear and for a while was chased by a cloud of smoke. Eventually it disappeared and I felt things were going better. In describing it as 'Without a doubt the most exciting race of the day', *Autosport* reported that I '… suddenly started gaining on the (leading) trio …' After swapping positions once or twice with Mike McKee I passed both Mike and the second placed Tony Maggs and stayed there. I couldn't catch Jim Russell, but if I'd had a proper start I might have been up there with him. I did have the satisfaction of setting the first Silverstone lap at over 100mph in a Formula Junior car. In fact my performance rather went to Ted Robbins' head as he had that signwritten on the car!

Taking my two Lotuses to Prescott for the Bugatti Owners' Club meeting, it was good to be back on the hills and see some of the old faces again. I managed a 52.70 with the Formula 1 car, which took the class and BTD, and had a class win with the Lotus Elite as well. The old Cooper Twin had started sliding into the background rather, but it was nice that you could still take a top notch circuit car and do well with it on the hills. Not something you could easily do today.

After this we had an outing to Crystal Palace with the Lotus 18 and another really good ding-dong, just behind the leaders, with Jackie Lewis. I came off better in the end and went on to take third behind Roy Salvadori and Henry Taylor.

I didn't go to Crystal Palace much, but I do remember driving a Connaught sports car there for Peter Bell. It was a 1500cc Lea Francis engined car of which only two were built. It had a pre-selector gear box and a glassfibre body which seemed to be held on with self-tapping screws, so it used to shake, rattle and vibrate in the wind. But it was quite a quick car and, much to my embarrassment, I found myself on the front row of the grid next to Colin Chapman's Lotus-MG and Archie Scott-Brown's Lister-MG. My tactic was simple, to try and get to the first corner ahead of the others so they'd have the hassle of trying to pass me. I know I was ahead of Archie (who had a deformed hand which he put into a little cup on the end of the gear lever) because he eventually wriggled past me, switching from side to side. Whether this was his normal driving style or whether he did it to try and intimidate people I don't know, but I didn't want to get too close to him if he was going to drive like that.

All the top names were at Brands Hatch for the 76-lap Silver City Trophy race. I was around the middle of the grid on the fourth row. It was a good race, with people overtaking left right and centre then calling in at the pits as mechanical problems took their toll. At the finish it was Moss, Clark, Brooks, Salvadori, Gurney and myself, so all in all a good result. There was a Formula Junior race at this meeting won by another Moss, namely Bill, in a Gemini. I always took a bit of an interest in the Gemini. It was built by the Chequered Flag firm, who were specialist sports car dealers in Chiswick, West London and I drove one of their cars at Snetterton. It was a nice little car and unique in that it had inboard discs at the front with little drive shafts coming in to the brakes, but I seem to remember that I didn't drive it as fast as I would like to have done.

Back to 1961 and once again I sneaked a hill climb in amongst all the racing, taking BTD at Shelsley Walsh. Some of the old names were still around; Reg Phillips, Patsy Burt, Phil Scragg and one or two new ones too. Peter Boshier-Jones had followed brother David into hill climbing, there was Betty Haig of the whisky family and Arthur Owen in his Cooper. But in 1961 circuit racing was the priority and early in July we were at Silverstone for the 52 lap, 150 mile British Empire Trophy race.

At this distance I can't quite remember why but I was back in a Cooper Climax. It wasn't a very big grid – only 18 cars – and possibly because I was in the older car I was on the fourth row out of five. But as one might expect from a race of this calibre, I was in very good company. I don't remember it being a particularly exciting race although Bandini in the Centro Sud Cooper-Maserati and I swapped places a few times, with him winning out in the end and finishing seventh to my eighth. I did manage the sixth fastest lap in 1m39.4sec (three seconds slower than winner Stirling Moss) or 106.01 mph. One memorable feature of the meeting was that Juan Manuel Fangio dropped the flag to start the main race. He also appeared on the Formula Junior grid to chat with the drivers.

In fact the Formula Junior race had so many entries, 60, that they held it in two heats of 25 laps with the fastest time over the distance deciding the winner. I was in heat one and tried to stick to the back of Bill Moss's Gemini. I missed a huge five-car shunt on lap two and eventually passed Bill but the Cooper-BMC car I was driving for the Midland Racing Partnership suddenly slowed and we had to retire.

For the British Grand Prix at Aintree it was so wet that one of the local department stores completely sold out of plastic macs! In very exalted company I started on the eleventh row out of twelve in the Lotus. Von Trips, Phil Hill and Ritchie Ginther made it a Ferrari one/two/three, but it wasn't a particularly happy weekend for me, what with the weather and having to stop to change a plug fairly early on. In fact I couldn't even tell you where I finished that day.

Next came a typically hectic August Bank Holiday weekend with the German Grand Prix at Nurburgring immediately followed by the Guards Trophy race at Brands Hatch.

The German Grand Prix was a full Formula One grid with 26 of the best drivers there. I was in position 20 just behind my old friends Lorenzo Bandini and Jack Lewis. Jack was six seconds faster than me in qualifying – but that was put into perspective when you consider that Phil Hill in his Ferrari was 36sec quicker still; the only qualifier to get under nine minutes. In fact it was the first time the nine minute barrier had been broken at Nurburgring. But Stirling Moss won, beating the works Ferraris driving Rob Walker's privately entered Lotus in what many considered was one of his finest races. Once again, Fangio dropped the starting flag for a race which, for me, would turn into a bit of a nightmare.

I was way out in the countryside when the car stopped. Running, for some reason, without the bottom side panels in place alongside the engine I looked in there and could see that a wire had come off the distributor. The little terminal had broken. My problem now was how to get the insulation off the end of the wire and wrap it round so that I could get back to the pits for a more permanent repair. I resorted to running along the line of German spectators asking, in broken English, if anyone had a penknife! Eventually somebody realised what I was babbling about and we got the job done. This enabled me to get back to the pits, where we made a rather better job of it and I was able to resume racing. In those days we had rather more mechanical failures, so if you could get back out you did, to finish the race if at all possible. I did finish it, in fifteenth place (the last classified finisher), which I think was pretty good when you think that eleven cars didn't finish at all.

After Nurburgring it was a quick dash back to Kent where I was driving for Fred Tuck in the Guards Trophy at Brands Hatch. As I mentioned, Fred's racing was done on a shoestring and on getting to Brands I discovered the team orders were to do a few laps and then come into the pits because they hadn't put up enough starting money for a full race!

So after a rather disappointing race at Brands, as far as I was concerned, it was back to a few hill climbs. Having discovered how well the Lotus went on the hills I'd entered for the championship and the next event was Bouley Bay. Local Jerseyman Mac Daghorn won the event and: '...also beat Tony Marsh by 1.18 sec, no mean feat against so experienced an opponent', reported *Autosport*, saying that I was 'way out ahead in the championship' with three wins already.

Although hill climbing was still taking second place to the circuit racing in 1961, my next two events were also uphill. The first was at Shelsley, where I was pictured in *Autosport* setting a new record of 34.48 seconds with a borrowed BRM. The drive really came about during a visit to the Belgian Grand Prix at Spa earlier in the year and a chat with former British Hillclimb champion and BRM founder Raymond Mays. At Spa I'd wandered up the pit lane after practice, as was my wont, to chat with the BRM mechanics. Then later, while talking to Raymond Mays at the champagne party, he mentioned that Sir Alfred Owen had read them the riot act, telling them to be more self sufficient and to sell off some of their older cars. Mays thought the old 2.5-litre BRM would go quite well at Shelsley and asked if I would like to drive it there. So after I'd set the new hill record I felt rather obligated to buy the BRM. Part of the deal was that they would adapt the chassis at the rear to take a 1.5-litre Climax engine as well. That way I could use the 2.5 BRM unit for hill climbing and the 1.5 Climax for Formula One. So that was how my hillclimb BRM came about. However while they were beautifully made cars, they were actually very difficult for the private owner to work on.

In fact at Spa I'd had one or two problems with the Lotus in practice and didn't qualify for the Belgian Grand Prix. The Belgian team, Equipe National Belge, had even more problems than I did, but because they were the national team they automatically had entries. So they hired my Lotus and hastily sprayed it yellow for Willy Mairesse to drive.

But it was the F1 Lotus that I took to the National at Prescott, alongside my road going Elite. We took third in class with the Elite, behind Phil Scragg in his Aston Martin and Austin Nurse in his own Elite, but this was in the dry. It was still dry when I managed to set a new hill record of 50.70 seconds in the Lotus. Later on the rain came in and some drivers had difficulty in staying on the track. Normally the wet times are around four to five seconds slower, but I managed to stay within 2.5 seconds of my dry time with the Formula One car and, according to Patrick Benjafield, showed 'masterly technique'. Part of my success could have been down to my new German Dunlop road tyres; they were something else again.

Back to the circuits and to Zeltweg in Austria, where I put the new BRM, now fitted with the Climax engine, on the second row of the grid despite a lot of trouble with flooding carbs. Reg Parnell, manager of the Yeoman Credit Team, was tremendously helpful and we eventually discovered that it had the BRM high pressure fuel pump on it, which put out 10 lb/sq inch, instead of the usual one which just put out 3 or 4 lb/sq inch. Roy Salvadori and Wolfgang Seidel were alongside me on the second row with just a hundredth of a second separating us. After a moderate start I moved up to a rather comfortable third place behind Jim Clark and eventual winner Innes Ireland, when I had more problems with the fuel pump and called into the pits to retire. We'd been playing with the adjustment of the pump but the pressure release valve wasn't shutting off properly. Rather disappointing, and the BRM had to go back to have a new fuel pump fitted.

At Oulton Park for the Gold Cup, I put the car on the third row of the grid just four hundredths of a second behind the American, Masten Gregory. I was two seconds behind Graham Hill in his works BRM, but whereas his had been specially built for racing mine was, as I've said, a compromise. However, when it came to the start there was a big hole in the grid where my car should have been – the BRM mechanics were still working on it! Shades of things to come? Well, possibly. Eventually I did manage to start and although I had a quick visit to the pits shortly afterwards I managed to work my way up to seventh place, four laps adrift by the finish.

But for the second year running, I won the Lewis-Evans Trophy race at Brands at the end of September. The only real Formula One challengers were John Campbell-Jones in a Cooper, Tim Parnell's Lotus, Mike Spence's works Emeryson, Brian Naylor's JBW-Maserati and Keith Greene in his Gilby. Having qualified for pole position I got a good start and never really felt challenged throughout the race, taking the chequered flag and the fastest lap at 92.08 mph. This was the only race BRM won in 1961. Interestingly, looking back, Hugh Dibley was in the race running a 'stretched' 1475cc Ford Anglia/ Classic engine in his Lola Junior. I was later to buy an engine from Hugh for a rather special project.

After a hectic season's racing it was good to get back to speed events at the end of September, when I took the F1 Lotus to the Hagley speed trials at Chateau Impney. Here we beat course record holder Reg Phillips in his Fairley, although we didn't manage to beat Reg's record. It rather amuses me to read the *Autosport* report, which states that Mike Hatton in his ex-Christie car just beat Peter Gaskell in his ex-Marsh car. I would just beat Mike in the Hill Climb Championship, sharing second place with Arthur Owen behind 1961 champion David Good. While at Chateau Impney, David had a bit of bad luck, spinning on his first run in the dry then getting a wet run.

Finally, in 1961, I took the F1 Lotus on my first visit to Wiscombe Park in Devon for the 750 Motor Club meeting. Coincidentally, Hugh Dibley took his F1 Lola there too, for his first visit. As ever with a new hill I walked Wiscombe several times, and really enjoyed practice. However what I enjoyed more was breaking the hill record with my first timed run of 46.21 seconds. Even better was taking a bit more off with a second run of 45.80. David Good's challenge faded with a broken crankpin, but my time stirred Wiscombe veteran (the hill opened in 1958) Wally Cuff to new heights, who chased hard for 46.92 in his Cooper 1100.

1962 began with a report in *Autosport* that BRM V8 engines had been ordered by Jack Lewis and myself, with both to be installed in ex-works cars.

The people at BRM had agreed that I could have one of the latest V8 engines and they would put it into last year's Formula One car, which was an interim model. It was very similar to the 2.5-litre car I had but not quite the same as the F1 car they subsequently designed, although this one was modified to take the V8 1.5-litre engine. The first race of the year was to be the Grand Prix de Bruxelles at Heysel and even before we got there the fun began. BRM rang up and asked if they could borrow my car as Ritchie Ginther's had caught fire in testing. I said sorry, but Brussels is one of my better circuits and I really want to drive there. But at the end of the first practice session I had my first BRM hiccup – the gearbox casing had split. BRM had a spare, and said that if Graham Hill didn't need it I could borrow it. Graham was duly asked, he didn't want it and it was fitted to my car, which I put on the second row of the grid behind Clark, Moss, Hill and Mairesse. Both Moss and myself made really good starts with Stirling winning out. However at Chaussée Romaine corner Stirling's front brakes locked up and he shot up the escape road, leaving me out front.

This didn't last too long, especially with Hill having the very latest V8 BRM with fuel injection. Both he and Mairesse in the V6 Ferrari passed me fairly early on. Stirling had rejoined and was doing his very best to get back up to the front. Eventually, he too passed me but no one else got by and I finished Heat One in fourth place; behind Hill, Moss and Mairesse but ahead of John Surtees, Jo Bonnier, Innes Ireland and the rest of the field.

Now came heat two. In those days the regulations stated that Formula One cars should be self-contained and have their own on-board starter. We had to drive to our grid positions and stop our engines until a special board, in addition to the various minute boards, was held up to indicate that engines should be started. Both Graham Hill and myself tried like mad, but neither of us could start our cars. Now came a hiccup in the translation of the regulations. BRM seemed to have the English regulations from 1961 which allowed push starts, whereas the Belgians had their own regulations, which didn't. We could be pushed back to the pits for repairs, but not push started.

Nevertheless Graham and I were push started and we both set off in hot pursuit of the field, only to be black flagged at the end of our first lap. It was a shame really – I think the organisers were looking to help eventual winner Willy Mairesse in the Ferrari. Willy was a Belgian and obviously they wanted him to win, even to the point of failing to notice that he reversed on the track (which definitely wasn't allowed) and even though he hit and damaged Trevor Taylor's Lotus. I think there was a bit of favouritism going on, but Heysel was an interesting event even if it was a bit disappointing.

On 15th April, we went to Debden for the National Speed

Trials where my BRM powered Marsh Sprint Special took BTD from Patsy Burt in her Cooper-Climax. This wasn't the car's first public outing as I'd called in at Wellesbourne near Leamington Spa on my way back from testing the car at Finmere where, according to Paul Watson's Seasonal Survey for 1962 in *Autosport*, I'd given '...a shattering demonstration of things to come.'

This first Marsh Special came about through the problems with changing between the 2.5-litre BRM engine and the 1.5-litre Climax. With the Cooper and the Lotus you had, say, this hole and that bolt and you just put the two together. With the BRM nothing was that simple. It all had to be perfectly lined up, the bolt had to be machined just the right size to fit the hole. You couldn't just throw it together. You had to be very precise – it was really quite a hassle. So my mechanic and I had decided that, for something to do over the winter, it would be quicker to build our own chassis for hill climbing, using the 2.5-litre BRM engine, and leave the 4-cylinder Climax engine in the BRM proper. And what was known as the BRM powered Marsh Sprint Special was the car that we built. It was such a good car – a superb car I should say; I think it won every hill climb I entered it in.

Debden was a bit frustrating in a way, even though we did take BTD. It was a straight line sprint where I averaged 99.9mph over the half mile. It would have been so nice to have rounded it up. During the day, Jenks (Denis Jenkinson) offered me a ride round the perimeter track on his sprint motorcycle. Having set me off he suddenly remembered that it was set up for going in a straight line, not round corners! Fortunately nothing untoward happened...

Then it was off to France again, to Pau in particular, with the V8 BRM. This was an Easter meeting so many of the top British names would have been at Goodwood – including, of course, Stirling Moss who would sadly end his F1 career there with the crash at St Mary's. Nevertheless, there was a good turnout at Pau. With Jim Clark, Ricardo Rodriguez and Jo Bonnier on the front row, I was on row three alongside Lorenzo Bandini's Ferrari and my old sparring partner Jack Lewis in his own privately entered BRM.

The first practice session hadn't been without its drama when the clutch went silly on me. If you want to stop you press the clutch, but I had to do the reverse – if I wanted to stop I had to take my foot off the clutch and to go, I had to press it. With the BRMs being so beautifully made, clearances were absolutely minimal. Grit had got into the bell-housing and jammed the clutch thrust race on its shaft. The road circuit at Pau required gearchanges every two to three seconds and as the sticking thrust race worked ever closer to the fingers, eventually the clutch went over centre and worked backwards.

It was surprising what petrol sloshed into the bell-housing would do and we managed to free it off. Then, just to be difficult, the car stopped dead in the next practice session. My analysis was that it had to be electrical, not fuel, so we started looking round. Unlike the modern car there wasn't much to look at, and when we took the cap off the Lucas distributor there was no rotor arm, just a lot of dust and some bits and pieces.

Wilkie Wilkinson had been sent over to look after Jack Lewis and myself because with the other BRMs at Goodwood, we were the works entries at Pau. But although I was a works entry I didn't even have a spare wheel. How things have changed. And I think BRM were even on 10% of the enhanced starting money!

This would be a difficult one, said Wilkie, because the distributors had been specially made for BRM. With only one per engine it would be no good phoning round for another one because there weren't any. I went round all the garages in Pau trying to find something to adapt but with no luck, so we carefully retrieved all the bits and pieces of rotor arm, got out the Araldite and stuck them all back together before doing a slow bake job in the oven.

Another problem with the car was that those early V8 BRM exhaust systems had individual pipes all pointing up into the air. The engine obviously had a vibration period as every time you took your foot off the accelerator they'd all shake about and every so often one would fall off. I'd spied this old bicycle frame in somebody's back garden and when nobody was around, I climbed over the fence and 'borrowed' it, using the tubes to make up stays to support my pipes.

After all these trials and tribulations we eventually got to race day and after various mishaps, Trintignant won, Rodriguez was second, Jack Lewis finished third and I was fourth. Once the race was over, Wilkie wanted to take off the cover to look at the engine. It was then we discovered a big crack in the cylinder block, right in the centre of the vee. Only later did I learn that BRM had already fabricated a steel plate to try and strengthen these blocks.

During the race in Pau I did have problems with Bandini in the second Ferrari. He was holding me up and in the end I had to resort to tapping him on his shoulder, just to let him know I was behind. He still had the dent in his tail when he appeared at Aintree. Also, it's interesting that *Autosport*'s Continental correspondent, Gerard 'Jabby' Crombac, said that I'd felt unwell during most of the race having tried some fancy French food the night before. Now I do remember that we went out for supper, but I think it was more a case of me trying to wind him up about his country's reputation for fine food.

From Pau it was more or less straight up to Liverpool for the Aintree 200, so there was no time to do anything about the V8 BRM's cracked block. I'm afraid I just did the nuts up a bit tighter, turned up as a 'starting money special' and very early on in the race retired with no oil in the engine. Obviously the engine was just pumping the oil out, which made one wonder how much further I could have gone on at Pau without running into mechanical troubles.

After all this it was quite a relief to get the Marsh BRM out for Prescott where it took BTD in 48.84 seconds, setting a new hill record. The meeting was rather a Marsh benefit I'm afraid, because I also took the old Climax engined BRM and ran second BTD with that too. And, now I look closer at the *Autosport* report, I see that Peter Gaskell had his picture in there, running my old Cooper-JAP.

The next meeting was the Silverstone International Trophy, where Frank Gardner in a Brabham-Ford beat my 1961 Formula Junior Lotus record by 1.2 seconds. Immediately after Aintree the V8 had gone back to BRM to be repaired, but during practice at Silverstone I was totally disgusted with it – I could have gone faster in my old Formula Two Cooper. My car was on carburettors whereas the works cars, driven by Graham Hill and Ritchie Ginther, were on fuel injection. I had a big grumble to BRM who sent for their carburettor man from Bourne. He had a quick look and said no wonder it was bad; the petrol levels were all over the place. Now that engine was supposedly straight off the test bed! It did make me wonder, because at the Brussels Grand Prix I'd got to the first corner before Graham Hill in the works car. I'd sort of apologized, saying that I'd done one of my hill climb starts, but I think it had been noticed. They put the carburation right for second practice at Silverstone and the car went a lot better after that, though not quite as quick as Jack Lewis's BRM. I did get my revenge on him during the race though as I finished in seventh place to his ninth and I managed 51 of the 52 laps, to his 50, so I'm sure I would have enjoyed lapping him even if his fastest lap was 105.37 mph to my 104.54. And bearing in mind my comments about the exhaust pipes, Graham Hill won the race at Silverstone but was down to one exhaust stack on one side and two on the other.

After Silverstone the car went back to BRM once again, but more of that later. My next event was Wiscombe Park, with the Marsh BRM. This was my second visit to the hill, which seemed very well suited to the car, and we managed to break the record on successive runs. But although this was a British championship event, my new record of 45.49 seconds wasn't in any danger because soon after, down came the rain. I took BTD with the new record but only managed fourth in the championship runs behind Ray Fielding's ex-works 1960 BRM, Josh Randles and Arthur Owen.

A week later at Shelsley, Ray took the honours again with 34.65. I climbed in 33.96, but was only on a demonstration run. This was because I'd originally hoped to compete at Monaco but by now, Jack Lewis and I were involved in a wrangle with BRM about the suitability of their cars for the private owner. Jack and I had also been due to drive in the Belgian Grand Prix at Spa but, again, this didn't happen.

So my next event was Prescott with another BTD on 50.14 seconds in the Marsh BRM. It was a new class record, even if we couldn't beat my existing course record of 48.84. But then came another notable weekend of motorsport. Notable, as we competed at Bo'ness hill climb, near Edinburgh, on the Saturday before driving down to Evesham Automobile Club's sprint at Long Marston on the Sunday. Well, we'd got to drive home at some stage and Long Marston was only a little bit further (such is the enthusiasm of youth). Bo'ness was another resounding success for the Marsh BRM, even if I hadn't driven there since 1954. We took BTD with a new record of 30.99, beating Arthur Owen, Ray Fielding and Ian McLaughlin along the way.

I wasn't the only person to make the quick dash south to Long Marston, which was well worthwhile from my point of view. In the half mile sprint event I took BTD in 18.48 seconds, only to be beaten by Sidney Allard in his famous dragster in the 440 yard *Autosport* Trophy runs. Sidney did a spectacular 11 seconds dead, while I could only manage 12.17. This was when drag racing was just getting off the ground over here and dragster classes were tied in with other speed events.

At both Bo'ness and Long Marston we were noted as having created a lot of tyre smoke wheel-spinning off the line. This was partly due to the characteristics of the BRM engine and did influence us when we later started to build the 'baby' Marsh Special. If you dropped the clutch at 5000 rpm the 2.5-litre BRM would probably stall, whereas at 5500 rpm you would sit there with tyres smoking. There was such a narrow rev band that to avoid stalling you tended to err on the high side.

After another long trek north with the Marsh BRM, to Rest-and-Be-Thankful, my second timed run took BTD with a 52.52. But it was on my first championship run that disaster struck. At Rest-and-Be-Thankful there's a hump where you take off, but when you're going at a rate of knots you go quite high and land with a serious thump that bangs the sump on the ground. This run was going to be a good one and I was all geared up for a record-breaker. I'd realised that because of the road camber, if I drove a little bit off the centre-line I wouldn't be flying so high. This meant putting the nearside wheels just on the edge of the grass. But this time we landed a bit too far to the left, shot off to the right, up the bank, bounced back into the centre of the road, bounced again and landed on a little stone wall on the left. Later inspection showed this was just short of a marshal's telephone, so he must have been getting quite excited. After teetering on this stone wall, slowly the car fell off, away from the road. Fortunately the Marsh BRM had a very big cockpit and I ended up sitting on the grass with the seat on my head.

My rescuers were quickly on the scene and were very enthusiastic, but unfortunately they didn't hang on to the car when they pushed it off me and it rolled down the mountainside. It could have been repaired but we were now well into the season; if we were doing a major job we would, in the light of experience, have built the car differently. So there didn't seem much point in burning midnight oil when we'd have probably thrown the car away at the end of the year. In retrospect (which is always a wonderful thing) it was rather a shame because I could easily have won the championship again – the car was invincible. I have always put this particular mishap down to driver error, but was it a coincidence that the left steering arm was broken at a weld? Who knows…

So there I was, with just one competition car left to me; my old 2.5-litre BRM with the alternative 4-cylinder Climax engine. It didn't let me down. At Shelsley Walsh in August I took the championship points (with a 38.48) from Chris Summers in his Cooper-Chevrolet and Peter Westbury's Daimler V8 powered Cooper when the weather improved. Our timed runs had taken place in rather wetter conditions and the class results had been an exact reverse of the championship positions. David Good double-drove my car that day as I'd not quite finished fitting my Climax engine, which he'd bought, into his Cooper. I had a guest drive as well, as Ian Sievewright had asked me if I'd like a go in his Tipo 625 Ferrari, the same car in which Maurice Trintignant had won the 1955 Monaco Grand Prix.

Ian might have known what the answer would be and driving this 1950s 'upright' GP single seater was jolly good fun. I managed a 46.03, not bad considering the weather and the fact I'd never driven the car before. Some time later, I heard, the car was lying around unused and was virtually given away, before ending up in an auction down in Monte Carlo where it achieved its full value.

I enjoyed the opportunity to drive other cars although I was always conscious that they belonged to someone else.

Then it was off to Prescott for the final hill climb of the season where, despite many class records falling, my old course record remained intact. David Good had his first official outing in the Climax engined Cooper and went extremely well to give me a good run for my money in the championship runs. I did hold him off to take both BTD and the top championship points and we were the only drivers to get into the 49s that day.

So at the end of the hill climb season it was Jerseyman Arthur Owen that won in his 2.5 Cooper-Climax T53, followed by Ray

Fielding in his BRM, myself and then Ian McLaughlin's Cooper-JAP.

But there was one final meeting to attend - the Brighton Speed Trials. Chris Summers took top honours that day in his 4.7-litre Cooper-Chevrolet powered Cooper with a new class record of 21.69, but I did hang on for second BTD with 21.77.

But other things had been happening in 1962, notably the problems with BRM.

Jack Lewis had been having similar experiences to myself. His father, a hard headed business man, wasn't happy about the way Jack had been treated and asked if I would join them in taking BRM to task. We'd handed the cars back after Silverstone in May knowing that if litigation was to be involved, things weren't going to happen very quickly. Jack and I were intending to take BRM to court because we weren't getting the support we needed from the company and the cars were very difficult for the private owner, even with specialised facilities, to work on. At the eleventh hour, BRM owner Sir Alfred Owen came on the telephone inviting me to a meeting. The eventual outcome was that BRM agreed to take the cars back, so a nasty situation was avoided.

The other major thing in my life during 1962 was a move from Kinver, where Di and I had been tenant farmers on one of the family farms, to our own property at Petersfield in Hampshire. In fact it would have been very difficult for me to have a full season's racing that year as we'd bought the farm at Petersfield in March and were trundling backwards and forwards from there to Kinver, sometimes as many as three times a week, for many weeks. This went on until the autumn, so during that summer I was never quite sure which place I was living at. The car transporter came in very handy as a removal van!

In the Midlands my mechanic had changed and my new mechanic Ted Jeffs and I had built up a little business repairing other people's cars and rebuilding engines. We had our own dynamometer and our customers included Count Carel Godin de Beaufort and Wolfgang Seidel. We overhauled both their cars for the coming South African season, but until we got known to the people round Petersfield it was going to be a bit more difficult to keep Ted fully employed. We decided to buy a little filling station at the top of the hill. Froxfield filling station had four pumps and a kiosk, with a house attached. We built a workshop there and it became Froxfield Service Station, where we started building up a bit of a reputation amongst local people with multi-carburettor cars who weren't otherwise being looked after satisfactorily. Ted was the ideal man for the job.

The grapevine did its work and just before the Motor Show I had a tip-off from a friend of mine who worked for Roy Salvadori that I ought to go round to the BMW stand. There they asked me if we'd become BMW Service Agents, saying that with our state-of-the-art workshops we could become BMW dealers if we had a showroom. So one was duly built and we became the first dealer/distributors in Hampshire.

While I was looking for a suitable site for the new venture, Ted wasn't fully employed. He was really a motorcycle man and had worked under Joe Craig of Nortons, and Ted suggested acquiring a Formula Junior car and sponsoring a driver. This idea had definite appeal and we ended up sponsoring Paddy Driver, a South African who'd come over for the 1963 season. I'd got friendly with Paddy while racing on the continent and he and Ted used to go off to race meetings both in this country and abroad, so that kept Ted out of mischief until the garage was bought and the workshop built.

At the end of 1962 Ted and I had wondered what to do next. We decided to build a car which ended up as the little Marsh Special, and this entailed me sitting on the garage floor with some tubes laid out alongside me so that measurements could be taken. One of Ted's many attributes was that he was rather good with pen and paper. He drew up some plans and we started work on the car during the winter of 1962/63. I'd only got a tiny little lathe and some of the parts required, particularly for the suspension, we needed in quantity so we decided to farm the job out. We looked around for a local engineering company and found one in Petersfield itself that was already doing work for Lotus. We would take over drawings, they'd produce the bits, and with the way one thing leads to another I ended up as Chairman of the company. But that's another story…

Meanwhile we'd expanded the BMW business, started selling cars and BMW had spread a few more dealerships around. After the one in Portsmouth folded up we expressed an interest in it. BMW weren't very keen on this idea, even though we'd built up quite a reputation with Portsmouth-based customers coming to us for service We'd drop them at the station to catch their commuting train to London and pick them up later. BMW wanted us to take on a place at Chichester, but we weren't keen on this idea.

In addition to the Portsmouth/Chichester debate we felt that BMW were hounding us in other ways. They were regulating the expansion of our business in that they restricted the number of cars we could have according to postcodes, which was fine until you realise that we had a lot of cows in our area but not a lot of people. There was also a vast increase in the amount of paperwork and they wanted us to install a computer, to help cope with this and to order spares. On the front of the premises they wanted us to have what we called a tombstone; a big, freestanding BMW emblem. This would alter the whole appearance of the place and we didn't think would go down very well, especially with the local planners. We had already had problems with the garage and workshop developments, at one point being refused permission for the workshop as it would have been too high. No problem - we reduced the height by lowering the base into a large hole in the ground.

In the end BMW told us things could get very difficult if we wouldn't open the place in Chichester, so we told them we were finding it equally difficult to meet all their requirements and that it would be better to say goodbye.

After we'd finished with BMW we had to find something else, but this proved difficult for our service station manager to cope with. We tried Citroen, but he'd grown up with BMWs and found it very difficult to put his heart and soul into the new enterprise. It wasn't the same, with customers arguing over the price of a new choke cable when you were used to dealing with a £1,000 parts bill for a BMW. He lost his enthusiasm and I decided to pack it all in and sell the place. Just recently, it has all been knocked down and three or four nice houses have been built on the site.

Having digressed a little, let us go back to motorsport and 1963. *Autosport* decided to do an article on the new Marsh Special and sent Patrick McNally along to find out all about it and take some photographs. He seemed quite keen on it, giving out all the vital statistics of our new spaceframe car, with its Shorrock supercharged 1500cc Climax FPF unit and Citroen gearbox, which we'd built in around three months. Two of the photographs printed showed the German made Dunlop SP tyres very well. They were fabulous tyres in the wet and while the normal Dunlop racing tyre would probably have been better in the dry, the SPs were pretty good all-round tyres. Bear in mind that we didn't have several sets of wheels and tyres to chop and change like we do today.

The first public outing for the car was Debden Speed Trials where we came second in the 1500cc racing car class, a quarter of a second behind Elsie Price in her 1.5 litre Mk 6 Lotus. Patsy Burt was a further quarter-second away in her Cooper Climax so it was all pretty close. I also used to enter the Dragster class at Debden, run over a quarter of a mile, coming fifth on this occasion with a 14.86. Mike Eyre's Cooper-Buick won in 13.21, so I still had a bit to do even if I was quite pleased with our first outing.

I took the 2.5-litre BRM to Mallory Park on Easter Monday and won the Formula Libre race. John Taylor tried his best to get his Cooper ahead, but averaging just over 90mph I kept him about ten seconds behind for most of the twenty laps. I also had the fastest lap at 52.2.

Although I still had the 2.5 litre BRM to race, having the new car to play with I think I made an unconscious decision to do more hill climbing in 1963. The first of these was at Loton Park where we took the first round of the hill climb championship on the newly extended (to 900 yards) course, run in those days by Severn Valley MC. It wasn't the best of days, rather wet at times with cold winds. Even so my first timed run was 37.38 which Phil Scragg's BRM just managed to beat by 0.13 seconds. On the second runs I improved to 37.03 and Phil's time was looking good, but he fluffed a gear change so the win was mine. Not bad considering the car was virtually straight out of the box – except that we built it ourselves and it didn't have a box!

Apart from the Marsh BRM we really didn't have a lot of experience in building cars from scratch, but the Marsh Special just worked. We were looking after other people's cars when we were at Kinver, which gave us the opportunity to study them minutely. And we did have a nice flat, concrete pad for setting up suspension on so we could relate the measurements to the way we knew the cars handled. This all helped to design a car that would suit me.

The 2.5 BRM engine's characteristics, combined with the fact it had quite a lot of horsepower, had made the Marsh BRM difficult to drive, particularly in the wet. We decided that if we had a small car, the track would look bigger and we could have less horsepower, because a small car would weigh less and have the same power to weight ratio as the bigger car. That was the theory, but the problem was that we couldn't scale the driver down enough to match it! As it turned out, we scaled the car down a little bit too much. It was a tad twitchy and I think the centre of gravity was a bit too high, because of the relative size of engine and driver. However, to get a bit ahead of the story, we were second in the championship in the car's first year.

After Loton I took both cars to Prescott. Unfortunately I nominated the Special as the car for the championship, as the BRM wasn't running quite right. It proved the wrong decision as the Special wasn't as fast and while I took BTD with the BRM in 48.68, I was only fifth in the championship runs with 50.90 in the Special. However, even with its peculiarities I was quite au fait with driving the BRM by now, whereas I was only just learning to drive the Special. The BRM also went off colour at Rest-and-be-Thankful, which turned out to be a broken valve spring. Wilkie Wilkinson came down from Bourne to the farm at Petersfield to change it which I remember well; it was harvest time and we had Wilkie out driving a tractor, helping with bale carting.

I also took both cars to Wiscombe Park, where the BRM went extremely well to take BTD and the championship win. The Special wasn't quite so lucky that day. I mentioned that it could be a bit on the twitchy side and Wiscombe's no easy hill to drive – the car got away from me slightly and we went straight into the bales at the Gateway, denting the front bodywork. The incident started at Bunny's Leap (as so many do) where the faster you're going the more you need to control it – a bit like the finish S-bend at Gurston, where in a less powerful car you can straight-line it but when you have more power you have to drive it as a corner.

Before Wiscombe, we'd decided to change the 1.5-litre

supercharged Climax engine to a similar, unblown Climax unit bored out to 2-litres. The 1.5 didn't develop quite as much horsepower as we expected and this was quite important to our power to weight ratio theory. All in all another steep learning curve for the Special!

One of the good things about building your own car is that you know it, literally, back to front, so it didn't take long to repair the damage. After the shakedown of the new engine at Wiscombe we were off to Barbon Manor in Westmorland in the middle of May. The car proved its worth here with BTD and the top championship place. But we didn't win our class. That honour went to Peter Westbury, who had been pushing me hard all day in his new Felday-Daimler. Once again I'd taken the BRM along, so I suppose you could say that I was having twice as many runs and therefore should be at an advantage, but as they were totally different motor cars I don't think that argument necessarily holds water.

After Barbon came Shelsley and while I shattered the overall hill record, Agnes Mickel set a new Ladies Record in her 2.5-litre Cooper-Climax, the car in which Arthur Owen had won the championship the previous year. Again I had both cars there and although top honours went to the BRM in 33.54, the Special won its class with a new record of 34.50. After his first timed run in the Felday Peter Westbury had the bad luck to break a crownwheel and pinion, but his time of 34.80 was good enough to hold onto second place.

The Whitsun Prescott saw another BTD and first and second in class. I suppose it could have started getting a bit boring, but these BTDs weren't quite as consistent as it might seem and we also had the challenge of developing the car, as we knew it had still more to offer.

Then it was Long Marston near Stratford on Avon and while Sydney Allard took top honours in the 440 yard straight-line sprint I took the half-mile win with 18.54, beating the record I set in the Marsh BRM in 1962. It's interesting that Sydney's 440 yard time was 10.76, mine was 11.94 and on this occasion Mike Eyre, in his Cooper-Daimler, couldn't better a fourth place 12.63. What a difference a day makes.

In the middle of June came the long drive to the Kinneil Estate in Scotland for the Bo'ness hill climb, where I was on good form and took BTD with the BRM in 31.16. This was achieved in the championship runs with only Ray Fielding, Gray Mickel and myself managing to get under 32 seconds that day. I did take the Special along too, but couldn't better 32.23.

After Bo'ness came Rest-and-be-Thankful again and here, partly due to that broken valve spring, I only managed second in the championship runs, half a second behind Peter Westbury, who set a new hill record in his Felday. The weather was a bit iffy and a drying track meant falling times during the day. Peter narrowly beat my first time before David Good came along and beat both of us. But in the dry championship runs Peter, myself and Ray Fielding were the only ones under 52 seconds, which wasn't bad considering it was my first run there since the accident in the Marsh BRM.

Next was one of my lessening commitments to the race track and a Formula Libre race at Silverstone. The weather was awful and as a result the main event, the Martini International Club Trophy race, was cut from 50 laps to 30. 'Not such a dry Martini!' as the *Autosport* headline said. Now the particular characteristics of the engine in the 2.5-litre BRM, which I've mentioned before, combined with the bad weather meant I didn't make a good start. It may have even been this race when I spun the car when driving in a straight line! Whatever happened, shortly after the start I was down in eleventh position but by lap three I had worked my way up to third. And I've always said, this ability to drive a little better than some in the wet was due to a good grounding in car control at Trials and Driving Tests. However, because of the lead they'd already pulled out I hadn't got much chance of passing either John Taylor's Cooper-Ford or the Hon Patrick Lindsay – in second place with the vast, pre-war Napier Railton – in the remaining ten laps so I stayed in third place. Even so we were the only three to finish all ten laps, the rest of the field being at least one lap behind.

With the new farm and home to put in order, I wasn't finding quite as much time in 1963 for motorsport. I missed one or two championship events but following Great Auclum, Peter Westbury and I were tied for first place on 71 points. As I've mentioned before, Great Auclum was never one of my favourite hills. But I did go to a club event at Dyrham Park, near Bristol, where the Special took BTD in 34.11 seconds.

After this it was Shelsley and another wet meeting, this time in the Special. Bearing in mind how twitchy it could be, I couldn't manage any better than third in the championship runs behind Peter Boshier-Jones' supercharged, Climax-engined Lotus 22 and David Good's Cooper-Daimler.

At Prescott, the Special was definitely off song and got worse as the day progressed. We managed second in class, a second behind Westbury, but in the championship runs finished last and out of the points. Not one of our better days!

A week later came the final championship event at Dyrham Park, where the engine still wasn't sounding right. We did our best, but only managed second in class and third in the championship runs behind Westbury, who clinched the 1963 title with a new hill record, and Boshier-Jones.

The car still wasn't right when we went to Weston-super-Mare for the half mile speed trials on Marine Parade and we finished sixth overall. I always quite enjoyed driving at Weston. It was a funny place and the surface was something else. You'd think you'd got a lot of grip but you hadn't. And if there was a strong breeze and the tide was out, it used to blow sand off the beach and on the course, so it was rather like driving on ball bearings. In addition there was a lot of camber and after the start, when you were just building up speed nicely, you drove alongside a big, low building and caught quite a strong crosswind when you came out the other side – it could be quite exciting!

Still with a misfire, Hagley's sprint at Chateau Impney wasn't the best of days either but we took second in class, a tenth of a second behind David Good. The final outing of the season was at Loton Park and this was one of the few occasions I was disqualified. Well, disqualified might not be quite the right word for it. My mechanic had taken the car and transporter to Loton for me, the idea being that I would fly up later. I was delayed by low cloud and took my runs in quick succession. Later, when I was second BTD, someone protested this, the protest was upheld and out I went.

I think Loton was the first time the car was running half sensibly again and I remember that I'd had a problem or two with the Lotus 18 there. We'd done an engine rebuild on the Lotus and went straight off to Rest-and-be-Thankful followed, almost immediately, by

Spa. The car wasn't going well (this was the time I didn't qualify it and Equipe National Belge hired it from me for Willy Mairesse) and when we got it back home Ted put it on the Crypton machine. We found that the contact breaker had worn and upset the timing far more that I had realised. Running engines on the dynamometer at Kinver, we realised that ignition timing was crucial. I think the problems I had with the Marsh-Climax at the end of 1963 were similar to the one I had with the Lotus. It had been going downhill so slowly that I hadn't realised there was a problem until it was really not running well at all. After a session on the Crypton machine things could be made better.

Another contributory factor could be that in hill climbing there's a long wait between each run until you get to the championship runs, in quick succession. Then as the car heats up, the heat spreads to the ignition condenser which starts to object. When we got the Marsh back on the Crypton tester that's exactly what we found.

Chapter Five

I've mentioned flying a couple of times now, so perhaps this is as good a place as any to put some of those experiences on paper.

My flying log tells me that my first lesson was on 8 July 1963, which was during the second year that we lived in Hampshire. And it was really my father's fault that I took up flying.

Father had got an aeroplane again. He'd had a couple before the war, although he'd had a bit of a mishap with the second one. They were both open two seaters in which you sat fore and aft. He and a local doctor he was friendly with decided they would fly from Birmingham's Elmdon Airport down to Northolt, which was the London airport of the time. When they got back and were about to land, they could see that they would run over a patch of grass that had been re-seeded. To avoid making big grooves in what might have been soft earth, they decided to make use of the aeroplane's 'new fangled' brakes. They upended it and were left hanging upside down in their seat belts. The doctor was shouting blue murder because he could smell petrol, which was carried in tanks in the upper wing above the fuselage and which was now below them. All ended well, but as far as I know the propeller boss, complete with dents and soil, is still in the house at Kinver.

After the war father would sometimes charter a plane (a twin engined De Havilland Dove belonging to Tarmac, the road construction people) and a professional pilot from the local aerodrome, three miles from Kinver, to take him to London or Anglesey. So he decided he was going take up flying again, took his licence, and in addition to chartering the Dove he bought a small plane of his own.

In fact he later made the news in the local paper under the headline; 'Aerial Magistrate Nabs Poachers!' He was flying over his farms and woodlands one Sunday morning when he spotted the poachers. He radioed back to the airfield, who alerted his keeper to go and investigate. The poachers ended up in Brierley Hall Court, where father was Chairman of the Magistrates. Clearly he couldn't try the case himself or they might have received even bigger fines than they did!

Once when I was up at Kinver he took me for a flip round. I was so fascinated by being in a small aircraft. It was like a flying motor car really; I could look down and even see things like rabbits running about. When I got back home I made enquiries and ended up going to Thruxton for flying lessons.

I was in the fortunate position to be able to arrange my own schedule and used to go two or three times a week. I'd have an hour in the morning, let the mind unwind over lunch and then have another hour in the afternoon. The benefit of that was that you didn't lose your touch between morning and afternoon flights. And in fact I got my pilot's licence just over a month later. But in those days, if you went to a recognised flying school you only needed a minimum of 30 hours flying to obtain your licence, assuming that you passed your flying test. I had two or three hours to go before I got to 30 and had to fly around in circles using up the time before I could take my test.

I learnt to fly on a little Piper Colt, a two seater with tricycle undercarriage, so I felt that if I bought a plane it would have to have a tricycle undercarriage as well. I was thinking of buying a Cessna and wondering about an airstrip at the farm, and in fact that came along quite quickly as well. When father came down to view the property I'd acquired he flew into Thorney Island, an active RAF aerodrome at the time. He had a pilot with him on this occasion, who I took up the fields to ask his opinion on an airstrip. He said that if I filled in a ditch and took a hedge out I should just about have enough room, so that was all put in hand.

During my initial training I'd seen an old Tiger Moth at Thruxton, in its typical yellow livery. I said to my tutor, Derek Johnson, 'I ought to have a go in one of those as part of my education'. 'That could be sooner that you think', replied Derek and sure enough, after lunch we walked out to the Tiger Moth. On the way, Derek said I was going to do a revision in spinning. Sitting in this thing with a rip in a canvas side panel and no roof I did feel a little insecure, I must admit. But Derek said that it wasn't often he got to teach people in an aerobatic plane, and the normal teaching planes had their limitations. He asked if I was up for a loop, promptly did one and then invited me to have a go. The opportunity was too good to be missed and he talked me through it, although I must admit I do prefer flying the right way up. It seemed very strange hanging upside down with no roof and the ground was an awfully long way away. Mind you, there were certain advantages to having an open cockpit. Some time later I was able to fly a little training plane called a Beagle which had a cockpit canopy, and Derek did an inverted flight in that. We flew upside down for quite a while and all the bits and pieces on the floor came cascading down into the canopy.

Eventually I flew over the farm with Derek, who was a bit of a flying nut and used to go long distance gliding on his days off. He had a good look at the strip from the air when we'd got it cleared and the grass mown a bit. But before I'd got the strip really operational I discovered the limitations of a PPL (Private Pilot's Licence). You're very restricted as to what you can do. You can only take passengers with you if you've got decent weather, the clouds have to be above a certain height and visibility has to be a certain minimum distance. To fly in clouds you need to fly on instruments and as a preliminary to instrument flying I did what's known as a night rating. For this you need to be able to fly on instruments, or at least to make use of them. The training consisted of wearing a hood so that I could only see the dashboard, not out of the windscreen, and Derek would give me instructions.

I did the requisite training, got my night rating, and did my first night flying around September 1963. I know I'd completed it by 9 October because obviously one needed dark nights and opening hours at Thruxton were restricted. Also, Thruxton didn't have a runway, just a grass airstrip, nor did it have any landing lights. You may remember the old road mending gangs that used to light their road works with a thing like a watering can with a wick; well Thruxton used those to mark the runway. I was taught to land without using the landing lights on the aircraft, so in the final bit it was quite difficult to judge your height above the ground. It was all good experience though.

By 23 October I'd done about nine separate landings at night and that included an hour and three quarters of night flying. This was enough for my night rating which allowed me to take passengers, but which only lasted for a year. If I'd wanted to take passengers after that time I'd have to renew my rating fully, or at least show I'd flown at night during the previous year.

As I said, to get this rating I'd had to do some instrument flying but I decided to continue training on instruments. On one occasion Derek said he would give me a simulated GCA (Ground Control Approach). He would simulate the radio controller in the tower and give me instructions. I was reading the instruments like mad and the altimeter was slowly unwinding; 1000 feet, 750 feet, 500, 400... I was nicely lined up at 400 feet and then continued going down and down. I thought: 'He's going to tell me to look up at any minute'. But the wretched chap never did. 'Ease the throttle and pull back on the stick', he said, and I actually touched down. 'Open the throttle', he said, and off we went again – just a touch and go. It did go off nicely and Derek seemed very confident, but he probably had his hands hovering over the stick all along.

In fact there are two different types of instrument rating. One is for commercial pilots and involves quite a lot of work, but it allows you to fly in airways. Then there is an instrument rating for private pilots, which allows them to take passengers in inclement weather. With this, you can get permission to cross through airways and go in special aerodrome zones.

As far as instruments themselves are concerned there are a number of different types. The altimeter works off barometric pressure and for airspeed, you have a hollow tube underneath the wing which points forward and the airspeed indicator operates on the pressure of the air as you fly along. Your engine speed indicator is obviously a mechanical instrument too, but there are other instruments such as, say, your gyro compass. You actually have two compasses, a conventional one and a mechanical compass which you set up according to your magnetic instrument. You also have a turn and slip indicator because if you turn sharply, in effect you reduce the aeroplane's wingspan and it tends to lose height, so this double instrument has a finger hanging down which tells you whether you're banking left or right. Under the finger is a curved tube with a little ball in it, so if you started to slip sideways the ball would run up the tube. So the finger tells you how steeply you're banking and the tube and ball indicates rudder correction to help maintain your height. The final instrument is for the rate of climb and descent, in feet per minute.

I'd done some flying on the 'limited panel' as they call it, in which some of the instruments that could go out of action due to mechanical problems could be covered up so you couldn't read them, although you still have all the basic instruments. On this particular afternoon Derek told me I was going to do 'recovery from unusual attitudes'.

Now before you attempt anything other than straightforward flying you have to make sure you have enough fuel, enough height and enough visibility. We checked these and then climbed to about 5000 feet. I had the hood on and several instruments had paper discs stuck over the dials. Derek took control of the plane and told me to close my eyes. I could feel the aeroplane climbing, then I could feel it descending. But next time we went up we were turning at the same time and after two or three of these passes the mind loses track a bit. 'Right', he said, 'there you are, recover from that'. Well, I think he'd slowed the engine right down but the airspeed rating was much more than it ought to be, so that suggested we were going down. Also we were in a turn so were spiraling. But in fact we weren't going down, we were going up, because although he'd gone down for a bit to get the speed up, when he handed the controls back to me we were climbing. So from there, I had to assess what was going on from the limited number of instruments I could see, and then sort it all out.

Eventually I got the IMC (Instrument Meteorological Conditions) rating for when the weather wasn't so good and it was quite easy to keep that current. I began to feel more confident, but during the winter months I didn't have so many specific journeys to make. So if it was a nice Sunday afternoon I'd take the opportunity for some flying practice, perhaps round the Isle of Wight, because flying is something you must be able to do automatically.

By now we'd bought our first plane, a four seater Cessna 175 (Golf Alpha Romeo Whiskey Mike). Derek was still at Thruxton (he would eventually leave to start a new flying club at Blackbushe) and the next step was to bring the new aeroplane to the farm. We'd done an overhead recce and a dummy run, so Derek had summed it up and got me practising short field landings at Thruxton, on a small grass triangle with roadways on the sides, as opposed to on the full field. Eventually he thought I was ready, agreed to come with me to see me in and off we went. We were just going down over the house and he said 'You're committed now, because of that big hill in front of us. You've either got to land or have a mishap.' So I landed it, took off and landed it again. After that I was on my own with it.

It was always interesting landing at Soal Farm because the prevailing wind is a side wind. Depending on whether it's from the west or south west, there could be a tail wind element to it as well and some days I was touching down rather faster than I would have liked. Of course to take off, I had to turn the Cessna round and go the other way, but at least we had a slope to help. The other thing I had to watch out for was the dog. If he heard the Cessna coming he would rush up to the landing strip to greet me and that could be a bit disconcerting. Sometimes I would have to stop the engine, open the door to let the dog in and start up again before I could taxi back to the barn.

Round about October 1964, when I'd done about a year's flying, we did a trip to Dusseldorf for the wedding anniversary celebrations of our au pair's parents. This meant going up to Gatwick to clear customs and Gatwick at that time had its own set of buildings for private planes and a special parking area. You went in there to get your weather forecast and file your flight plan; the details of your onward journey, which way you were going, your predicted flight time, how many people you had on board and all that sort of thing. You also had to say what instruments and safety equipment you had on board. This was all telexed down the line, so the air traffic controllers were expecting you. In fact the people meeting us at Dusseldorf were very excited when we got there. They knew we'd arrived because they'd heard 'The next flight arriving from Gatwick...' over the public address system.

It was a bit awe inspiring leaving Dusseldorf. We were given taxi clearance, I trundled off down the perimeter track and found there were a couple of enormous jets in front of me. I kept my distance in case they opened their throttles and blew me over. My plane had a small rear window and as I turned round to mention this to the people in the back, I saw another huge jet looking down on me from a great height. I felt very out of place.

I went to Dusseldorf twice (the other time was for the au pair's wedding) but I think it was on the first trip, coming back into Gatwick, that there was a very strong side wind. All the way in the controller was telling me the wind strength and how it was fluctuating, so I purposely kept the speed up about 10 miles an hour so I'd be still flying when it subsided a bit. The runway was so wide in comparison with what I was used to that I could almost have landed across it. I decided to land on the left hand side and it was just as well I did. When you have a side wind like that you're coming in skewed and into the wind a little bit. You tend to touch down on the one wheel, straighten up quickly and touch down with the other one before finally putting the nose-wheel down. By the time I'd pulled up I was way over on the other side of the runway. It was all quite exciting.

During those fairly early days of my flying career I was still buying cows for our dairy herd. There were some heifers (young cows until they have their first calf) for sale up near Shrewsbury, where a farm was having a dispersal sale of excess stock, so I decided to fly up and have a look at them. I was just coming in nicely to RAF Shawbury when the controller's voice came over the radio: 'Can you pull your finger out a bit, I've got a jet landing right behind you'.

We saw the animals and I arranged to buy a few, then we were taken in to have some refreshment by the chap who was also running a home for disturbed children. Some of the children came into the sitting room to meet the visitors, including a little boy who just stood there and said nothing. I was told he didn't speak at all but he understood everything said to him. The children came to look at the plane before we went and one or two sat inside the plane. I asked this little boy if he would like to sit in it too. 'Oh, yes please', came the reply. That was the first time they'd heard him speak, so we all went home most satisfied.

I had rather an odd experience when I flew to another sale with a nearby aerodrome. It was a very foggy day, so I rang up to enquire what their weather conditions were like. I was told that they weren't very good but they had radar, so if I could get there they would guide me down. Just after I landed and was taxying down the runway, the controller came on: 'I can't see you on the radar any more, where are you? Can you take the next left, please?'

In 1966, my wife Diana decided that she was going to take up flying as well. We would fly up to Blackbushe, she would go off with Derek, have her lesson in our plane and then we'd fly home again. She was doing very well and had got through some of the PPL steps, and the next one was cross country flying. First you fly to an aerodrome you don't know and do a landing, then for your qualifier you have to do a triangular trip, two landings in different aerodromes with a total journey of around 100 miles or so. That was going to be Di's next step, but she got held up by inclement weather. When she finally got around to doing it, Derek noticed she was pregnant and thought it advisable to postpone things.

After that, Peter was born and Di was so busy with the distraction of looking after a baby that she never took up flying again. But it proved very useful because with her experience so far, she could sometimes take control while I was map reading or doing calculations. Eventually I bought a simple autopilot, but it didn't do everything. Where it came in handy was, for example, if you're looking at the map and using the calculator with one hand on the stick, eventually that hand becomes very heavy and you're not going where you ought to be. A simple autopilot would tell that the plane was banking a bit and level it off again. Then there are others that check the height and correct it if you start to go up or down a bit. You can go to another stage and couple the autopilot up with one of the navigation radios, so that when you reach a certain point on your journey it will automatically turn you onto a new course. But I didn't get that far.

I did find the plane quite useful for motorsport, because it meant that my mechanic could take the car and transporter to a meeting and I could follow later. For instance I went up to Rest-and-be-Thankful, flying up to Glasgow, and was back for lunch on Sunday. And for Prescott we flew to Staverton aerodrome and would come back for the Saturday night after practice. It was also quite useful when I was building the four-wheel drive car, the final development of the Marsh Special. I used to fly up to White Waltham, near Reading, and Mike Hewland used to come and pick me up from my 'heavier than air' machine, as he used to call it.

One significant flying date I remember was 22 March 1967, when I flew to Gurston Down Farm just outside Salisbury where the BARC South West Centre were building a new hill climb course. They had asked me to go down and give them the benefit of my experience so I flew down, landed on the top of the hill near to where the finish line now is, gave my advice and then flew home.

After the Cessna 175 I had a slightly bigger aeroplane – and I blame my father for that too. He had a similar plane to mine but it was fitted out with every conceivable type of radio and was in fact licensed to go on airways, providing the pilot was too. There are two categories of radio, the ordinary common or garden one and a super accurate one for airway flying. Father had wanted to sell this plane but was having some difficulty, because it was rather more than the average club flier would want. So we decided to sell my plane and I would have his. And that was how I acquired Golf Alpha Romeo Juliet Tango, a Cessna 182 Skylane. After I picked it up from Oxford, I called in to Blackbushe to do two or three landings to get used to it and then took it to Soal Farm. Once I'd landed I decided I'd turn the thing around, take off and then land again, just for a bit of practice. As I opened the throttle there was a big bang and clouds of smoke came from underneath the engine cowling. So I shut everything off, got out and lifted the little dipstick flap. Clouds of smoke came out of there too, but it seemed to be dispersing. I decided to start the engine again, taxied back to the barn and then rang up the people at Kidlington, Oxford where it had just been for its mandatory engine overhaul. As it turned out, this had been done by Hants and Sussex Aviation who used to be based at Portsmouth, so they sent up their man who took the cowling off, took one look and said: 'Oh dear, oh dear!'

The engine was a flat six and each cylinder was quite separate, but each section of the inlet manifold is joined to the next one by a rubber sleeve and two Jubilee clips. One of these hadn't been properly assembled, so when I'd landed and opened up the throttle the mixture was weak, the engine was sucking too much air and this caused a backfire. It had blown back through the gap and set fire to the 'elephant's trunk' paper tube that takes the hot air to the heater.

Then on one of my trips to Plymouth, where Di and I had a holiday home, I had another problem. The family was already at Plymouth and I was going down for a long weekend, taking more provisions and produce from the gardens and greenhouses. There I was, sitting above the clouds, minding my own business and heading towards Exeter. Just as I thought I ought to call up the airfield and say I was passing to the south of them the whole aircraft, but particularly the rubber mounted dashboard, began to shake. I decided this wasn't particularly good so called Exeter, told them about my problem and asked to divert to them. They gave me a course to steer and further instructions to fly a particular pattern so they could confirm which blip I was on their radar, then positioned me for landing. When I got down through the clouds and could see the runway ahead of me, I could also see the fire engines and ambulances that surrounded it – just in case I had further trouble.

The engine would run smoothly for a while and every now and then it would start this terrible vibration, so no one knew what might happen next. I landed without recourse to the rescue vehicles and taxied to a hangar. Out came a mechanic and the first thing he did was to take the dipstick out. 'Well, there is oil on the end of it but only just,' he said. In fact the engine was very close to seizing. But bear in mind it had only done about 100 hours flying after its overhaul. What had happened was that a valve seat had started to break up and every now and then it would hold a valve open. Being a flat six, the engine would put three cylinders out of action so no wonder it was running a bit rough. It was a bit worrying, but even more so was that I was regularly flying up to the family holiday home or to business on Anglesey as well.

The Cessna 182 was a more powerful aircraft than the 175 and in the luggage area at the back there was a dickie seat, where two children could sit. So you could make it a six seater, which was quite handy for us. But after the Exeter experience I was always listening for an uneven engine note and thought perhaps I'd be happier with a spare engine. So I part exchanged the Skylane for a twin engined Piper Apache which had previously lived at Cambridge airport. It had belonged to one of the top men there but was hardly ever used. It lived in a heated garage and was used just for emergencies such as collection of spare parts. I went up there a couple of times to do a conversion to flying a twin, as you can't just hop from one type of aircraft to another. I had to learn to fly, and land it, on one engine.

I only flew the Apache into Soal Farm a few times. It was rather like flying a Jumbo into a small city airport and it was really too heavy for the undulations of my field, so I transferred it to Goodwood. Not quite the same as walking through the garden and just taking off, but Goodwood was only about 20 minutes away and the airport staff would have the plane out, fuelled and warmed up for a quick getaway.

Several times I took off when the clouds were on top of the surrounding hills and didn't see the ground again until I was approaching RAF Valley on Anglesey. I think the controller used to like giving me a GCA – he certainly got plenty of practice at it!

On the way up to Anglesey, controllers would have me on their radar until I was about to leave their air space, when they would hand me over to the next area controller. It was very comforting to have someone looking after you and to talk to when all you could see was cloud, cloud, and even more cloud.

Once I going up to Halfpenny Green, father's local aerodrome at Kinver, which meant flying over Brize Norton and then almost immediately over Little Rissington, by Stow on the Wold. These were both RAF stations and at the time Rissington was home to the Red Arrows. Trying to call them up was always a bit tricky because although they'd got our frequency, they were mainly concerned with military signals and sometimes you'd get no reply. On this occasion I could get nothing out of Rissington and moved out of one zone into another, so I wasn't quite sure what to do. It should have been alright because I was way above the circuit height where their aircraft should have been maneuvering. I glanced out of the window and there was one of the Red Arrows, throttled back and having a good look at me. That was rather unexpected and a bit off putting.

Another time, returning from Halfpenny Green, I'd negotiated Rissington and called up Brize Norton, where they said they had a thunderstorm brewing and would divert me round it. Well, sure enough there was an almighty storm on the way and it got so dark that I had to put the instrument lights on. Suddenly I noticed the altimeter was going up and up and up. We were climbing. I pushed the stick forward to try and maintain my height as I was crossing the edge of the airfield. I even resorted to throttling back and still couldn't get the thing to come down, as I was being sucked up in the thermals of the storm.

Then there was the time when Diana and I had been invited by a friend to go to their box at Cheltenham races, where we could land the plane in the middle of the racecourse. When we opened the curtains in the morning there was snow on the ground – a proper amount of it! So what were we to do? Eventually our tractor driver came to the rescue by driving up and down the airstrip, packing down the snow.

I suppose I would have carried on flying for a number of years but in 1972 I had a heart attack, and the authorities get a bit excited about people flying around with dicky hearts. When you get to 40 (at the time I was 41) you have to have an annual medical to be passed fit to fly. I went to see a flying specialist at Cosham and told him I'd had a hiccup, but instead of throwing the form away he said he'd do the medical in any case as he'd heard of people in similar circumstances who eventually regained their licences. This was now six months after the heart attack and I was keen to have a bit of an overhaul to see how I was going on. At the end of it all, which included an ECG, the doctor said that if I hadn't told him about the heart attack he probably wouldn't have picked it up, even from the ECG. So that was quite encouraging.

He told me to wait a year and then have another medical, after which he sent everything off to the CAA and made a case for me. The powers that be insisted on a second opinion before they gave me my licence back, but even then there were two conditions. The first was that I had a co-pilot with me until they saw how things went on and the second was that I couldn't go out of the UK. It would have been a big drawback to have a co-pilot. If I was going, say, to Anglesey for the weekend, what was I going to do with him? Also I had to take a refresher course because it was now a couple of years since I'd flown and I would need to re-do all the night flying, etc. So I didn't take it up as I didn't seem to have the same need for an aeroplane that I used to. I wasn't going to motorsport meetings any more and so didn't need to travel quite so much.

The heart attack took us all very much by surprise as I'd never smoked and I drank very little. Working on the farm, too, I was fairly active physically. But I think I was an unconscious worrier and had recently taken on responsibilities at the local engineering company that had done work for us on the Marsh Special. I ended up as Chairman, but the company needed someone to wield a big stick to get it all sorted out. Not being a businessman by nature I found this all rather worrying.

In some ways the heart attack affected Diana more than me. She found it difficult to come to terms with and accept – she also realised she could have been left on her own with three young children to look after. Anyway, after all the looking after me and all my convalescence we discovered that we'd drifted apart and fallen out of love. On holiday in Alderney we talked things over, then came home and consulted our solicitors.

After a short period of my living on our boat and then in digs, Diana moved to a small farmhouse about five miles away. So it was quite easy for me to go on seeing the boys. It was a bit of a hassle at Christmas but like many other couples before and since, we managed.

My parents had also divorced and it was after this that I started spending a little more time with my father. We used to go shooting and boating together but those stories are for another part of the book.

Chapter Six

1964 was an interesting year for me as this was the time that Ted Jeffs and I were developing the Marsh Climax. Midway through 1963 I'd sold the BRM to Ken Wilson, so this was now the only competition car I had. We did quite a bit of work on the car over the winter, lowering the seat in an attempt to lower the centre of gravity, moving pedals and generally making the cockpit a bit more comfortable.

Our first outing in 1964 was to Debden. This year, instead of the usual blast straight up the main runway we did two laps round the one mile circuit with four cars on the track at the same time, released at ten second intervals. It proved popular with everybody. The spectators had a bit more to keep them amused and if you had a reasonably fast car you could try and overtake a few people, which was good sport. I took BTD, though *Autosport* reporter Paul Watson did wonder whether my 2-litre Climax engine would have the steam to keep up with the bigger 2.5-litre cars, not to mention the V8s, in hill climbs.

Well, 51.60 at Wiscombe certainly wasn't quick enough with Peter Westbury putting in a time of 49.62 in the four-wheel-drive Ferguson P99, and Peter Boshier-Jones taking BTD in his supercharged Lotus Climax 22 with just 46.83 seconds. In my defence I have to admit that the weather did play its part, which it so often does at Wiscombe.

Westbury was on top form at Loton Park with BTD in 35.56. Despite a spin at Fallow I managed a class win with a time half a second slower and a marginal improvement in the championship runs gave me second place, just clear of Tony Griffiths' BRM. So was Paul Watson's theory holding up?

As things turned out he was probably somewhere along the right lines, although I probably wouldn't have admitted it this early on in the season. We'd made the car a bit quicker but it was still very twitchy because of its short wheelbase – when I was pushing the car to its limit, I often found it!

But on my one and only visit to Brunton for the BARC Southwest Centre's hillclimb, I took BTD with a first run time of 27 seconds dead. Once again the weather wasn't very good to us with a lot of mud being carried on to the track from the paddock. However *Autosport's* Michael Ware reported that a new timing system the 'boffins' had been working on enabled the club to nearly double its entry, to 120 starters.

At Prescott, Westbury and the Ferguson were just too quick for us, again taking BTD during the championship runs. It was close – I was just eight hundredths behind him with Boshier-Jones a couple of tenths further back. And to show that you could still take more than one car to a hill climb, Phil Scragg won one class with his Chevrolet powered Cooper Monaco and another with his E-Type!

Another BTD for the Marsh-Climax came at Longleat in May. It was my turn to drive two cars that day as I also appeared in Arthur Rusling's Reliant Sabre Six – taking about eight seconds longer for the climb than I did in the Marsh! I'd been asked to test the Reliant at Goodwood and did one or two hill climbs in it. It had a Ford Zephyr engine with a triple SU Raymond Mays conversion. I wasn't over-enamoured with its road holding and traction, but I always enjoyed driving different cars.

I managed to beat Peter Westbury by a hundredth of a second in the championship runs at Wiscombe, although he'd already set BTD with a new hill record during the class runs. I always quite enjoyed Wiscombe although the racing car paddock, on a grass slope like all the paddock arrangements at Wiscombe, could still do with some attention today. It has a big hollow where you can ground the car and if it's wet, you have difficulty turning into your parking bay. And the start always seems something of nothing. You put a lot of effort into getting off the line, then immediately have to brake for the first corner.

From Devon it was all the way to Westmorland the following weekend, for Barbon Manor. After setting another new course record during the class runs, beating my old record by 1.5 seconds, Peter Westbury and I were both inside my old record during the championship runs but this time it was Westbury's turn to beat me. We were the only two in the 27s and ahead of Boshier-Jones, John Macklin's Cooper-Buick and Tony Griffiths' BRM. But it was, as it is still today, all very close. Quite commonplace at today's meetings but rather a novelty in those days was the speed trap before Lafone

Hairpin, which the Ferguson went through at 96.4 mph as opposed to my 95.2.

The end of May saw my first visit to the BARC Yorkshire Centre's hill climb at Harewood. I obviously enjoyed the course as my very first ascent broke Boshier-Jones' hill record by nearly three quarters of a second. This didn't count of course, being only a practice run, but I made sure of things in the first runs with an official record, which 'Bosh' promptly re-took by a tenth of a second. The second runs brought more excitement with 'Bosh's' supercharged Lotus suffering a seized engine and my finding another three quarters of a second to snatch back the record in the Marsh-Climax. But that wasn't the end of the day's sport. BARC Yorks had organised a single-run competition in which the four fastest touring, marque sports, sports, sports-racing and racing cars would compete for the Montague Burton Trophy on a class run improvement basis. Obviously everyone was keen to take the trophy but, equally obviously, I didn't really stand much chance. We gave it a good shot, but the trophy ended up with Allan Staniforth in his Mini.

At Prescott's BOC Members' meeting, despite rather inclement weather we took BTD from Peter Boshier-Jones. This was quite a coup as the car was still rather twitchy and wet weather could have been our downfall if I hadn't got things just right.

Shelsley Walsh was next on the agenda, where I was again driving both the Reliant Sabre and the Marsh-Climax. Third in class with the Reliant was rather gratifying, as it wasn't the most obvious choice for a hill climb car. Also, the GT car class had David Good and George Keylock driving George's lightweight Elan. David and George were great mates and often used to fool around together. I particularly remember one very enjoyable evening during an event at Bouley Bay, with a party round someone's swimming pool when a lot of larking about went on

The Marsh-Climax also did very well at Shelsley despite (as we discovered later) a broken chassis frame tube, winning its class and coming second in the championship runs behind Peter Boshier-Jones' new hill record of 33.35. In fact Bosh and I were the only ones under 34 seconds that day. I didn't take my second class run, preferring to save the car for its championship run, which proved a good move.

However, a chassis failure was no problem for Ted and me – a couple of minutes with the welding torch and we were back at Bo'ness at the end of June. Peter Westbury and the Ferguson P99 did their stuff again with another championship win in addition to taking the class win, BTD and my old hill record along the way! Peter climbed in 29.87, a time which none of us two-wheel drive competitors could match even though I beat my old hill record of 30.99 by a couple of tenths. The Ferguson's 4-wheel-drive would have been an advantage as the track at Bo'ness (which is now a housing estate!) was a bit on the rough side.

Peter Westbury missed the Rest-and-be-Thankful round and Peter Boshier-Jones took the win in Argyllshire, with another new hill record, while I had to settle for third place behind Ray Fielding's Cimax engined Lotus 21. Some consolation came with another win back at Longleat, but then it was business as usual at Bouley Bay. Westbury took top honours here for both BTD and the championship runs, even though I managed to beat Peter's hill record in practice. It was a close thing once again with Westbury, myself and Boshier-Jones all covered by half a second. At Bouley you could find yourself driving right into the sun, which I always found a bit disconcerting. Even worse, when I first went there back in the fifties the track was terrible. It had been sprayed with tar then laid with what seemed like pebbles off the beach. They were so smooth you only needed a sea mist to come in and the road became almost impossible to drive on. It was only later that a proper tarmac surface was laid.

After Bouley came Dyrham Park, where we set a 31.42 course record before heading off to Great Auclum. The shortest hill in the championship and what an exciting event with Westbury, Boshier-Jones and myself swapping places all day. 'Bosh' won out in the end with a new record, with Westbury second and myself third.

Then one of my few visits to Northern Ireland and Craigantlet wasn't the best of events for me. To start with, a radius arm came adrift coming to the line in practice so I had to use my first timed run as my practice run. Third after the first championship runs behind Westbury and Boshier-Jones, with everything to do on my second run I had to give it all I'd got and I gave it a little bit too much, spinning on the first corner after braking a bit too hard on the rubber-coated surface. Never mind, these things happen.

With Peter Westbury away at the St Ursanne hill climb in Switzerland (where, on the 4½ minute climb the Ferguson lost out by just half a second to Charles Vogele's Brabham for BTD), at the August Shelsley I had a class win and second in the championship runs behind Boshier-Jones before going to Prescott in September, where the Marsh Special's twitchiness nearly caught me out. The car snapped sideways at Ettores and I spent a few very precious moments sorting it out. I wasn't the only one though as David Good also had a 'moment' or two at Ettores in the Elan. So again Peter 'Bosh' was on the top spot but this time Peter Westbury sneaked ahead of me for second place in the championship runs.

I didn't get to Harewood for the penultimate championship round, but Peter Westbury made sure of his second successive British hill climb title with a good BTD in the Ferguson. However we did make the final round of the 1964 season at Dyrham Park where, again, it was a slightly disappointing third in the championship runs for me. I was the first person to beat my old record that day but it was beaten more comprehensively by the two Peters – Westbury and 'Bosh' – in the championship runs. The new champion making it his eighth outright record of the year.

1964 hadn't been a bad year considering it was only the second season for the Climax engined Marsh Special, which had been up against much more highly developed cars. Development of the Special itself, though, was still very much in the minds of Ted and I.

Over the winter we installed a 4,160cc Buick engine in the Marsh Special. I'd bought the engine from Hugh Dibley and rumour had it that Hugh, an airline pilot by profession, had brought it into England as hand luggage on one of his trans-Atlantic flights. It was quite a torquey engine and we'd replaced the old Cooper Citroen gearbox with a four-speed Hewland HD4. We'd also lengthened the wheelbase by eight inches and fitted Dunlop R6 Yellow Spot tyres.

We'd decided to replace the engine simply because we weren't getting enough power out of the Climax. But the first event of 1965, a non championship event at Longleat, was a little disappointing as I broke a wishbone and went off onto the grass, which curtailed the day's activities. Still, it was much needed practice in the re-engined car.

But at Wiscombe I managed second BTD, albeit some way behind Peter Westbury in the works four-wheel-drive F1 BRM. This was the car that Richard Attwood had driven – briefly –in practice for the previous year's British Grand Prix. Imagine a Formula One team entering a hill climb today! It was a horribly wet day which no doubt amplified the traction advantage of the BRM which was designed, incidentally, by future top hillclimb car constructor Mike Pilbeam.

It was damp, too, at Loton Park for the first championship meeting of the year. Conditions worsened as the meeting progressed so that Tom Clapham took BTD in his Lotus-Climax Seven on only the second run of the day. Tony Griffiths took the class win while I took the win in the championship runs. In those days, the surface of Severn Valley MC's 900 yard course wasn't quite as smooth as it might have been even by the standards of the time, which meant it could be quite hairy in the wet.

Prescott's Cutty Sark Trophy meeting was in early May and at last we had better weather. Back on the winners' trail again we took the class and BTD during the championship runs, to extend my championship lead.

Before the next event we decided to make a few modifications to the car. One problem was that I hadn't realised just how much I drove the car on instinct. All right, you look at your rev counter on the first practice run in particular, but I was confused by the rather wooffly sound of the V8. It never seemed to be revving. You'd hear four cylinders on the one side and four on the other, so I put the two tail pipes into one – rather like a Porsche – so that I could change gear by the engine's sound again. I also altered the throttle layout slightly.

So when we went to Wiscombe I was interested to see how things would go and as it turned out, they went very well. We made BTD in 43.33 seconds, slightly down on my time the previous year, but by the time we took the championship runs (which I also won) it had started to rain. However we were the first car ever to be timed on Castle Straight at over 100 mph. Only 1 mph over in fact, at 101 mph, but it was enough to win the magnum of champagne on offer.

But at Barbon Manor, Peter Boshier-Jones brought my

championship lead down to just one point. I took third place in the run-off behind 'Bosh' and Peter Meldrum's supercharged Lotus-Ford 22, which set FTD, but rather late in the proceedings I'd discovered that I wasn't running on all eight cylinders, which didn't help things at all.

Having sorted out one or two little problems with the car we went to Prescott for the Bugatti Owners' Club meeting at the end of May. Here everything seemed on song, even though we now had to have oil catch tanks for the first time and there was a bit of a mix up over the regulations concerning these. That sorted, we rocketed to the top in 48.15 to take Peter Westbury's outright hill record.

At the Diamond Jubilee meeting at Shelsley, hill climb history was made when I broke the record twice during the meeting, bringing it down to 32.98. There was a slight damper on the meeting when Peter Westbury announced that he would not be able to defend his championship title as Sir Alfred Owen, who was rather religious, did not want the BRM cars to compete on Sundays. For this reason, Peter would also not be able to contest the European Mountain Championship. I suppose there were definite advantages to being a private owner rather than a works driver!

Although not allowed to compete in the car at Shelsley, Peter did manage a demonstration run or two as part of the cavalcade of cars and to give us something to think about during these demonstrations, Peter Boshier-Jones and I decided to swap cars.

Another BTD at Bo'ness and the Marsh Special was just two hundredths outside Westbury's four-wheel-drive record with the Ferguson. But to show just how much faster the Marsh was at that event, Peter Boshier-Jones was six tenths down in second place. Halfway up the hill at Bo'ness stood Kinneil House where, it is said, Stevenson did most of his work on improving the steam engine. I wonder what he would have made of hill climbing!

We missed Rest-and-be-Thankful that year as I thought the car needed a good check over, which it hadn't had for some time and which in any case was rather advisable when developing a car. It's surprising how things move and become stressed. Also, it would have meant another trip to Scotland only a week after Bo'ness and I could have probably done with a rest myself.

The weather played its usual trick of slowing things up at Wiscombe, or at least it did for some of us. Peter Boshier-Jones managed a slightly drier run than most and took BTD, although my best time was good enough for the class win and second overall.

According to Patrick McNally in *Autosport* we made the trip across the water to Bouley Bay with great finesse. You see, at this time my father had got a rather nice motor yacht, the deck of which was just big enough to take the Marsh Special. So we borrowed the yacht, packed all our gear and drove down to Weymouth, where the Special was craned onto the deck and lashed down under tarpaulins.

Whether or not it was because we had our own private accommodation I don't know, but Bouley was good for us that year with me taking 1.25 seconds off Peter Westbury's record in the class runs with a time of 45.13, just ahead of Peter Boshier-Jones and Peter Meldrum, who were also both inside the old record. This was good enough for BTD and I also won the championship runs, although the time was two tenths slower.

Back in England, and to Longleat, where we bettered the hill record by 1.28 seconds with a time of 36.76 for the 1200 yard hill. 'This is in no way a reflection on the other drivers,' said Richard Feast in *Autosport*, 'more a yardstick for assessing the current domination of Tony Marsh plus Marsh Special.' The report also pictured David Good in his new Lola T70, which I'd converted to a left hand gear change for him. Naturally I had to give it a little test, so I put some trade plates on it and took it up the hill near Soal Farm, which is effectively the side of the South Downs.

The next event on the British calendar was Great Auclum, but I missed that as part of my one man protest against keeping it in the championship. I felt that it wasn't really the best hill for these bigger cars and there were a number of other, newer hills that were better championship hills than Great Auclum. I suppose some could say that it was more of a challenge to get a big car up the little 440 yard hill quickly, but it wasn't my idea of fun and if I didn't enjoy a hill I wouldn't go.

With only Peter Meldrum and Tony Griffiths making the trip to Craigantlet, it was back to Shelsley and my 33.54 in the championship runs was just four hundredths slower than my class winning BTD. It was a significant run though, as it regained my first British Championship title since 1957 - just as well, perhaps, for a week later at Prescott's Gold Cup meeting I retired on my second run with a broken driveshaft.

The original driveshafts in the Special were BRM items which I'd had shortened by cutting and rewelding and this one broke at the weld. After that we did a little bit of a modification and fortunately they never broke there again.

Then, at the final championship round, at Dyrham Park, I missed the championship runs with a broken camshaft. The V8 Buick/Oldsmobile engine was really an 'everyday' sort of unit and in what I always considered to be 'sports' tune, with an extra knobbly camshaft. I'd started the engine and walked away, leaving it to warm itself up as I usually did. When I returned it had stopped. On investigation I found the camshaft was broken and although I had to get a replacement sent over from the USA I'd replaced it in time for our final event for 1965, a 750MC 'clubbie' at Wiscombe Park. It was a good end to the season, with another class win and BTD in the special run-off for the Martini Trophy in a time of 42.60 – just seven hundredths outside Peter Westbury's hill record.

So we'd finished the season in first place in the RAC Hill Climb Championship, which was most satisfying in a home-built car. Satisfying too, because it came exactly ten years after my first championship title. I suppose some people would say that it might have been a different story if Peter Westbury had been competing and yes, I would have liked a bit more competition, but Peter wasn't running in 1965 and championships aren't won on 'what ifs'. Of course most people in those days were competing in a car they'd bought and then modified in some way, but Peter's 1963 championship winning car, the Felday-Daimler, named after his company, Felday Engineering, was very similar to the Marsh Special in that Peter built it himself with a few friends in his back yard.

I think that my use of a V8 in 1965 encouraged a number of other people to order similar engines for their cars for 1966. Certainly there were more of them on the hills than before. And it was interesting to see *Autosport* were now referring to the car as the Marsh GM. It started off as the Marsh Oldsmobile, then became the Marsh Buick and was now the Marsh GM. I think availability of column inches may have had something to do with that...

The beginning of 1966 was memorable for more than just motorsport. On January 15th our first son, Simon, was born. There's a story behind that, too! The baby was due to be born at the Grange Maternity Home in Liss, so Di and I did a dummy run there in the car to check out the route and see how long it would take. What we hadn't catered for was that the level crossing we had to go over was a manual one and was closed at night, so on the day I had to make rapid alternative arrangements. As it turned out there was no particular panic. I left Di at the hospital and went back again later, when I was put in charge of holding the gas and air mask for her. After the birth, though, I did manage to put my foot in it. Someone asked what I thought of it all and without thinking I said it was all very similar to what happens in the cowshed. I wasn't too popular!

Simon's birth didn't really affect the motorsport and we started the 1966 championship season in the best possible way at Loton Park by setting the pace in practice, the class runs and the championship runs. The 35.81 BTD for the Marsh Special, with very little in the way of modification from 1965 except for new, lower profile, Goodyear tyres, was just a quarter of a second outside the course record. Then, at a very wet Prescott, I managed a 55.61 in the class runs to take BTD despite a big slide at Ettores on my first run. It was also another ten points for 55.63 in the championship runs. These weren't my only driving opportunities at the event. Mike Hawley and I drove one of the new Johnny Walker Formula 4 cars, together with constructor Walker himself who had brought three of these 250cc Triumph motorcycle engined cars along. Having been invited it would have been rude to refuse, although we didn't come anywhere in the class, which was won by Paul Hill in a 1-litre Cooper Vincent Mk 8 on 59.74. I was the fastest of the three Johnny Walker cars with 63.99. Some people might have thought it rather odd that the reigning champion was playing about in cars like this, but the new Formula 4 was about to be introduced at Brands Hatch and besides I could rarely resist the temptation of driving anything on four wheels – or two, come to that. And in some ways driving that little car was like going back to my motorsport roots.

In fact one of the few times I didn't accept an invitation to drive a different car was at Gurston Down on July 20th, 2001. This was my 70th birthday and my brand new Gould-DFR was due to arrive at the event direct from Gould's factory at Newbury, but due to unforeseen circumstances it didn't get there. John Forsyth and several other people offered me a drive in their cars, but it was difficult to know which one to accept and which to turn down. Somebody would inevitably have been upset that I hadn't driven their car, so I declined all the very kind offers.

Wiscombe Park produced another class win and BTD, but the competition was hotting up a bit by now. Bryan Eccles had run me close at Loton, in his ex-John Bridges 4.5-litre Traco Oldsmobile Brabham BT14, and Mike Hawley was pushing hard in his Ford Twincam powered BT16. This must have been the first year that Jack Brabham had his own cars out on the hills; and he must have been busy over the previous winter because there were several of them. Tony Griffiths, too, was out in a new Westbury built Felday 6, with 4.7-litre Ford V8.

Barbon was another wet day, which inevitably affects performance and times. So much depends on whether it rains all day or whether it comes and goes. If the latter you might be lucky and get your run just before another shower – but then again you might not. At Barbon I didn't do much in the class runs and was almost two seconds away from winner Peter Meldrum's 31.42 in the supercharged Lotus 22, while Griffiths didn't even qualify. But my second championship run of 31.37 was good enough to take BTD. As fifth fastest qualifier, this may have been the time when the engine was not running on all eight cylinders, but the penny dropped, we put in some decent plugs and away we went. I think Peter and I were the only ones to get below 32 seconds.

According to Richard Feast in *Autosport*, I surprised everyone by not taking BTD at the Newton Oils Trophy meeting at Prescott in June. This honour went to Mike Hawley with a time of 49.21 although I did take second BTD, sixteen hundredths behind him. But this was just about the time when I started to feel up against it – a bit of pressure here and a bit of pressure there.

Shelsley was another event where rain came into play although this meeting was one of those 'wet and dry' affairs. Peter Boshier-Jones was there and gave me a good run for my money in the championship runs, still in his Lotus Climax 22, now fitted with a new 1460 long stroke Climax FWB engine and still supercharged. Peter Meldrum won our class in his own, supercharged Ford powered Lotus but by this time I was not worrying about the class results so much and keeping a bit in reserve for the championship runs. I finished up with BTD and the top championship points, almost a second clear of 'Bosh' and Peter.

Bo'ness saw my first championship defeat of the year. Bryan Eccles did the business with the Brabham Oldsmobile to take BTD, although he did have a bit of help from the weather. Not to say that Brian wasn't a good driver, he certainly was, but I was hampered by the weather more than some people that day and it was Peter Meldrum who took the top championship points with me second ahead of Peter Boshier-Jones.

As usual the week after Bo'ness came Rest-and-be-Thankful, but I decided not to stay in Scotland for that event, preferring to come home after Bo'ness. Sometimes I stayed up and we had a bit of a holiday between the two events, but not on this occasion. I didn't miss out though, as after the results from 'The Rest' (won by Boshier-Jones) were published I found I'd managed to keep the lead in the championship and was still eight points clear of Eccles with Hawley third.

At the next Bugatti OC event, in true Prescott fashion the weather had something to say about things. It stayed dry until halfway through the first class runs, when Phil Scragg set a new 50.13 class record in his Lola T70 which was good enough for BTD. I did manage to take the class win, well over eight seconds slower, but it was very much an uneven playing field that day.

For the next event the hill climb circus moved to Jersey once more and a rather damp Bouley Bay. It rained up until the class runs started so we were lucky to have a drying track, although it was still far from dry in places. It was a good day for me as we took the class win from local driver Brian de Gruchy's Forward Cooper-Daimler. The championship runs were also good for me (although Bryan Eccles had a bit of a discrepancy with Radio Corner) and I drove the twisty, 1011 yard track in 50.21 seconds – good enough for 10 points and BTD. Jerseyman Brian Moody competed on his local hill in a Jaguar powered sand racer and Brian is still hill climbing today, supported by wife Audrey and usually sharing his Ralt RT3 with son Adrian when the latter's work commitments allow.

Continuing this somewhat damp 1966 season, it was yet another wet day for the Sunday of West Hants and Dorset Car Club's two-day Wiscombe event where I took BTD, over two seconds ahead of Saturday's winner Ian Swift. You'd think we'd have all got used to driving in these conditions by now, but it's rather ironic that after I installed four-wheel drive on the Special I don't remember doing any wet event where it would really have come into its own!

The weather failed to relent for Shelsley where the rain was so bad that they nearly abandoned the meeting. However the V8 had a bit too much power on that occasion and we only came third in the championship runs, three tenths short of Mike Hawley's BTD time of 40.17 and a few hundredths adrift of Peter Boshier-Jones.

After Shelsley came Prescott and, would you believe it, another wet meeting. To combat this I wore an all-in-one waterproof suit complete with hood over the top of my overalls and helmet. According to Simon Taylor in *Autosport*, I looked like an abominable snowman. There was rather a lot of opposite lock in use that day and more than the usual number of slides as drivers battled to balance power, traction and speed. At the end of the day Peter Boshier-Jones took top honours in the championship runs with me just under a second behind. But despite being beaten by 'Bosh' on the day, this result clinched the 1966 British Hill Climb Championship title for me – my fifth championship in eleven years.

It was at this Prescott meeting that I had my first experience of driving a Haggispeed Imp in the small sports, touring and GT class. This was great fun. Roger Hickman won the class in his Mini Cooper S with John Rhodes second in a very special supercharged Vitafoam Mini, less than half a second behind him, and me third only a tenth behind Rhodes. A very close result indeed.

The championship then went to Harewood, but as I'd already made certain of the title, I didn't make the trek north. I did, however, go to the much closer Dyrham Park a week or so later for the final round but despite the dry conditions couldn't manage any better than fifth in the championship runs. This was when I had trouble with the condenser and the distributor started to 'go off'. The hotter the car got the more it didn't want to go, but once we'd diagnosed the problem back home on the Crypton machine and changed the condenser we didn't have any more trouble.

The final meeting in 1966 was the 750 Motor Club's meeting at Wiscombe where there were a number of interesting motors including the first appearance of a Ford GT40 at a hill climb in the hands of John Macklin. I didn't do anything much, coming fourth in the meeting's finale; a two run run-off for the fastest ten competitors. I also finished second behind Bryan Eccles for the Martini Trophy, awarded for the fastest aggregate times at two separate meetings during the season.

And so, with the fifth hill climb championship in my pocket, ended 1966 and the first year that the championship had been won by an American engine.

I'd been thinking for some time about a four-wheel drive car and in fact I'd been offered the loan of the Ferguson P99 in which Peter Westbury subsequently won the 1964 championship. But I'd thought this would bring an unwelcome 'professional' element into the more amateur world of hill climbing. I'd love to have done some demonstration drives in it but Ferguson Research wanted the car to actually compete and so Peter, who of course had won the championship the previous year in his Felday-Daimler, was offered the drive.

So with four-wheel drive in mind, over the winter of 1966/67 I built a completely new chassis for the Marsh Special which was longer and wider than the previous version as I had to make room in front of my feet for a front differential and inboard front brakes. The car still had the Buick/Oldsmobile/GM engine and one or two other bits from the old car and I thought I'd got most things sorted out. However, due to an odd technical hitch the four-wheel drive didn't materialise until halfway through the 1967 season.

Hewland had done the modifications to the gearbox and calculated the relative speeds for the front and rear wheels, which were different sizes. But when we came to test it all it just locked solid. I jacked the car up, found that the transmission was free, so we put chalk marks on the wheels and with the car in the air, rotated a back wheel and found the front wheel was doing its own thing. Eventually we worked out there was a 2 in 1 error between the speeds of the front and back wheels. So I rang Mike Hewland and said 'Somebody's made a boo-boo!'

The long and the short of it was that Mike had given the job to an understudy. He gave the understudy a thumbnail sketch and left him to do the calculations and then draw it all up. The young man had drawn it up and taken it back to Mike, who'd said 'If you do this and that you can simplify it a bit'. The understudy went back and simplified it, but didn't adjust his calculations. So he was sent hot foot to Soal Farm with his notepad, confirmed what the problem was and within two weeks Hewland had produced a little gearbox to alter the front/rear wheel ratio. They'd made a pattern, had a casting made, machined the casting and produced the gears and internals all in two weeks, which was pretty good going. And this little gearbox, which replaced one that I'd crudely manufactured from some combine harvester parts, was also the heart of the four-wheel drive system. It was the bit that allowed you to have two or four-wheel drive and Hewland incorporated the principle into this little gearbox – very much simpler and more of an engineering job than my original device.

In the meantime we'd missed Prescott and with only two-wheel drive and one or two electrical problems, I didn't have the best start to the season.

At Wiscombe we had a misfire over 4000 rpm but even so we managed fourth BTD with just two-wheel drive and I also took fourth in class with the Haggispeed Imp.

The first round of the hill climb championship that year was at Loton Park. We were still only two-wheel drive, but managed second BTD and second in the championship runs, a quarter of a second behind Bryan Eccles' new hill record of 35.37. I also had another drive in the Imp which unfortunately had fuel-injection problems on its second run and the engine died, but we finished second in class from our first run, behind Sandy Hutcheon's Mini. The Imp was quite a quick little car but stripped of absolutely all its internal fittings it was a bit of a rattle-box!

In May it was back to Wiscombe where, yet again, the weather was horrid and much more like winter. Phil Scragg took BTD in the Lola on a 44 while David Good, driving the1964 four-wheel drive BRM, won the championship runs on 48.98. I was fourth with a rather twitchy 51.20 but I'd taken the class win in the Haggispeed Imp with a quicker time, which again shows how much the weather can affect things.

As I wasn't particularly keen on going to a meeting with a car that wasn't right, not to mention getting things prepared for the four-wheel drive system, we missed the fourth round of the championship at Barbon and a club meeting at Prescott. But this was also around the time that that Di gave birth to our second son, Peter, on June 15th so I wouldn't have wanted to be away from home. I was present at the birth, as I had been when Simon was born, and fortunately this time we didn't come across any unmanned railway crossings!

By the June Shelsley meeting Peter had arrived and the car was ready, so now we would see what four-wheel drive could do. Only just, as it turned out, because the gearbox casing didn't arrive until the Friday evening and we burnt a bit of midnight oil getting everything ready.

For once the weather was good, the hill had been resurfaced and slightly widened and records were broken something like 60-odd times, which must be a bit of a record in itself. The new system in the Marsh worked beautifully and we drove the hill in 31.23 seconds which was 1.71 seconds inside my previous record. This gave me BTD and 10 points for the championship run off which put me in third position in the championship behind Peter Boshier-Jones and David Good. Everybody was in good spirits at the meeting with the possible exception of Reg Phillips. Reg, an old sparring partner from my trials days, turned up with a Mini Moke which he called the Fairley Poke. Bryan Eccles and I decided this thing looked a bit like a trailer, so thought we ought to try and load the back of it with some straw bales. Poor Reg, he'd gone up to the starting line and was completely engrossed in what he was doing so hadn't noticed our antics – but as always, 'Smiling Reg' took it all in good part.

At Rest-and-be-Thankful for the sixth round of the

championship, Peter Boshier-Jones took BTD with a dryish run while I took the championship win ahead of David Good, Bryan Eccles and 'Bosh'.

After this we all trooped off to Bouley Bay and the Marsh Special once again proved its worth with a superb run to take BTD, the championship win and a new hill record, which gave me the championship lead. According to Paul Watson in *Autosport* the Marsh Special was 'Deceptively slow on the corners and indecently fast on the straights ...' However, this cool, unflustered approach is the only one to adopt if you want a good time. It can still be seen when records are broken by today's top runners.

Then came the official opening of Gurston Down hill climb, which at the time, shared with Great Auclum the only downhill start in British hill climbing. Gurston was, of course, much longer and faster. Having advised on the hill during its construction it was rather nice to take the first BTD there and establish the first record for the 1160 yard course in 35.50 seconds.

In fact Great Auclum was the eighth round of the championship and despite knowing I could probably do with the points, I stuck to my one man protest and didn't go. So Shelsley was my next outing and here we had more problems with the car sounding very rough. Bob 'Haggis' Le Sueur helped me change the plugs, which I think had been in the car since the previous year, but this didn't entirely solve the problem. The other worrying thing was that the driveshaft between the front and rear gearboxes had started to twist so you had to be aware of that too when you were driving. Even so I managed to take second BTD and get second in the championship runs to Bryan Eccles for a much needed nine points. Incidentally, by now the name of Roy Lane is starting to appear in the reports. Roy started, I think, in a Cooper but by this time he'd bought Bryan Eccles old Brabham BT14 chassis into which he'd installed his supercharged Lotus Twincam engine.

The penultimate round in the championship was Prescott where Eccles, my nearest opponent, had a nasty shunt in the class runs. This left me to take top honours and maintain the lead in the championship. However, Bryan could still beat me to the title if he managed to repair his car in time and beat me at Harewood.

Well, Harewood dawned and Bryan had managed to get his car straightened. Only one point separated us in the championship. What an exciting day – if you weren't driving, that is! Peter Westbury held the course record in the Ferguson P99 with 44.45 and in our first runs I missed it by less than two tenths, pursued by young Peter Lawson in the ex-David Good four-wheel BRM that he'd purchased only a few days before. On the second runs Lawson got the record with a 44.02 with me a quarter of a second behind him and Eccles just outside the old record. Then, in the all-important championship runs, Lawson took the lead at first with a mid-43 while I took 44 seconds exactly. So, on the second championship runs it was all still to play for. However experience counted that day and while I snipped more off the record with a 42.94 to win the run-off and the 1967 title, Lawson could only manage 43.27. I say 'only manage' but this was an amazing feat in a new car by a promising young driver. That promise was fulfilled when he took the title himself the following year in the BRM, but unfortunately the youngest ever champion didn't stay long in hill climbing.

On that last run I had to experiment a bit with the handling of the car. At Harewood you go through a number of typical right-angle hill climb bends and then uphill between some farm buildings. Then comes Farmhouse Bend, a very long left-hand, uphill corner which opens out and it was here that I was losing time. Understeer, oversteer; I had the lot and in the end I rather took the bull by the horns. I went into Farmhouse very fast to make the front end break away, then put the power back on and kicked it in an oversteer situation – that was the run that counted.

So there we are, still at the top of the points when we got to the end of the day and my sixth hill climb championship. It also marked my second hat-trick, exactly 10 years after my first.

But Harewood wasn't the last hill climb of the season.

First came another Wiscombe with both the Haggis Imp and the Marsh Special, and what a day it was too. The Imp and I managed to take the class win despite the car not sounding at its healthiest. Then on the second runs in the Special I broke my class record. And in the Top Ten contest for the Autosport Trophy, with the track still showing one or two damp patches I took the Special up in 41.70 to take the trophy and become the first competitor to climb Wiscombe Park in under 42 seconds.

Finally, there was an invitation hill climb at Gurston just two days before Christmas when, at very short notice, BARC South West Centre put on an event to be included in the BBC's Grandstand programme. Unfortunately this was during the foot and mouth outbreak and so no cars were allowed from infected areas, which put Mike Hawley and Tony Griffiths out of the running. And with a number of cars in the process of being rebuilt the field was further depleted. But we put on a fairly good show (after we'd all been disinfected!) with only the odd misdemeanour, and at the end of the day I'd taken BTD with 30.6 seconds – 4.9 seconds faster than the record I had set at the inaugural meeting. And so ended 1967.

In March 1968, *Autosport* sent Simon Taylor along to do another piece about the car. I had intended to compete on a limited basis, just wanting to do the hills I really enjoyed driving because I was getting back into the boating scene and they're both summer sports. I was also getting a bit tired both of the constant pressure of being expected to perform brilliantly and of the adverse comments if I didn't. So I did one or two events, but found that without the constant driving practice in the car the times were becoming slower and it wasn't as satisfying. In the end I found that the change in pace from boating to motorsport was becoming more and more difficult to achieve satisfactorily. I sold everything, stopped taking *Autosport* and concentrated on other pursuits.

However there's one final little story to tell about the Marsh Special. Everyone was very curious to know how the Marsh four-wheel drive system worked, so I did a little 'visible modification'.

As I mentioned, Hewland had built me an extra gearbox positioned between the front and rear wheels. It was mounted next to the driving seat, which made it possible to have a 'bend' in the transmission line to the front wheels. It also contained the Marsh four wheel drive 'secret'. Just to confuse everyone, the box had a brass terminal which everyone could see and a wire running along a chassis tube to the dashboard, on which was mounted a small on/off switch. Even Major Tony Rolt of Ferguson Research was fooled. 'Ah,' he said,

'I think I can see how the four-wheel drive system works. It must have an electrical clutch.' I replied merely with a knowing smile, as if to suggest he'd discovered my little secret.

In fact there was only a freewheel device such as one might have on the back wheel of a bicycle, which operated when one turned into a corner and allowed the car to become two-wheel drive. When the car was straight it automatically became four-wheel drive again for when the power came on. So simple really, but I won't bore you with how it affected the handling, or didn't, as the case may be.

Although this appeared to be the end of motor sport in my life, it turned out not to be the case. It would be about 18 years before I returned and it would be the Marsh Special that brought about that return.

Chapter Seven

Having finished with motorsport, I could now spend more time with Diana and the boys and indulge in my other interests of sailing, shooting and ski bobbing. I'll come back to sailing and shooting a little later because ski bobbing came to fulfill my competitive needs. In fact ski bobbing and sailing could take place concurrently, as ski bobbing was very much a winter sport and sailing a summer one.

My first experience of skiing was with Tom Threlfall, who was also from a family of motor sport enthusiasts. I went to Scotland with Tom, in a Dellow, for a weekend's introduction to skiing. I'd borrowed a pair of skis which my sister Judy used when she went to Switzerland with the Palethorpe family the previous year. My ski boots were leather, purchased at a sports shop sale in Birmingham together with some 'skins'.

We stayed at a little pub and in the morning drove to a car park at the foot of a mountain. There was a ski club hut nearby, but no sign of a ski lift. Tom explained how to fasten the 'skins', which had rearward facing short hairs, to the underside of the skis. They allowed you to walk uphill or ski gently downhill, and generally instilled a false sense of security.

After climbing for what seemed ages through low cloud, which reduced visibility to perhaps 20 yards, we came across a hollow which was sheltered from the wind. Tom said we should stop here and have our packed lunch. This allowed room in our backpacks for the now rolled up skins, so we were ready for the big descent. Without the friction of the skins, the skis seemed to develop a mind of their own. After a few yards I discovered that one could descend on one's back, side or front and that the snow in Scotland was not dry and powdery, as it was in the Alps. I was soon soaked through, cold and miserable, but had to keep going because only Tom knew the way down – at least I thought he did.

At last we came out of the mist and returned to the pub and a hot bath. All that night I was grumbling to myself for having let myself in for this horrible, miserable sport. But the next day I was raring to go again and determined to master these skis. The weather was better, I could actually see where I was going and I finished the day with a better outlook to life on the mountains.

My interest in winter sports developed further when I was keeping company with Eunice Griffin who, you remember, drove my cars on one or two occasions and who passengered for me on trials. Eunice was working as au pair for the Porter family; they had skiing holidays each year and I was invited to go along. We acted as excess baggage carriers in my much modified Ford Thames van and set the pace, followed by David Porter with two sons and a school friend in his Bristol. Rosemary Massey took Nicky Porter (later a hill climb and Classic rallying Mini driver of some note) in her Jaguar XK140 and brought up the rear. I can't say my skiing was the most stylish as I was basically self taught, but I did enjoy whizzing about on the snow.

After Diana and I were married, we'd decided to have a winter sports holiday in Kitzbühel as our honeymoon. It was the first time Di had tried skiing so we spent quite a lot of time on the nursery slopes, although I did go off onto the mountains on my own at lunchtimes when Di liked to laze in the sun after our meal. Going up on the ski lift one day we saw a couple coming down the mountain on what looked like bicycles with skis and with short skis on their feet. Di felt sure she could progress a bit faster on one of those, enquiries were made and one was hired for her use. So off we went together and she did indeed progress faster. It wasn't long before we were off onto the mountain together. Di still liked her sessions on the verandah after lunch, so I borrowed her ski bob and found it really quite exhilarating as it allowed me to travel at a more satisfying speed.

Ski bobs reputedly first made at the tail end of the 1800s, when a postman thought it might be an idea to take the wheels off his bicycle in the winter and put skis on it instead. And in certain areas it did prove better than a standard bicycle and others took up the idea. One such who took out a patent on his design was the father of a man I was later to become very friendly with, Erich Brenter. Erich and his brother Willi were both champions in their time and Erich still manufactures ski bobs. Basically his business builds things like wooden balconies for houses and hotels but with little demand for those in winter, ski bobs proved a useful sideline.

The ski bob really does look like a bicycle without the wheels. When you sit on it, you're about the same height off the ground as when sitting on a settee. You have a handlebar and little skis on your feet.

Di and I enjoyed our new found freedom on the mountains on our honeymoon and shortly after getting back home, we turned on the TV to discover there was a ski bob race in Switzerland. We sat glued to the screen when the event turned out to be a British racing drivers' annual winter jolly! Watching them, I thought that I could probably do just as well if not better. Then, when an article appeared (in either *The Field* or *Country Life*) about the British Ski Bob Association, Diana decided to join. Large envelopes appeared with lots of paperwork about ski bob racing, which prompted me to get in touch. The Association was very enthusiastic, as it turned out they knew much more about me than I did about them. They thought that with my racing experience I could be a very useful member of their fledgling team.

I bought a British made ski bob (which as it turned out was a horrible thing) and off I went with the British Team, who made a slight 'error' on my entry forms. I was still 39 when they put me down as 40. They thought it would be an advantage to have me in the class for 40-year-olds and over, so I became an 'honorary' 40-year-old. So that was the start of it all – I got hooked on ski bobbing, started making my own ski bobs and started racing quite regularly.

It was about this time, 19 November 1970 to be exact, that another notable event occurred. Our third son, Paul, was born. He was due to arrive at home but the District Nurse had one or two reservations and sent Di to see a specialist, who decided that the birth should take place in hospital. I told the staff that I very much wanted to be present for the birth. They rang me quite late one night but by the time I arrived it was too late, Paul had already been born, so that was a bit of a disappointment.

Back to the ski bobbing, and I had just poked my toe in the door of the racing scene when the racing drivers' weekend came along. In 1971 it was being held at Crans Montana and I was invited to go along. The deal was that you had to get yourself there and back, but after that there was no expense, not even a cup of tea. All the people at the top end of motorsport were there and the first event was an ice hockey match – drivers v the press. They'd also organised a driving test on the local ice rink using Dune Buggies, converted VW Beetles, and every driver had a member of the press to assist him. It was only semi-serious – things like barriers had to be removed and put back by the passenger and the test culminated in him having to fetch a tray with two glasses, bringing it back to the car so that the contents of the glasses could be disposed of. We came second in that behind a motorcyclist named Giacomo Agostini...

The following day we had to assemble on the local golf course (not that you could tell it was one) for snowmobile races. These snowmobiles were like scooters with caterpillar tracks and a means of steering; either one big ski at the front or a pair of smaller ones. We went round the course two at a time and I was drawn against a rider called Hans Muller. On the second lap he suddenly appeared in front of me. He didn't overtake, but he'd realised that visibility was so poor that he could cut a big corner off the course and nobody would know. In the second heat I picked up a straw bale on the front ski but I finished somewhere reasonable and was in the prize money.

After all this excitement we finally had a ski bob race. The ski bobs were built by Porsche, very cunningly designed and obviously for the tourist market. Halfway down the course the handling altered when the monocoque box frame broke in half. When I got to the bottom the whole lot was quickly removed from sight since it wasn't a very good advert for Porsche. In the end they let me ride my home-made ski bob, which I'd taken just to make sure I could go ski bobbing whenever I wanted to, and I won the ski bob race.

That evening there was a big banquet and prize presentation. It was an embarrassment really. There were prizes for more or less everything and everybody. I came away with a Porsche ski bob, a pair of very nice desert boots, a jumper and an anorak. You name it, they were handing it out. I also got the award for the overall winner, worked out on a combination of all the points I'd won. Not only was it a bit embarrassing but many of us had to go home via the local airport, which was a bit difficult with all this stuff. But it was a really good outing and the only thing that marred it for me was that I'd gone on my own; Diana had not been allowed to go with me. I suppose they had to limit numbers because everything was paid for, but it would have been nice if she could have come too.

The following year I felt I ought to defend my title. The plan was that Di and I would drive down for the competition and then on to Alpbach in Austria. This meant that Jean, our Girl Friday, could fly out with our eldest boy Simon and we could have a family holiday after the competition. Di would then fly back on the return part of the ticket and Jean and Simon would come back with me in the car. While we were driving down to Villars in Switzerland for the competition the BMW's windscreen shattered. This wouldn't have mattered too much, except that it was pouring with rain and we had about an hour's drive to the nearest BMW agent.

Unfortunately, too, on the first day of competition I was feeling a bit groggy and thought I had a cold or flu coming on. There was nothing to do except press on and this year, instead of the event on the ice rink, they gave us a cross country race. This involves walking on very narrow skis and at the end of it I was huffing, panting and wheezing. Still, I persevered with the competitions, won the ski bob race and collected more trophies at the farewell feast, although these were easier to deal with as we had our own car this time.

Then Di and I went off to Alpbach where we discovered the British Army was having a ski bob race. The thinking at the time was that it was easier to teach British soldiers to ski bob than to ski and they could, perhaps, carry a bigger payload. Anyway, myself and another member of the British Team were invited to take part in this race as a yardstick, if you like, for the army to measure themselves against. However I was still suffering from this wheezing, puffing and panting.

After I got home I went to the doctor for some antibiotics to shift the infection. He wouldn't give me any as he thought I had a heart problem. Pull the other leg, I thought! But I had to admit to being rather out of breath if I walked too briskly down the High Street. He gave me some pills and said 'If you get an attack, put one under your tongue and see what happens. I'll see you again in a few days time.' But before I could go back, I was sitting in bed one night feeling very disturbed and uncomfortable to the point Diana switched on the light and asked whatever was the matter. I'd been off to the loo a couple of times to try and be sick, but couldn't. I was sweating like a pig and absolutely ashen white, so Diana called out the duty doctor who gave me an injection. He also gave me instructions to stay where I was until my own doctor came in the morning.

Morning came and I realised I was supposed to be going to a board meeting at the engineering company I was involved with, so I thought I'd better do something about it. I phoned up my secretary, said I was confined to bed and asked her to get everybody to come up to my bedroom. We had the board meeting, followed by a visit from the doctor. He wasn't best pleased and said he wanted a blood test but he was pretty sure I'd had a heart attack.

Apart from my being rather concerned at the thought of having had a heart attack, it was rather frustrating because of the things I now wasn't allowed to do. I certainly wasn't allowed to shoot pigeons from the bedroom window and after a couple of days, the doctor discovered I was having a hot bath every morning. The bathing was definitely out but he did allow me to go to the bathroom and have a cool shower, although it had to be assisted and I had to sit down and be dried off before going back to bed. This went on for at least a week, and then the heart attack was confirmed.

Back in 1972 the treatment for heart attacks was a bit different from what it is today. I didn't go to hospital, I stayed in bed for a while before being allowed to sit in a chair and then to go downstairs for a short while for gradually extended periods, but when downstairs I had to rest up. And so I recovered from that although a little damage had occurred in the heart muscles. But I must have recovered quite well from the attack because the following year we went as a family for a winter holiday. However I did have a young fellow along who my father insisted I employed as a general factotum and baggage carrier, so we had quite a nice holiday.

Although it was obviously quite scary for me, looking back I think my heart attack probably had a greater effect on Diana. She had to do so much for me in the early days after the attack that at one time I think she thought I was going to be an permanent invalid. And for quite a long time afterwards I was very anxious about going to bed. I think this was because the attack happened at night, which rather stuck in my mind. No doubt about it, for someone who had always been quite healthy it was a major disruption in my life and a big worry for some time afterwards.

Back with ski bobbing, when we started the sport the equipment was quite basic really, in fact somewhat crude. Later the ski bobs became a bit more high tech with coil spring dampers both front and rear. They didn't give much movement to the skis, but just took a bit of the shock out of going over some of the lumps and bumps. It also added a bit of illegal weight, because a heavy ski bob was an advantage as you could accelerate more quickly.

By 1976 I'd recovered quite well from the heart attack and went out with the Ski Bob Club to the British National Race in Berchtesgaden. The club chairman, David Spry, knew a family there, the von Tolls, who would host us and we stayed at their pénsion. I flew out and caught a train, eventually finding myself outside the Berchtesgaden station with ski bob, ski boots, large suitcase and so on but with only two hands. I discovered the pénsion wasn't far away and walkable, so I ended up carrying two items, putting them down and going back for the others. Eventually I got there.

Organized by the army, it was a good weekend which gave me valuable experience as I was getting a bit more interested in the racing scene. This was also the year they managed to organize an indoor British Championship at one of the ski shows in London. We had a short course on an artificial mat and I appear to have finished third, judging by the little medal I have.

The following year the London event was upgraded to World Championship status and a number of continental competitors flew over to compete. On that occasion I seem to have won; always very satisfying.

Initially I did only the odd race but one year I was particularly keen and had about six solid weeks of competition. I'd become very friendly with the Austrian von Toll family and stayed with them at a very advantageous rate. The wife, Annie, was a Ladies Champion and her son became the Schoolboy Champion. They were very kind to me, as was a ski bob manufacturer called Herr Kampf. This gentleman also owned a multi-story car park in Munich and he very kindly used to let me park my car there free of charge. He even used to ferry me to the airport. Sometimes he would join my partner of the time, Jane, and myself for supper as he liked to practise his English. Many people were very generous with their time or facilities and it was much appreciated.

In 1977 I won the Seniors class when the British Championships were held at Hinterglemm in Austria and in 1978 the SAGB (Ski Bob Association of Great Britain) went to Soll where I won a gold medal. I also went to Hallein in Austria where I finished tenth in a Giant Slalom race, but that was an International event.

Ski bobbing was very much a family sport although it had two levels. The national level involved different countries with teams, managers and uniforms but there were other events, more like family outings with classes for everybody. The national championships were just for the elite, who were usually 18 to 30 years of age, very quick and who took it all very seriously.

I suppose I was really at national level as for many years I was either in the British team or, in fact, I was the British Team! Originally there had been David Spry, who'd come across the sport when he was studying in Switzerland. Then he managed to rope in the army who were very keen on winter sports; they used to have places in the Alps where soldiers could do a short tour of duty and learn to ski. We got some of them ski bobbing and most were very good. Then along came Harold Wilson with his various cuts and squeezes, the army found it very difficult to supply any team members and the team dwindled until I was the only one left.

Most of the races were held at minor resorts because skiing and ski bobbing didn't necessarily go hand in hand – ski bobbers could to be rather enthusiastic. We tended to go flying past the holiday-making skiers, who used to get upset in case we mowed them down. And with ski bobs you didn't need ski schools to make a start, which adversely affected the local economy. So we used to go to small ski resorts with perhaps just three lifts and monopolise the village for the weekend. The village liked it as it was good for trade and they used to put on an evening do, usually it was a torchlight procession through the town. The kids would carry banners, there'd be 'Grosse Bretagne' on a placard in front of me and another kid would carry a Union Flag. We'd march through the town to the civic centre or the bandstand, where the Mayor would welcome us and we'd all drink Schnapps. The locals would lean out of their bedroom windows to watch us go past and listen to the band. Once, when 'Dad's Army' led the procession, they had very antiquated equipment including what looked like a battleaxe. They'd also brought a cannon, firing off volleys with lots of smoke. Everyone had a good time. I'm not really a party person, but I very much enjoyed the social side of ski bobbing and all the ceremony that went with it.

Practising on Friday and Saturday, I could actually run over the mountains and ski runs that we were going to use in the competition. There were no poles out to define the course, but you could find out where the bumps were. Often you'd find someone sitting on a ski bob on the next hillock and go tearing down, pulling up on the wrong side in a flurry of snow. You'd be joined by two or three others and eventually someone would decide it was time to move on and we'd all sit there rather like cars at the traffic lights, seeing who was going to be first away.

As you can tell, it was all very much more lighthearted than skiing. You need to be serious about skiing or you're going to fall over and hurt yourself. While you could easily come off a ski bob, especially if you got out of control by going too quickly, you just rolled off and there were no skis to get crossed up. Before things became more organized we just hired ski bobs, took some friends and they did the best they could with them. Once or twice someone would be heading downhill, freeze up and be unable to slow down. It wasn't until they got chucked off that they stopped – sometimes hundreds of yards downhill. But towards the end of my time in ski bobbing we had proper instructors, in fact my three boys and myself became instructors. It's much quicker to be taught to ski bob than to learn by experience like I had to. I initially taught all three boys, having built a miniature ski bob which each of them used in turn. But I have to admit that ski bobbing with the boys was terrible. We'd be skiing down a mountain path and I'd be leading the way, perhaps because I knew where we were going, then I could hear them coming up behind and knew they were trying to get between me and the mountain to edge me off the path.

The British Ski Bob Association used to have a 'National Week' out in Austria. We'd all go out and teach new people to ski and end up having races. I used to win as a matter of course and so was National Champion a number of times. It sounded very grand but it wasn't really. Some of the bigger races where I got the odd medal were really worth doing but there was a lack of opportunity to do enough of them. As in my motor racing, some days I'd got the devil in me and others I was much more circumspect and quite happy to drive quickly. But you got a bit of a rough ride on the ski bobs, unlike in skiing where you have a very good in-built suspension arrangement from hip down to ankle. On the bob you've only about four inches of movement on the skis, so potentially you were in for a very hard ride. In a lot of places we were actually getting off the saddle and running on our little foot skis.

People used to say to me: 'All very interesting, but where's the handbrake?' There are no levers at all, of course, but it's exactly like conventional skiing in that you turn to slow down or stop.

For our races we had little starting cabins, just as they do for skiing. We'd do the same type of racing, too, such as Downhill, Slalom and Giant Slalom. In the same way, we'd come out of the starting cabin and push off to try and get an extra bit of momentum. We'd sit astride our machine, dig in with our little foot skis and push off with these for the first few yards, after which we'd be sitting with our feet up so as not to cause any drag. In fact we used to have footrests so we could put our feet up on a straight section. You used the skis on cornering and the principles are very similar to actual skiing. It's all about getting the ski on its edge so it'll turn of its own accord and, of course, weight distribution comes into it as well. In a sharp turn you'd only use one foot and the other one would be well out of the way.

We didn't crouch down over the handlebars much – well, the real whizz kids would but then they used to have body-hugging lightweight suits for the downhill races rather than an anorak flapping in the breeze. I'd got a race suit, but you needed more than that while waiting around on top of a mountain. You ought to leave your anorak behind, but how was it going to get to the bottom? You really needed someone to bring down the accessories.

I was once invited to a race in Southern Germany. It was just after the Winter Olympics and they were trying to get ski bobbing as an Olympic discipline, but compared with skiing ours was a very minor sport. The race was held in the hope of catching some of the journalists on their way back from the Olympics. The idea was to represent as many different nations as possible and while it was really the German Nationals and above my level, they said 'never mind, just come along and enjoy it'. We started off with the Slalom and worked up to the Downhill, which was very exciting. The winner would average 60 mph over just two minutes, so you had to be fit. I was determined to do the race even though I knew I'd be glad when it was over. I'd be looking out for the next gate knowing that I would have to turn and kill some of the speed and I wouldn't say I was in control all the way. It was more a question of trying to stay with the machine.

But I always enjoyed going to the competitions as you got to know so many people. It was rather like hill climbing in that you turn up at an event, meet all your friends and have a good time together.

Now the SAGB was a very small, voluntary organization and at some point, I don't remember the date, I found myself Chairman. This was fine up to a point because I was still racing and had taken over from David Spry, who had set up the club. But by this time the SAGB had grown somewhat and was becoming an association of local clubs such as the Yorkshire club and the London club. We used to meet up in London at the Civil Service Club, where we could have a drink and play table tennis or snooker. And two or three members, who I think worked for the Civil Service, wanted sub-committees, and committees to run the sub-committees, and so on. I'm afraid that's not me. I want a decision now. I remember getting quite irate at times and making the beer glasses jump a bit on the tables.

I survived being Chairman for a number of years, but found that the only way to get things done was to do them myself. So I became editor of the newsletter and organiser of the National week and nearly ran myself into the ground. But it was fun in many ways and the racing was becoming more prominent. I remember going to a place called Gries am Brenner for a World Cup event and I have a gold medal from the slalom race there. I also won a cup for the combination of the Downhill and Slalom. I also went to Gries am Brenner again after Di and I were divorced. I took my two eldest boys, Simon and Peter, my nephew Richard and Judith Yates, my girlfriend of the time. We had a week's holiday and the boys were going frantic on the last two days. They nearly wore the mountain out because we only had a week's ski lift pass. They knew how much each run cost if they took them individually and were trying to make sure they had their money's worth.

At a competition in Dorf Gastein, in the Gastein valley, I came second in the Downhill, second in the Giant Slalom and first in the ordinary Slalom. This gave me a combination of second overall, which is pretty good. And after one visit to the Gastein valley I went on to the European Championships at Destne in Czechoslovakia.

I'd been told that Destne was a dreadful place to go, with all the humbug of the border crossing; form filling and obtaining a visa beforehand and so on. So I decided to cut the trip short and stay for just three days. This caused concern because the paperwork said five days and I'd had to buy five days worth of money, which was non returnable, in advance. All the equipment had to be unloaded onto the customs forecourt and inspected, but eventually I was allowed through. When I got to the state operated hotel at Destne, the first thing I had to do was put on a pair of overslippers so as not to wear out the carpet. The room was adequate in that it had a bed and something like a heater, but this had obviously overheated while drying some clothing and showed evidence of a fire. You could take a shower, but it wasn't very welcoming and when you arrived for breakfast at the appointed hour, your meal was already on the table complete with the regulation squirt of mustard on the side of the plate!

Outside, instead of salting the roadways, the Czechs used what looked like the ash from a power station so all the roads were very black and the cars got absolutely filthy. The ski lift was a hand-me-down from another resort and very antiquated, but it did have one very nice touch – an attendant who brushed the snow off the seat for you. I also caused something of a problem when I left Czechoslovakia. I had won a vase for my efforts there, but the customs people weren't quite sure if they should let it out with me as I hadn't brought it in...

Looking back I see I must also have been to the German Championships, as I have a silver medal from those. And at the World Cup meeting at Krispa-Gaissau, I had some success at senior level in the Downhill and won a bronze medal in the Giant Slalom, which also netted me a bronze for the combination. I enjoyed all the races but I wasn't quite so happy with the Downhill. You could practice for the Slalom or Giant Slalom every day but to actually race down a mountain with skiers coming and going wasn't really on. It would be just a bit too hair-raising at those sort of speeds.

My eldest boy, Simon, and I went to a race in the north of Italy and the whole thing was nearly disrupted by snowstorms. We finished on the Saturday and were coming home on the Sunday because Simon had to be at work in Guildford on the Monday morning. We spent two or three hours driving from the hotel to the mountain pass and when we got to the top the customs man said 'You'll have to go back down again. I'm afraid the French haven't got their side open yet and they won't work overtime.' We were a bit worried about time, but he told us there was another pass to the south that we could use. He even made a telephone call to make sure that it was open, so off we went. I'd cut things a bit fine with currency as I didn't want to take a whole boxful of lira home with me. We had enough petrol to take us over the pass, but I didn't know if we had enough to get to the next one. We just made it, so the first thing we did was head for a filling station. Simon went for baguettes while I was filling up, as after spending all morning on the mountain it was getting late and we had to get to Le Havre by midnight.

After a couple of hours driving Simon worked out that by going from east to west and picking up a main Autoroute we might just make the ferry. I drove like a madman – why I wasn't picked up I'll never know – but we just made it in time. Unfortunately our troubles weren't over. An official came over and said 'The boat won't be back tonight as they've got a problem with it. We can either give you the money to put up in a bed and breakfast, or you can drive up to catch the Calais boat. You'll just about make it if you hurry.' So we hurried up to Calais, just managed to catch the boat and got back to Dover in the middle of the night before driving back down to Petersfield. The odd thing is that I'd driven 1100 miles virtually non-stop and Simon was in bed sooner than if we'd caught the boat from Le Havre. Mind you, neither of us was much good the next day! But I supposed I was used to the odd spasm of marathon driving. After all I'd once done the German Grand Prix on a Bank Holiday Sunday, then driven back and raced at Mallory Park with the same car on the Bank Holiday Monday.

But back to ski bobbing. All the major countries had their

national teams. And within the teams there would be a team leader or manager, a coach and someone who saw to jobs such as the waxing of the ski bobs. They had proper uniforms, a coach to get them to events and it was all very professionally done. They used to have their own National Championships to which they would invite guests. I was invited to a number of these championships and remember coming out of the pénsion one morning where the German team was also staying and finding my ski bob already waxed and in good order. It was very good of them as, by this time, the British team had dwindled until it was often just one member, me. I think they were very appreciative of the effort I put in to get there and compete. Sometimes you would have 70 or 80 people competing at a meeting which might be broken down into Children's classes, the Elite, Ladies, Seniors and Veterans. I have tried to suggest a similar system for hill climbing but they don't seem very keen to give an age allowance!

I should also mention Erich Brenter again as he and his wife were very kind to me. I often stayed with them for a day or so before going on to an event, which allowed me to get in a bit of practice. Just as I learnt hill climbing by watching Michael Christie and Ken Wharton, Erich used to take me up the hill and I'd learn by following him down. He'd set the pace and used to take me by surprise sometimes. Once I was following about a yard or so behind him when I realised that he was sitting there looking at me, going backwards on his ski bob. He is a great character and quite a joker – occasionally he'd do 360° pirouettes all down the mountain, which I eventually learnt to do.

It was a shame the team dwindled because at one time there were four of us who used to have a great time together. Ann White was quite prominent on the racing scene and very good, as were the Osbaldeston brothers, Bill and Denis. Between us we'd hire a minibus to take us and all our gear to the events. But I suppose that like all good things, it had to come to an end sometime. The sport continues, of course, and my eldest boy Simon is still racing. In fact he was the 2005 British Senior Champion and interestingly, one of his fellow racers is Denis Osbaldeston.

If you'd like further information on ski bobbing I suggest you look on the SAGB website, which is *www.skibob.org.uk*. In addition to manufacturing ski bobs, Erich Brenter has moved into the Health and Safety aspects of skiing and ski bobbing and if you wish to ski bob in Britain today it has to be the 'Brenter Way'. This involves having a Brenter passport which shows you have undergone basic training.

The Brenter Way is very good in many respects as I did have one incident with a skier myself.

I'd gone away to meet an ex-German au pair of ours as she and a number of friends were having a skiing holiday. I'd taken the ski bob to do some training and I'd stopped towards the edge of the slope above the restaurant where we were going to meet for lunch. It was about a hundred yards or so wide and I'd made a point of stopping some distance from the edge, as I always did, so that if any skiers were on the slope they had the choice of which side to go round me. Except that this particular one didn't. I remember sitting on my ski bob watching for my friends and the next thing I knew I was flat on my back with faces peering down at me. I realised something wasn't quite right and was told to stay where I was until the 'blood wagon' came. This turned out to be a stretcher like a very flat banana with the top half cut away. You lay in this thing, strapped in and covered with blankets, while two skiers, one in front and one behind, took you down the mountain. My main concern was my ski bob, which some people very kindly took charge of. When I got to the bottom I was recovering from what had been quite a heavy blow, but they wouldn't let the skier go until they found out if I wanted to take the incident further. Well, I didn't want a fuss and there was the language problem to contend with, so I left it at that. But later I was going off to Zellamsee to pick up some ski bobs to take back to England. When I got there I was obviously walking rather badly. Most fortuitously, the man who'd got this equipment was also a radiologist. He took me off to X-ray me and have a better look at things and discovered I'd cracked one or two little bits off the bottom of my spine. He also put a dye in my bloodstream to look at my kidneys. Fortunately I was only badly bruised but it took a little while for things to settle down again. To start with, getting dressed was a bit of a trial and I remember sitting on the bed, dangling a sock in front of my foot and wishing things didn't hurt quite so much. But I was back on the squash court just a few weeks later.

I don't really remember when I finally gave up ski bobbing, although it was 1991 when I gave up the Chair of the SAGB. I do know that we had a number of lovely family holidays which incorporated ski bobbing either for pleasure, with the Association, or for events. All three boys became very proficient, qualified as instructors with the SAGB and took part in races. I was very proud of their achievements.

And while I hadn't planned a return to the slopes, Simon phoned one evening on his return from the last European Championships. 'Dad, there were any number of people asking after you, why don't you come out with us next year?'

Chapter Eight

I make no apology for recounting my sailing life now, rather than returning to motorsport. I was out of motorsport for eighteen years when ski bobbing and sailing took up a lot of time. As you may have gathered, boating and sailing have been in the family and have formed a big part of my life.

The sailing interest started, and was fostered, at the family holiday home at Rhosneiger on Anglesey where the family owned the local lifeboat house. This was also used to store assorted boats for holiday home owners and father had an arrangement with a local fisherman to look after the boats and store them during the winter. I was very keen on boating and whenever anybody was going out on the sea I'd be there.

My very first boat was made for me by the carriage works at Marsh & Baxter and I remember going up to the works with father to have a fitting, to make sure the seat and rowlocks were in the correct position. Our first holiday after my boat was finished was just after the war. Petrol rationing was still in place, but my father and my uncle Ron (father's brother) had put their heads together, bought a small farm on Anglesey and applied for a petrol ration to go and see the farm and manage it. This petrol ration was put into father's horse box together with all the excess baggage, including my boat.

Once at Rhosneiger, my boat was unloaded onto the lawn where I had to sit, do the rowing motions and get co-ordinated. When they considered I'd done enough damage digging up the lawn, we took the boat down to a little pool which was filled from the local lake and then drained off down the beach, where I was allowed to paddle about. That first little boat was called 'Icanopit' (I can 'op it!).

My uncle Jack Palethorpe had a very nice little sailing boat on Anglesey, kept in the boathouse, which father was allowed to use when he was there. I used to crew for father and learnt something about the art of sailing.

Father also had a little fishing boat, about 16 or 18 foot I suppose, with a big, single cylinder diesel engine. We used to go out and put down lobster pots round the rocky coast, which was always exciting and actually just below the headland where the Anglesey sprint course at Ty Croes is today. In those days it was an army camp where they practised shooting at a target pulled by a light aircraft, although I don't remember seeing any hits.

There was another small boat there, a bit bigger than Icanopit, called the Bantam. It wasn't long before I graduated to the Bantam, which was a very light boat and could be dragged about the beach – very handy for one person to paddle out to collect a bigger boat anchored up elsewhere. One year a family friend, Vi Eveson, was staying with us. She was quite a large lady. I was delegated to take her out to the fishing boat in the Bantam and when Vi sat in the back, I had to sit as far forward as I could to balance the boat. I was so far out of the water that I could barely reach the sea with the oars.

Being out and about a lot on holiday, we always had very healthy appetites and would get through a full English breakfast, a big lunch and then tea, followed in due course by dinner. After breakfast we usually went to look at the lobster pots to see if there was anything to contribute to the kitchen. After lunch we'd go for a walk, go out on the sailing boat with father, or out on the fishing boat for mackerel. Those who couldn't manage all this activity just lay in the sun waiting for teatime, when the cook would bring out delicious cream sponge cakes. We usually managed a walk after tea before preparing for supper which, again, was usually a three course job. We all went home like fat pigs but they were wonderful times.

During the war we went to Anglesey on holiday by train. A whole group of us would go with Granny, a maid, a dog or two and all our luggage. We used to change trains at Crewe, then the local taxi would collect us from the station on Anglesey and shuttle us to the house. This vehicle was something like a Rolls Royce or Armstrong Siddeley for which the owner had a number of bodies. It could be a taxi, a lorry or even a hearse. The driver would back it up to his shed, hoist one body up and replace it with another. That's how life was in those days.

It must have been fairly early on in my life that grandfather Marsh came on holiday with us. There were a number of other Midland families with holiday homes nearby and someone organized a tennis tournament. When it was in full swing grandfather called me saying 'Tony, come for a ride in the car with me'. The chauffeur brought the car round and off we went to the village, where he was given instructions to park outside the barber's shop. I had very light, flowing hair when we went into the shop where grandfather asked 'Can you trim him up a bit?' I was a bit dubious about this because I hadn't had many haircuts, and when grandfather saw the result he must have had a bit of a guilty conscience because we stopped on the way back for the biggest ice cream you could buy. But the flak started to fly when we got home. Grandmother Ceney was staying with us too, so both grandmothers had a go at him. Mother wasn't best pleased either, but of course by then it was too late.

Back on the water, when I'd done a little more sailing I was entered in a small regatta. I still wasn't quite as au fait with the art of sailing as I could have been and had to be towed back. Nevertheless it was a bit of an adventure.

What with our fishing and the lobster pots, I suppose we used to catch about a third of our meals on those holidays. As I grew a bit older I was allowed to do the steering when we went out to deal with the lobster pots and was nicknamed Skip or Skipper. Later on, while I was at Uppingham, father read my school report and was a bit dubious as to what qualifications I might achieve. There was an agreement that if I got a reasonable School Certificate he would buy me a boat, except I couldn't have the one I really wanted as it wasn't suitable for bringing round to the little village where the house was situated. I ended up with what is known as a Menai Straits One Design. There were about two dozen of these boats built, all identical except for the colour scheme.

I was about 17 and quite excited when we went to Anglesey for the summer holidays that year, I even took my School Certificate to remind father, who came with me to the boat builders to collect my new acquisition. While there they explained various features before going out for a trial sail and father told me to pay particular attention to all this.

With myself as skipper and father as crew, we had entered the One Design in a race on the Menai Straits just the day after we took delivery and were staying on father's boat, anchored off Bangor. Race day dawned and to save getting another boat out, father decided I needn't go ashore to declare my entry; we would just tag along after the other boats. The race started and after a while we found ourselves out in front. But because we hadn't declared the entry and attended the briefing, we didn't know which buoy to go round next. The other boats headed off at an angle so we followed them, rounded a buoy and headed back down the Menai Straits with the wind behind us. This is the point at which you put up your spinnaker (the big, parachute-like sail at the front) and father, being the crew member, went off to do this. After a short while he came back to relieve me at the tiller – unlike me, he hadn't been paying attention at the boat yard and didn't know how the spinnaker worked!

There was a bit of sadness attached to one of our boats. Father had bought an American Chris-Craft with twin engines, quite a high speed boat. After we'd been out one afternoon and come back to Rhosneiger for tea, the water level in the harbour wasn't high enough so we had to anchor it out. After supper, my father and a friend decided to go and retrieve it, taking the boatman with them. They up-anchored and brought the Chris-Craft into the harbour, with the boatman on the foredeck to catch the mooring buoy. Suddenly he slipped and went overboard. It was dark, but they could see the boatman with the searchlight. They threw life jackets, but in those days not all seamen could swim. This one couldn't, neither could he catch the life jackets and, sadly, he drowned. For days afterwards we scoured the headlands using binoculars to try and locate a floating body. Eventually a prawn fisherman found the boatman under a mound of seaweed in the harbour rocks.

After that the Chris-Craft wasn't very popular, Father sold it, bought a boat called 'The Derson', and this was the boat subsequently requisitioned by the Admiralty at the beginning of the war. It was about 38 feet long and had twin Morris Navigator engines. These were the standard Morris engine that might have been in a big van or small lorry and which had been 'marinised', with modifications added such as seawater cooling. During the war The Derson was fitted with a Lewis gun on the foredeck and taken round to Holyhead as a harbour defence boat. After a while Father got a letter from the Admiralty, with a cheque enclosed, saying that they had bought the boat. Father rather assumed that the boat had been sunk until one day he saw The Derson in Holyhead harbour. He made enquiries and the skipper invited us both to go out with him to a Q-ship. This was a very innocent looking cargo boat but once on board you could see that all the cabins had flap sides. On lifting these sides up, the boat was bristling with guns. The theory was that it would confuse the Germans who would think it was a sitting target, go alongside to put a crew on and get themselves blasted out of the water.

At the end of the war Father bought back The Derson. He'd worked out what he ought to pay the admiralty allowing for depreciation and by that time it had been fitted with new engines. These were two grey marine engines, bigger than before and the boat was quite a bit faster. And, as I recounted earlier in the book, it was on the Derson that my school pal, Tony Nixon, and I went off to the Isle of Man one school holidays to visit an old school pal.

Another school pal, Mike Manley, once came to stay on Anglesey. Mike was also interested in shooting and at the beginning of September we used to go out on early morning duck flights, but it's a boating incident that mainly brings Mike to mind. We'd been out one afternoon catching mackerel and when we came back to the little harbour, the tide had come in. This meant we could take the fishing boat right in, as opposed to using the dinghy. We decided to drop Mike off at the dinghy so that he could come in behind and pick us up. We'd moored up and got ready to come ashore, but there was no Mike to collect us. Looking back we could see him rowing furiously but making absolutely no headway at all. 'Try pulling the anchor up!' we shouted...

I kept the Menai Straits One Design until I discovered the Dellow. Then as I needed the cash the boat was sold, as was my motorcycle, a 650cc Triumph Thunderbird twin.

But it wasn't long before I took to the water again. I suppose it must have been in the mid fifties. I'd rather missed my summer sailing, so I bought a little Merlin Rocket sailing dinghy and used to take it out on the Severn. Once I put it behind the transporter and took it down to Goodwood for a bank holiday weekend meeting. The timetable for Goodwood was to practise on Saturday, have Sunday off and race on Monday, so I took the boat down to the beach and a friend came out with us plus a couple of Alsatians. The dogs were fascinated by the rubber mooring buoys and would lean out to try and grab one, so we had to hang on to them.

After a while I changed the Merlin Rocket for a general purpose boat, more of a family craft with a bit of deck round it. But now father had acquired his big boat, the Wild Venture, and invited Di and myself to Scotland for the launching party.

To describe Wild Venture as a boat is a bit of a misnomer, it was more like a ship really and so solidly built it could have been a battleship. It was built by a company that specialised in fishing boats and was 72 feet long. Up in Scotland the ceremony was all very traditional. We were taken into the building shed where there was a raised wooden platform for the launching party to stand on. Looking down you could see the door the boat would eventually go through into the water and it seemed as though it might be rather a tight squeeze.

My stepmother (by this time my parents were divorced and father had remarried) said all the appropriate words, wasted the champagne – and nothing happened. One of the boat builders looked down at the boat sitting on its cradle, saw that the last securing staple had been taken out and just leaned on the boat, which then slid down into the water. All quite dramatic in its way.

Then, of course, we all went on board and had another look round. That night father gave a dinner at the local restaurant for the boatyard workers and all the people who'd been associated with the build. Virtually the whole village was there as nearly everyone had done something, even to making soft furnishings or fitting carpets. Then came the proving trials; the boat was brought down as far as the Isle of Man where the boatyard provisioned it, following which it would be father's problem.

Father kept his new boat in the Menai Straits. Although I think he was very pleased with it, to my mind it wasn't the best sea boat. With the two big masts that my father had wanted it was a bit top-heavy and used to roll a bit. To try and appease my stepmother he had some stabilisers fitted which calmed it down a bit, but stepmother was never a very good sailor. She tried every seasickness pill going but always ended up asleep on her bunk.

Every year before Cowes week, father would get the crew to bring the boat down to Plymouth where they would wash all the salt off, drain the tanks and fill everything up again as the Plymouth water was very soft. Father would join them there and come up for Cowes week.

It was on Wild Venture that he took me to compete at both Bouley Bay and Craigantlet. For Bouley the crew brought it down to Weymouth, where there's a dockside crane. We tied the car down, covered it with a tarpaulin and off we went. Somehow it had become known that I was arriving in the Channel Islands by private boat and the TV cameras and quite a crowd of people were there to meet us. This was a big deal for the local motor club and gained the event some good publicity.

The Channel Islands have enormous tides that rise about 40 feet. Once the car was unloaded, to get off the boat ourselves we had to go up a stepladder set into the harbour wall. Then there was the problem of Simon in his carrycot. In the end we threw a rope down, tied the carrycot on and hauled him up. Of course, at the end of the meeting we had the whole process in reverse, except that it was raining pretty hard. Father had no waterproofs with him and stuck my crash hat on to try and keep his head dry.

Despite the rain, we finally got everything loaded and repositioned ourselves in the harbour for a quick getaway. But in the morning there was a knock on the cabin door. It was the skipper, telling us the shipping forecast wasn't good and the hydrofoil ferry from St Malo had been cancelled. Nevertheless, father said that perhaps we'd better go out and look for ourselves, so off we went. The skipper was a professional seaman who, before working for father, had taught navigation at the Sea Cadet Training School at the Marquis of Anglesey's house. However, he'd made such a fuss about going to the Channel Islands that father hired a local man to meet us in Weymouth and take us across. Not surprisingly, the return journey wasn't that good. We were all sitting in the big open cockpit at the back when father appeared with a large gin and tonic, not in the least concerned by it all. The skipper wouldn't have gone out had it been left to him, but that didn't stop father.

The trip to Craigantlet was another big occasion. We loaded the boat up from the jetty at Menai Bridge and set off, but when we got to Belfast there was a big kerfuffle. We couldn't just use their crane, we needed a crane crew as well and ended up with about eight men hanging on to ropes to stop the car swinging round. Quite a rigmarole.

We drove to Craigantlet, did the hillclimb, loaded up and came back across the Irish Sea through the night, offloading the car early the next morning. After their weekend on duty the crew just put the boat back on its moorings and left it. When they returned the following day to clean the boat they couldn't believe their eyes – it was gone. They immediately rang father, who contacted the coastguard at Puffin Island. 'Oh yes,' they said. 'We saw your boat going by early this morning, heading for the Isle of Man.' Father promptly rang the Isle of Man coastguard, asking them to give him a call if they saw it, then he rang the police as one of the Great Train Robbers had just absconded from Winson Green in Birmingham and there was a ports and airports alert out for him.

By this time it had all become quite serious stuff. Two and two were put together and the authorities thought Wilson, the Great Train Robber, could have taken the boat and he clearly needed to be stopped. Then the coastguards rang back: 'Your boat's been seen heading for Ireland.' So that was passed onto the Navy – they only had a submarine in the area but said they would keep a look out.

In the meantime the grapevine had been working overtime. One of the daily papers had got hold of the story and decided they were going to charter a plane to look for the boat. It so happened that Father used to fly out of the local airfield at Halfpenny Green and his plane (as I mentioned earlier) was fitted out for commercial flying. The paper chartered his plane for their search and struck lucky. Father's pilot knew the boat and spotted it over the Irish Sea, still heading for Ireland. This information was radioed to the Navy's submarine, which surfaced and radioed back that they could see it but that although they were probably not the best boat to apprehend a large yacht, they would keep it under surveillance. There were, they said, no signs of life on board and the yacht was getting quite near to the path of the Holyhead to Dublin ferry, which was also alerted.

Finally, the ferry crew caught sight of Father's boat and decided they could board it without too many problems. They sailed round it a few times, blew their hooter and made a big disturbance in the sea before they went alongside.

All this noise alerted the 'crew' – two young fellows who had been in Borstal at Weymouth and had read about father's boat. They were keen to go to America so they absconded, made their way up to Bangor, lifted a boat off the beach and used it to get out to Wild Venture. I thought they were quite enterprising as they'd found out how to start the engines and actually sail the thing. They were equally enterprising when they came up before the local magistrate – they asked if they could be sent to prison rather than Borstal. Whilst in prison they could study navigation, which wasn't on the Borstal syllabus!

Some months after the incident there were posters up at the south coast ports for one of these lads. He'd absconded again and taken another boat. But either he or the boat didn't like the weather. He had to turn back and got nabbed. I don't know what happened to him, but I thought at the time that if only someone had taken him on and given him the chance he needed he would probably have made a decent life for himself. He was obviously quite talented.

As I mentioned, father used to come down for Cowes week each year and Di, the boys and I used to do a little summer cruise with him over to France. We also met him most years at the Boat Show where I acted as his technical advisor, arguing technicalities with manufacturers.

Camper and Nicholson were boat builders in Gosport who did work for the Royal Family. I'd seen their boats out on the Solent and one year father and I met on their stand as I wanted to look at a particular model. But you didn't just walk onto the stand and look round the boats, you were given an appointment. So while I was looking at a 34 foot boat father went off to look at a 38 foot motor sailer. Eventually he reappeared, stood back looking at them both and said 'Well, which one do you like?' I was caught on the hop a bit and said 'It depends on what you want it for'. If it was just for me I'd have preferred the single masted 34 footer because I could race that, but as a family boat the slightly bigger one was better. Then you could have knocked me over with a feather. No sooner had I said that than father asked the Camper man how soon we could take delivery.

We were taken into the office, drinks were poured and shortly we were joined by some Midland friends, who had also made an appointment to view the Camper and Nicholson boats. It quickly turned into a boozy party, but it was agreed that I would go down to the company office after the boat show and sort out details such as equipment.

Over lunch, father announced that it would be useful to have a boat on the south coast because if the weather was inclement in the Irish Sea he could come down and sail in the Solent. But I knew the real reason. It was a nice boat, he wanted to buy it, but didn't really need it so it ended up with Di and me. We called it Syanora, after Di and I had seen a James Bond film, part of which was set in Japan. The word 'Syonara' means goodbye, which the Geisha girls said several times to 007. We rather liked the word, even if we didn't spell it correctly!

My next problem was how to say thank you for such a gift. Somehow it didn't seem appropriate to write a letter, after all how do you write one big enough? I thought the best way of thanking father was to get out and use the boat, which we did an awful lot. One weekend we'd go over to France or the Channel Islands with friends, the next we'd take the boys somewhere local, then after that we'd have a weekend on it by ourselves, and so on. And in the summer we went on joint cruises with Father, which we all enjoyed tremendously.

For his holiday father just wanted to go somewhere, anchor up and have a few days rest. Trouville and Deauville were two towns on either side of a little river in Normandy where we went. One was more of a fishing village and the other rather more well-to-do. One evening Father decided to take us all out for a meal. To him, if somewhere had a fancy name it had to be good, so we went to the biggest hotel in Deauville. We'd sat down, ordered our meal and eventually the waiter came to carve it. After he'd retired to have a sticking plaster applied, he finished carving what can only be described as a terrible meal. I would much rather have gone to one of the fisherman's cafés, which I thought far more genuine and wholesome.

We had many happy trips with Father and the two boats, but after a number of years things became a bit difficult for him financially. He'd been given some good advice, which was to put a lot of his wealth into trust funds for his grandchildren but when things became a bit more difficult he couldn't take any out again. He used a little Renault 5 for running around and laid up the boat for a time. After a while he decided to sell the boat rather than keep it in store any longer. It was brought down to Gosport for the TV presenter Hughie Green to look at. Eventually it went off to the Mediterranean but it was rather a shame that father didn't keep it, because it was built very much to his own specification.

After a few years my own family had started to grow and eventually we found the Nick 38 a bit small. I rang round a few of the boat yards to ask what was on offer within my size and price requirements and received details of boats being built in Hong Kong. These were not a lot of money for what they were and I ordered one. It was the first one in this country, built by Choey Lee.

Choey Lee were better known for their motor cruisers although they did in fact have two boat yards – one for yachts as well. Di and I decided to have a pretty basic boat with no niceties, not even covered upholstery. It seemed silly to send out all the bits and pieces we wanted, have them fitted in China (possibly not quite how we wanted them) and then bringing it all back again. It seemed much more sensible to have it fitted out on the Hamble with all the English bits and pieces. Eventually it was all ready to go and, because I'd recently had my heart attack, a young man who was working for me at the time helped me take the boat round to Chichester where we had a commissioning party. This boat we called Syanora II.

I kept that Choey Lee boat getting on for 20 years and went everywhere in it. At one time I had thoughts of sailing it to Monaco but when I started to work out how long it would take I changed my mind. It would have been a week to get to Gibraltar and probably another week to go across to Monaco. Then, of course, you have to come back again. When I came to measure them, the distances were much greater than I'd previously imagined. So that idea went out of the window. But I did get around quite a lot, bearing in mind that the longest I could afford to be away was two weeks and an extra weekend.

We went to the Dutch canals on a Whitsun holiday and time was a bit limited, but it whetted our appetite for more and the next time we went over to Flushing. This is a big port, but just inside it we turned into one of the canals and went through the salt water lakes right the way round to Europort, Antwerp, and that was quite interesting. I repeated that journey one summer holiday with the boys who were rather envious of the young Dutch lads and their wind surfers. In fact after my long term companion Judith Yates and I had learnt to wind surf later that summer, the boys also learnt on our windsurfers.

On one of our journeys through Holland we had a little adventure with a lock and a motorway bridge. They'd built the lock right underneath the bridge and you had to make an adjustment for whether the tide was in, out or halfway. Having already assessed the state of the tide I wasn't quite sure how tall my mast was but thought we'd be alright, proceeded with care and the lock keeper started to fill the lock. About halfway through I looked up and could see the little flag on the burgee staff flickering about in among the bridge girders above us. We hollered to the lock keeper, who turned off the tap while we tried to sort ourselves out. The problem was that the motorway above us was curved so our side of the bridge was closer to the water than the other. Fortunately the relief lock keeper came on duty, saw what the problem was and let us through properly. We ended up with a bent burgee staff – fortunately the radio antenna below it had just escaped.

Another journey, too, was a bit more complicated than it need have been. In settled but very murky weather with very little visibility I'd gone below to get a bit of sleep, leaving the autopilot on and Judith looking out for a particular buoy. Poor Judith never saw it so when I came back up I wasn't really sure where we were. Having done aerial navigation I found it quite easy to adapt my skills to the water. I got all the gear up and running and by using a hand held compass fitted with an aerial, turning onto different headings and listening for radio signals, I eventually discovered where we were and took us into Calais for the night. It's not easy when it's foggy, your sense of direction disappears.

Before we went on continental trips with the boys I would take the boat round to, say, Ramsgate so we could get maximum time abroad during their holidays. On one occasion we'd taken the dog with us and weren't allowed to moor up in the harbour. So we had to go out again, land Judith and the dog on the beach a little way up with the tender and take the boat back in. We moored up, found Judith and the dog, but he wasn't allowed into the harbour from the land either. In the end the watchman looked after him while Judith helped unload before we made our way home.

Once, just as I started getting back into motorsport we took Syanora II to Bouley Bay. We sailed to Alderney, had a couple of nights in Guernsey and then had a most wonderful trip across to Jersey, sailing virtually the whole way without having to touch the wheel. The sail and the wind were just balanced so the boat would steer itself.

From a hill climb competitor's viewpoint Bouley Bay is a very attractive bit of water, but to sit on the water there for any length of time isn't very peaceful. You tend to get a bit of a swell coming in which rocks the boat a bit, but it's still a nice trip to do.

Having had one or two holidays with father when he brought his boat down to the South Coast, one year we thought we'd return the compliment and sail round to have our holiday with him. Judith and I took the boat round in four days and four nights. Of the four nights we spent two of them under way but it was quite a good trip. Then the boys joined us and we sailed straight across the Irish Sea. The little port we were heading for in Ireland had a very long sandbank, perhaps four or five miles, running north to south outside it. We'd spotted a marker buoy, but it was just getting dusk when we arrived at where I thought the harbour entrance should be. I could see lights in front of us and decided, using radar, that was where we should be heading. I could see twin jetties coming out towards us but not their flashing lights, which should have been visible seventeen miles or so away. I decided to go in, we found a canal and tied up for the night. Next morning the harbourmaster came round to greet us and I mentioned I'd had a job picking out the harbour. 'Oh yes, well you would do,' he said. 'The light's not working'. 'What about the secondary light?' I asked. 'Oh well, you wouldn't see that either,' he replied. 'We lent it to someone when their own light broke down'. Somehow that seemed typically Irish.

From there we followed the coast round and went into a big harbour on the south east tip. Father often used to go in there and we watched all the hotel and restaurant people buying their fish straight off the quay. After that we decided to drop off at the Isles of Scilly. Neither of us had a chart of the Isles themselves, only a big chart that showed their position. I had a Shell guidebook that showed the ports, but it did contain a note that it was not to be used for navigation. We decided to give it a go anyway, had no problems and as we rather liked it, we decided it could be the feature of another summer holiday with the boys. On one of our visits to the Scillies we went ashore to do some shopping and left Paul, my youngest son, waiting outside a shop with the dog. When we came out, Paul said a policeman had just been talking to him. Apparently someone had seen us come ashore with the dog and wanted to make sure we hadn't come from France.

The very first time I'd been to the Scillies was by air. Di and I had flown over from Plymouth, while at our holiday home in nearby Newton Ferrers. I'd called up the airfield, who gave us a few tips for landing, but when we first saw the grass airstrip it looked very short. After you'd landed, the strip went over a hill and down the other side. Landing was alright, but when we came to leave I had to open the engine right up. Even so, there was no way the plane wanted to leave the ground until we had crested the hill and started going down the other side.

We did any number of French trips in Syanora II, or trips to the Channel Islands via France. I remember David and Ginny Good came once and fascinated by the radar, David asked how useful it was. To prove a point I went from Alderney to Cherbourg just using the radar. I was able to go into the harbour and even into a small canal, only looking up to see the last couple of hundred yards.

After a while Di and I sold the house in Newton Ferrers and bought a little bungalow on Alderney to use when we sailed over. The very first time we walked up the High Street we bumped into a couple we knew from the Midlands. He had been the chief salesman for Marsh & Baxter and a fishing companion of my uncle. We got to know them quite well and used to take food out to them from the cash and carry. Food was rather expensive in the Channel Islands, due to the double shipping involved.

We kept the bungalow for about three years and bought an

old Land Rover to run about in, but it was on a trip to Alderney that Di and I decided that the best thing for our marriage was to split up, so we sold the bungalow.

Once things had settled down after the divorce I advertised for crew for Syanora II. One man who replied was Syd the Sextant. At least that's what we always called him; his real name was Syd Henson and on one trip came armed with his sextant, because he was learning navigation. It turned out that Syd, a Midlander, was competitions manager for Ferodo. So as we had a lot of reminiscing to do it was just as well he came on quite a number of trips with me. He also made rather a good fruit cake and I still use his recipe.

I also met two fairly long-term lady sailing companions through adverts in the yachting magazines, whose names have cropped up elsewhere in this narrative. The first was Judith Yates, who I met in the summer of 1977 and whereas a lot of ladies were looking for an easy weekend out, with sea air and sunshine, Judy actually knew about sailing. She'd had her own dinghy and knew what made a sailing boat go. She became a regular companion, soon virtually every weekend.

Judy was about 12 years younger than me and had a flat in Wimbledon, which was quite handy for me when I went abroad ski bobbing. I'd stay overnight at Judy's and she would take me to the airport. She also became interested in ski bobbing herself and came on a number of family winter holidays. In fact Judy and her current partner still go ski bobbing with the London branch of the ski bob club.

Judy also came down for winter weekends; one day was usually sunny enough to do something with the boat and on the other she would go Christmas shopping.

On one of our holidays with the family we'd gone to a little bay just round the corner from Cowes. We had a pair of windsurfers, so either Judy and I or Simon and Peter would go off with them, as Paul was too small then to pull up the sail. On this occasion Simon and Peter had gone with strict instructions only to go as far as the main channel, because the way the wind and tide were running made it very choppy there. Judy and I took Paul ashore to buy an ice cream, while keeping one eye on the Solent. I could see the boys were getting to the stage where it might be prudent to go back to the boat. The long and short of it is that they'd been across to the English side and run out of steam on the way back. Peter was sitting on his board, being swept down towards the Needles and waving furiously at any boat in sight. Simon was very put out when I shot past him in the tender having decided that Peter, having gone furthest, needed rescuing first. I did collect Simon on the way back, though!

Generally the boys were good sailors and could be relied on. As we went past Penzance and Land's End towards the Scillies, Peter would perform watch keeping duties while I went below for some sleep,

I found Judy a very good companion. After one summer holiday, when she was between jobs, she stayed on at Soal Farm. However, living together on a full time basis was when things started to go downhill. Judith moved back to London around 1982, but the downhill part of our relationship was allowed to go a little too long and soured things a bit. She was a lovely lady, but her timekeeping was atrocious. She would also arrive with her luggage in half a dozen plastic carrier bags and it could sometimes be difficult keeping track of her. Once, just as we were booking into a hotel, I couldn't seem to find her at all – she'd already been distracted and was a dozen or so paces behind.

We still keep in touch and although it's mainly Christmas cards these days, I did call and see her when I'd been to Wiscombe Park for a hill climb event.

My next long term companion was a lady by the name of Jane Blyth who I met in September 1983, but Jane was under a bit of a misapprehension. She was looking for a permanent partner and I was looking for a sailing companion. We got on quite well though, she was another terribly good companion with whom I spent a number of holidays. Like Judy, Jane learnt to ski bob so we had a winter interest as well as a summer one.

Jane moved in when the lease on her flat ran out. But once again, living together full time was really when things started to go wrong. It became obvious that there was a significant difference in our finances, which I think Jane resented a little. After I'd bought back the Marsh Special, thinking it would be good for us to have another summer interest in addition to the boating, I got it in the neck because

I hadn't installed a new kitchen. I'm not sure whether the kitchen was badly designed in the first place or whether it was due to the influence of another woman, but Jane wanted a new one. In fairness it may not have been a brilliant kitchen and Jane had worked in an architect's office, so knew a thing or two about design. One of the things I shall always be grateful to Jane for, though, is making me look up.

When I competed at Loton Park, Jane and I stayed in Ludlow. It's a lovely old town; I went along looking at shop window level and it was Jane that made me look up. I realized I had been missing half the beauty of the town and her ability to point out things like this was a definite plus for me. I think we'd been together about eight or ten years before we drifted apart and later on my eldest son, Simon, married Jane's daughter Ariadne.

On one trip home from the Channel Islands I was a little more on edge than usual. I had seen a lovely Capo Di Monte scene of a gypsy camp and went back at the end of the season to see if it was still there, and maybe discounted a little. One of my crew members was a salesman. He saw me looking at this scene and pondering, because it was still well in the three-figure price range. Having ascertained I was genuinely interested, he went in and twisted someone's arm a bit so the price came down and I bought the piece. The shop people packaged it up in a big polystyrene box and brought it down to the harbour in the back of their estate car. I moved Syanora alongside the slipway and the box was handed over. The next problem was to get it into the cabin, as it wouldn't go through the door. I suppose I could have lashed it to the deck but having just spent something over £500 on it, I didn't want any harm to come to it if we had inclement weather. In the end we took the top half of the box off, took out all the polystyrene chips, slid things through the door sideways and reinstalled everything in the shower tray. Then we had to reverse the procedure when we got back to Gosport.

In June 1975 I did a motor sailer race. Starting from Brixham, in Devon, the first leg was a short hop round to Plymouth and the following day we raced across to Guernsey through the night. We spent a lot of time on the radio exchanging weather information, with half of us heading over the north of the island dropping down to St

Peter Port and the other half going to the south and coming up. It all depended on what time you anticipated arriving there and the state of the tide. From there we went to St Malo and then raced back to Brixham for the finish, before coming home via Weymouth. We were allowed to use our engines for a certain percentage of our overall time but until we got halfway there we didn't really know how long it was going to take, and therefore how long we could run our engine. There were quite a lot of calculations going on which all added to the interest.

Another trip that springs to mind is one we did to Penzance. With several boats anchored in the bay we chose our spot accordingly. Then we noticed another boat that had obviously just arrived, with people standing on the foredeck, peering into the water. We wondered what was taking them so long and found out when I dropped our own anchor – suddenly there was a disturbance in the water and the local dolphin came along to introduce himself. I think he used to scratch himself on the anchor chains. Later, while I was waiting in the dinghy to go ashore for supper, the dolphin came back and I could actually scratch his back from the boat. Later still, we were returning to the boat when there was another big watery disturbance – he'd come to escort us back to Syanora. Sadly we didn't often see dolphins, although we did see any number of porpoises on our trips.

I had very few problems with Syanora II in all the years I owned her. She was a big, strong boat and, handled properly, could go more or less anywhere, at any time. Looking back, maybe there were one or two journeys we perhaps shouldn't have made. But one problem we did have concerned the exhaust system and the water-cooled manifold. The Chinese, who had built the boat, didn't have much access to stainless steel and some bits were made from mild steel instead. We sprung a leak and water was running back down the exhaust pipe and into the engine. I managed to drain it out and repair the pipe, but the engine had quite a few miles on the clock by then and it was probably time for an overhaul. When I asked Camper and Nicholson how much it would cost, they said they'd have to take the cabin top off and all the dining area out; it would have been a big job. But I'd been thinking about things and had my own ideas about it. I hired one of their workmen and busied myself unbolting things.

The layout of the boat didn't make things very easy but we managed to haul the engine up with a block and tackle, drop it down onto a sloping piece of wood and using the sail winches and the block and tackle, drag it up to the cockpit. We managed to get the engine out in less than a day and used the Camper and Nicholson crane to get it onto the quay.

The engine people picked it up and in due course it was returned. Using the reverse procedure of sliding the engine down the sloping plank and then hoisting it up and down into position again, we started bolting it all together again. It was nearly midnight before I got it running, but I rang the engine builder next day to say that it had started straight away. 'Somebody's been working quickly,' he said. I couldn't believe how Camper and Nicholson were going to make such a big thing of it. It's amazing what you can come up with if you apply yourself to a problem.

During the late 1990s I had one or two major breakages on Syanora II, such as in the stainless steel ropes that hold the mast up, so I decided to sell it. I went to the local yacht agent in Gosport and found that not only would they sell my boat for me, they would also be pleased to sell me a replacement! After visiting their stand at the Southampton boat show I bought the boat I still have today. There was an introductory offer that I found hard to resist but, even better, shortly after I decided on the replacement I sold the Choey Lee. The buyers turned out to be some people I'd shown over the boat years before. They were very keen, bought it and took it to Southern Ireland.

The boat I have now is Syanora III, which is American built and known as a 'gentleman's motor yacht' or a trawler yacht. It's not a high speed gin palace, but it has all the comforts, a patio window at the back and is definitely a sea boat. It's not terribly quick in comparison with some; I suppose it'll do about 14 knots, but when you've only been used to doing seven or eight knots with a sailing boat this is quite good. I don't tend to take it much over nine knots unless I'm in a particular hurry, but it's a very comfortable boat to be on. On several weekends in the winter, my wife Liza and I go down to the boat with Boris, our Alsatian. Boris is very much a boating dog but he doesn't seem to mind if we go round the market at Gosport in the morning and then just toot round the harbour in the afternoon. In some ways we treat the boat rather as you might a country cottage, just popping down for a day or two.

Liza's also getting the hang of the boat although she found it much easier to take to motorsport than to the sea. Unfortunately she suffers with travel sickness and having tried various pills she's going to try acupuncture to see if that helps.

Syanora III is a comfortable boat with all the modern facilities; a microwave, a big oven, hot water and a generator which drives them all. There is an upper deck with big settees and a steering wheel. It's all very nice and we're lucky that there are any number of places to visit within a few miles of Gosport, where we keep the boat – Chichester, Langston, the Hamble, Southampton, the Beaulieu river and Lymington to name just a few. Lymington we like because there's a nice little village shopping centre there and a good fish shop too, where I have great difficulty in not buying crab for our lunch.

I hope you've enjoyed reading about some of my sailing and boating adventures. There are so many journeys and holidays to recount but it would take up rather a lot of room – after all, this is a book mainly about motorsport!

Chapter Nine

As I mentioned earlier, it was the pressure of top level competition during my last championship year in 1967 that caused me to give up motorsport, move on to other interests and spend more time with the family. I also mentioned it was the Marsh Special that was to bring about my return to motorsport.

In 1985 I had a phone call from Graham Galliers. He had come across the remains of the Marsh Special in the back of someone's garage, bought the bits and pieces and wondered if I had any drawings or photographs of its construction which might help him put it back together again, so I sent him what I could. In 1986 the car was finished and Graham did a few events in it. At the end of the year he kindly sent me an end-of-term report, but it was fairly obvious that the car had certain shortcomings. It was clear that several alterations had been made to the car before he'd acquired it. I helped him as much as I could and after a winter of work and another season of competition, the following end-of-term report was much more favourable.

I'd been able to call in at his Shrewsbury base and give him advice on one of my trips to Anglesey. In particular the suspension needed a little work and some of the chassis tubes seemed to be missing, particularly in the cockpit area. There were some little tubes that appeared to be merely supporting the bodywork, but in fact they were cunning little stiffening pieces, which was why he was grumbling about the car feeling flexible. So he did some more work and when he thought he'd got the car going quite well, he asked if I'd like a drive in it.

Now it wasn't like me to refuse a drive and I said yes pretty quickly, but with the proviso that it could be at Shelsley Walsh. Shelsley was particularly accommodating in having drivers such as Raymond Mays returning for the odd demonstration run and that was what I thought I'd like to do, rather than actually competing. So the arrangements were made, but of course I had to have some practice runs. Before the end of the meeting I was bettering Graham's times and only about two seconds away from the car's old record but with a slightly smaller engine. The original 4.2 Buick hadn't been available so it had a rather ordinary 3.5 Rover unit instead.

And that's really how it all started again. It was lovely going back to Shelsley where the atmosphere was just the same. I discovered many familiar faces in the paddock, albeit with a greater abundance of grey hair and, in some cases, rather less of it! The cars, of course, were very different with big, wide wheels, wings and all that sort of nonsense. But after that taster day, *Autosport* magazine was reinstated. This was really my downfall, as one always turns to the back pages to see what sort of cars and engines might be for sale.

Having given things a little thought before Shelsley I already had an engine type in mind, a V8 turbo, and I spoke with someone who was developing an engine up at Oulton Park. But then I saw an advert for Rovercraft in Maidstone, rang them and found they were developing just such an engine and would be delighted to supply one. In fact they were having a March 792 chassis modified to take the engine and as I always rather enjoyed messing about and developing the cars, they were very pleased to have me on board at the bottom of the ladder, so to speak. In the end I bought all the hardware, the chassis, the engine and the gearbox. Rovercraft were already in the process of doing the mechanical side of things and we went from there. What was to be unusual about this engine was the fact it had twin turbochargers.

At this point I must mention that I don't intend to list every meeting since my return to motorsport. Many of the venues are the same as before and many events, while very enjoyable for me as a driver, would make rather boring reading. The idea is to give a flavour of my 'latter-day' outings.

Before we actually got into full swing with the Rovercraft I had one or two more outings in the Marsh Special. One was at Prescott where I scored a personal best with a time of 47.20 – almost half a second quicker than when I set FTD twenty-one years earlier. Modern tyre compounds may have had something to do with that. There is a rather nice picture in *Speedscene* with me holding a screwdriver and studying something on the dashboard while sitting in the car at Prescott. The other meeting was at Loton Park where, unfortunately, I didn't finish the meeting. I had the unenviable embarrassment of spinning on my own oil at Triangle, which was just before the original start of the hill and where most of the spectators stand. There's a cover plate in the top of the Rover V8 engine, between the cylinder banks, which for some reason became distorted and let oil out. As I turned into the corner it ran out of the back of the car under the rear wheel.

In fact I did buy a car before the Rovercraft made its appearance. Graham Galliers told me he was thinking of selling the Marsh Special and would I like first refusal? I think he liked the challenge of rebuilding cars and competing in them for just a short while, before moving onto the next project. Having advised him with the rebuild, I appreciated the car more – it was a unique car and I thought I ought to buy it, if only to stop someone else from bending it.

So the Marsh Special came back to Soal Farm to live in the garage in which it was originally built, between outings to stomping grounds both old and new. One such outing was a demonstration run at Weston-Super-Mare's Marine Parade where the Marsh, a four-wheel-drive car of course, was the fastest car off the line all day.

And that really takes us up to the end of 1988. I was just dipping my toe in the water again with the Marsh, while waiting for the Rovercraft to be ready.

Now it might have been that I was getting older and didn't like the early season meetings so much, or maybe the Rovercraft wasn't quite ready at the start of the 1989 season, but my first meeting with the new car was at Gurston Down at the end of May. It could well have been the latter, as looking at the picture in *Speedscene* the Rovercraft didn't have my trademark white nose, or even an engine cover. To me it looked undressed without one and I quickly had someone make one up locally.

Also in May, as a former hill climb champion I received a car sticker or two from Russ Ward, the President of the Hillclimb and Sprint Association. Apparently the committee had thought it would be a nice touch to present stickers to all previous hill climb and sprint championship winners and I was given a small handful! This was at Prescott, where *Speedscene* reports that I was going 'faster than ever'. I think this was more to do with the improved technology as I found it very difficult, after the lay-off, to try and get anywhere near the required pace. I've always felt that I brake much too early for the corners these days. I can't quite believe that I'm going to get rid of the speed and get round the corner, but wide wheels and wings make many more things possible.

Then we went to a sprint at South Cerney, near Cirencester, where I just missed out on FTD (you'll note that we are now Fastest Time of Day instead of Best Time of Day) to Barry Giles in a normally aspirated March-Rover V8. I also had another driver sharing the car, a young lady by the name of Gillian Fortescue-Thomas whom I'd met at Shelsley. Now she's Gillian Goldsmith, but I met her when she was driving Terry Grainger's Lotus 23B and his HWM-Jaguar. She was an ex-works Ford driver and had also set a new Ladies' record at Shelsley in 1985 in Alan Payne's Anson-Rover. I asked her to share the Rovercraft at South Cerney and found it great fun, but it made the day much more hectic because her dimensions and mine are not quite the same. Our heights were similar, but we always seemed to be adjusting seat belts and no sooner had I come in that she was due out, so we were pretty busy. But it was interesting for me to see the car running as opposed to driving it. I think she was only about a second or so behind my times – very respectable.

After South Cerney came the Weston Speed Trials in October 1989, by which time I'd registered for the British Sprint Championship. The Rovercraft had only a 4-litre engine at this stage, which later became a 4.5, but even so we took seventh position with four points in the championship. And looking at the results I see that a certain Roy Lane took FTD that day in the original MP58 chassis, which he'd developed in conjunction with Mike Pilbeam, with 4-litre Cosworth DFL power. I had decided to register for the sprint championship mainly because I always like value for money and wanted the extra championship runs at no extra charge. This helped with the development of the car because the more driving time you had, the more experience you gained.

For our last outing in 1989 both Gillian and I went back to South Cerney where I reversed the results of the June meeting and took FTD ahead of Barrie Giles. Even if there wasn't a full championship type entry it was, nevertheless, very satisfying to take an outright win again.

In those very early days with the Rovercraft it was my middle son, Peter, who provided the original turbochargers for the car. Peter is a turbo specialist in his own right. He didn't start out by doing an apprenticeship, but got involved with sorting out the chips on car management systems and trying to get a bit more performance out of them. Then he moved to a turbo firm in Christchurch, who put him through their system and he ended up as their travelling trouble-shooter. When the firm was bought by Lucas and the factory re-located to the north of England, Peter decided to start up a turbo renovation company himself. The idea was that instead of having to buy a new turbo, you could buy a reconditioned one off the shelf from him in part exchange for your old one. He would then renovate the old turbo, which in due course would go onto the shelf for sale. He started off with all the popular sizes and has now done development work for Bentley. Garrett do all the production work, but Peter makes the specials for them to try out. He also works on turbos for the VW and SEAT touring cars, and for truck racing and power-boating. Part of the power-boating deal was that someone took him for a jolly round the Solent where he might well have seen evidence of other turbos he works on – those on the Isle of Wight ferries.

One of the problems we discovered with the Rovercraft was that if it had done a run and been left to stand for a while, on restarting it would push out clouds of oil smoke. This was because the turbos were mounted at the bottom of the side pods, very low in relation to the engine. Oil would drain out of the feed pipes, seep through the seals and sit in the turbos when they started up. I devised a separate little sump for the oil to drain into, which cured that problem.

My first meeting in 1990 was Prescott on April 8. I took the Marsh Special because Rovercraft had the engine back over the winter for development and it wasn't quite ready. At least I had the Special to play with and all along I have just enjoyed the driving, and indeed still do. The V8 Rovercraft engine had now been stretched to 4.5-litres, in fact the only bits of the old engine remaining were the rocker covers and the sump pan. I always referred to the whole car as the Rovercraft, because that was the name of Simon and Nick Law's company, but they always referred to it as a March.

Our next outing was to Shelsley Walsh for the Midland Championship meeting and while Martyn Griffiths took FTD in his Pilbeam-DFR, Andy McBeath and I had a good battle for the ninth run-off place, which Andy won in his 2-litre Pilbeam-Hart, leaving me with a solitary championship point. The commentator got very excited that I was in the run off – he should have known me better! But although 29.16 was nothing compared to Martin's 26.30, in fact anything under 30 at Shelsley was quite good in those days. The McBeath brothers, Andy and Simon, were very good opponents in their MP54 and we had many happy battles on the hills, particularly at Gurston which is our local hill and for which Simon is now the BARC South West Centre's press officer.

Talking of Gurston, that seems to have been my next event. But this time I had the advantage over both Andy and Simon to take FTD, twenty-three years after I had last won there outright.

The Brighton Speed Trials are always in early September and I always enjoy Brighton because of its tradition. It's one of the earliest motoring events in the country that's still running and the years when I didn't go to the event always felt incomplete somehow. On the other hand I'm always very glad to get home from Brighton because it's absolute chaos and bedlam! One thing that had changed was the distance. When I first went there with the old Cooper the course was run over a kilometre, but when I returned it was first of all half a mile and subsequently a quarter of a mile. But that year I was very glad to be back and the man I always wanted to beat was Roy Woodhouse in his March-Rover turbo. His was only a 3.5-litre engine, but he was running a lot more boost than I was at the time. He was over a second quicker than me but he'd had the car a long time, whereas we were still developing the Rovercraft.

Then on September 30, twenty-five years after the last hill climb at Longleat, Woolbridge Motor Club ran their first event at the Wiltshire wildlife park. I had taken FTD in 1965 and set a new hill record, beating Peter Boshier-Jones' supercharged Lotus-Ford 22 by 1.5 seconds. Amazingly, in 1990 I again took FTD, but this time in the Rovercraft. Woolbridge had asked if I would take the Marsh Special along to do a 'historic' demonstration run. After practice I found I was lying second to myself (!) and thought it would be rather fun if FTD actually went to a car doing a demonstration run, even if it couldn't be officially awarded. Just after the start you go over a brow before a slight curve to the right and here it all went rather out of control. I didn't know why, but the next thing I knew we were on the wet grass and away we went. It can, of course, be quite difficult to stop on wet grass and we were still going quite quickly when we got to the trees. Fortunately we were going backwards when we actually hit one, which we sheared off at ground level. However, it took its revenge and we ended up with a bent exhaust pipe, wishbone and chassis corner. It didn't take long to repair the damage to the car, it was just a nuisance really, but as this was supposed to be a demonstration run it was a little embarrassing. However I found it rather amusing that adjacent to the tree was a 'Motorsport is Dangerous' sign, which we moved slightly!

In the meantime the Rovercraft had done just enough to take FTD with a 43.48, which was very satisfying. Nowhere near my 1965 FTD of 36.76 but good enough on the day, which is what counts.

By now we were moving towards the end of the season and I finished third in the BARC (SW) Gurston Down Top Six Challenge. Andy McBeath took top spot with brother Simon second, myself third and Bexhill doctor Richard Thompson fourth in his Mallock Clubmans car.

Having taken in both hill climbs and sprints in 1990, I decided to concentrate a bit more on sprinting for 1991 and one of my first events was at Knockhill race circuit, near Dunfermline. This was one of the newer tracks and totally new to me. It was tricky because it was up hill and down dale with a variety of corners, some a bit blind, but it was one I thoroughly enjoyed and came eighth in the British Championship run-off, which was won by future British Sprint champion Chris Hill's Reynard-DFL. Driving his Hart engined SPA, David Render was just ahead of me in seventh and that wouldn't have pleased me as he was one of the people I was battling with at the time. There were three of us, Render, Guyson boss Jim Thomson and myself who looked upon ourselves as the three old men of the class.

Then came another couple of Gurston meetings where firstly John Meredith took FTD in his 5.4-litre Rover engined MP58, with his co-driver Rodney Eyles just three hundredths behind him and myself third, just a tenth behind Rodney. Although Rodney's a good driver and no fool in a car it was a little bit irritating to be behind him, but at least I was ahead of the McBeath brothers. At the second meeting John and Rodney swapped places and Barry Goode pushed me into fourth, but what I find more interesting is to see how many of the class winners at those two meetings are still driving and winning classes at Gurston today. Derek Mullis, John Forsyth, Colin Pook, Andrew Russell, John Frampton and Roger Cock, to name but a few, are all still in the forefront today as well as the McBeath brothers.

Wiscombe Park in September 1991 was the meeting when Martyn Griffiths clinched the hill climb championship. Martyn was a very good driver and this was his fifth championship title. He'd equalled Ken Wharton's four championships the previous year and seemed to be seriously looking at my six, but Martyn was the only one of us who had held the title in three successive decades. What would have happened if Ken hadn't been killed I don't know; he was a most uncanny driver as he could look at a set of regs and knowing the circuits as he did, could tell you what car you needed if you wanted to win. I must have started to get Ken worried though. On one occasion at Shelsley I spotted him on Kennel Bend with a cine camera recording my run, so I waved to him. Afterwards he came across to me in the paddock and gave me a right dressing down, telling me that if I had eyes on being a champion I should keep them firmly fixed on the road, not the spectators. It was typical of Ken that he would film someone else's run to examine it later, whereas the rest of us would just rely on our memories.

But I digress again. It was this meeting at Wiscombe where I had a little difficulty in practice. Between the Gateway and Sawbench is the Esses, a series of left-right swerves and a little crest. Going through this complex I realised I was a little close to the bank at one point. When I got to Sawbench the car felt unsteady and I could see that a front tyre was gone. So as not to hold up the meeting I proceeded to the finish where I discovered the wheel rim had been folded back, but I couldn't work out how. I went for a walk at lunchtime and found, in the Esses, the chopped off end of a tree root. It was no bigger than my thumb, but roots can be very tough and it was obviously what had done the damage. I hadn't a spare front wheel, I only had wets as an alternative. We tried to hammer it out but it wasn't having any of it. Even when I got the tyre off back home I still couldn't straighten it out.

My next sprint championship round was on a new circuit, at least to most people. Aintree was, of course, a racing circuit during my first session in motorsport and this might have given me an advantage for the sprint, except that it was perhaps twenty years since I had been there. Also as the event was on the club circuit, rather than the old GP circuit, we'd suddenly pop out on to a bit I recognised and then be on a bit I didn't think I'd seen before. Still, it was a good event even though I went out just after Ken Ayers had broken his gearbox casing and deposited oil all over the start line. I could only make tenth in the championship runs, but Jackie Harris took FTD on one of his trips over from Northern Ireland, he was a very good driver in his Hart powered Pilbeam and won the championship that year.

Jackie was over again for the Brighton Speed Trials, which was still a half mile dash, but with John Gray's 650 bhp Pilbeam Judd on record-breaking form – at 181mph over the line – it wasn't surprising that Jackie and I could only manage seventh and eighth respectively in the championship runs. We were obviously advancing the development of the Rovercraft as in 1990 I'd been quite a way behind Jackie, but this year there was just three tenths in it.

Weston-Super-Mare is another straight line seaside event but sadly, this was where Roy Woodhouse destroyed his March-Rover turbo. The right hand side of the course, the sea side, has a low, very solid wall where, at intervals, there are brick pillars with a gap so that people could walk on and off the beach. Roy ended up stuck in one of those pedestrian gaps. He very lucky in that he was, I think, virtually unhurt – certainly he was at the prize giving at the end of the day.

In fact Weston was quite a tricky course. What's so tricky about a straight line? Well, for a start it wasn't absolutely straight but a long, right-hand curve. The surface itself was peculiar, being a very coarse tarmacadam which got very shiny in the wet. Sand always blew on to the course and if there was a bit of a gale blowing, there was a nasty crosswind which hit you when you came out from the shelter of the swimming pool soon after the start. I think it was this that caused

Roy to get out of shape initially and at the speed he would have been doing, it's not surprising he couldn't hold it.

Curborough was another new venue for me that year and one that turned out to be not one of my best tracks. This was probably due to the characteristics of the turbo engine and the twiddly bits halfway round. However, I think I was quite well up in the order of finishers just behind Barrie Giles and *Autosport*'s Marcus Pye, sharing Barrie's Rover powered Ralt RT1. I was also just ahead of Paul Gething driving the Anson in which Gillian Goldsmith had broken the Shelsley Ladies' record. In deference to his Rover V8 Paul had a sticker across the back of his car reading 'Pushrod Preservation Society'. It is also interesting to note that this is the meeting where Tony Fletcher enjoyed his first outing in a single seater double driving Lesley Hickman's Reynard BDA.

Another Gurston, this time with David Grace taking FTD, and the end of another hill climb season. This year saw me in fourth place in the Gurston Down Top Six Championship behind winner John Meredith, his co-driver Rodney Eyles and Simon McBeath's Pilbeam-Hart.

After a final fling at South Cerney, where Gillian shared the Rovercraft with me again, it was time to put the cars to bed for the winter, or in our case time for more development...

In no time at all we were putting engines back in cars and preparing for April's Gurston double-header. And John Meredith did indeed make it a double with two FTDs to his name. This was particularly irritating for me in that he just pipped me on both days. However, for the championship meeting there in May we were running telemetry on the car for the first time, which caused a lot of comment. It was in the very early days of that sort of thing and was installed when the young man who helped Simon Law with testing and setting up the engine's ECU wanted to know what was actually going on during a run. So when my car sprouted a little aerial on the roll-over bar I told people it was so I could listen to The Archers. The young man was able to sit in his saloon car in the paddock and watch the run on his computer, which he found quite useful. I think this was the first time telemetry was ever run on a car at a hill climb.

We used the system two or three times in all, which helped in the development of both engine and gearbox. It didn't, however, help with the gearbox problems I had at Gurston which was down to worn dog rings. When this happens the car can hop out of gear as the dog rings driving the gears jump out of engagement. I'm certainly not alone in having replaced a number of them over the years.

On another outing to Curborough, both David Render and I got into the run-offs, but not the points. I think my problems stemmed from the turbo in the twiddly bits while David's were down to fuel pressure. He was driving the 3.9-litre Toleman-DFL V8 TG191, which I would subsequently buy from him. David had done really well in the 4-cylinder Toleman-Hart, but when he went up to a V8 he never seemed comfortable with it and didn't seem to do quite so well – although he probably wouldn't thank me for saying so. At any rate, when the time came he was quite keen for me to buy it.

Back to 1992, and on my second trip to Knockhill the development on the Rovercraft was starting to pay off with fifth place in the championship run off behind winner Chris Hill, who would go on to take his first title that year in the F3000-based Reynard-DFL 88D, John Gray's formidable V10 Judd powered SPA, Ken Ayers' Pilbeam-DFL and the 4-cylinder Ralt-Hart of Patrick Wood.

Now came another long drive, this time to west Wales for Pembrey's British Sprint round at the end of May. It was one of those dry practice, wet timed run events and we again finished fifth in the championship run-off behind Hill, Clive Harris's Ralt-Hart, Wood and Gray, so it was worth it. We were also ahead of both David Render and Ray Rowan, who was driving the little Formula Vauxhall Junior that his nephew Martin O'Connell drove on the circuits, so that was satisfying too. Hill was an amazing 5.5 seconds ahead of his nearest rival, which took some doing on a day like that. At that point we lay eighth in the sprint championship ahead of some good drivers such as Render, Rowan and Roy Lane so that was pretty satisfying too, even if there was still a long way to go.

Yet another longish drive followed, but this time it was for two events in the north and therefore more worthwhile. On the Saturday we competed at a non-Championship event at Aintree run, unusually, over two laps of the club circuit. This was a very satisfactory event as I took FTD by over 12 seconds. I must admit I did find the first corner, Country, very different the second time round when approached at quite a goodly speed!

Then we drove across to Three Sisters near Wigan for the first visit by the British Championship to the kart and bike racing circuit. It was another satisfactory outcome as we finished fourth in the championship run-off behind Hill, Terry Clifford's Toleman-Hart and Christian Mineeff's Pilbeam MP43 sportscar. I must admit to being rather put out by Christian, who turned up completely out of the blue (at any rate I hadn't come across him before) and took third championship place in a sports car! Not quite the thing, I thought, although I'm sure he enjoyed it.

Just a fortnight later we were back up north again, this time at Blackpool, where another long drive was rewarded with third place in the run-off. This time we were behind Ayers and Gray but ahead of Hill on what was not the most popular course in the Championship, reflected by the presence of only six British contenders. Again, a satisfying result although I did rather scare myself along the way.

The car was under constant development and we were now getting quite high on the horsepower scale. 'You might find it a bit tricky in the wet', said the engineers at Rovercraft, and provided me with a switch – up for wet and down for dry. I did the first run using the 'wet' position as with more horsepower I thought that might be wise. Also I was new to Blackpool, so I thought I'd take it a bit easy to start with.

The seafront promenade course at Blackpool is fairly straight and lined with concrete walls. Halfway along you're confronted with a road block, also concrete, as an artificial chicane through which you had to dodge left and then right, so it wasn't a place to leave the braking too late. On my second run I put the turbo switch into 'dry', which so startled me with the effect that I immediately flicked it back to 'wet'. I couldn't believe the difference. I went back, grumbled at myself and said this really won't do, get to grips with it. On the next run I knew what to expect. It went very well and I was clocked at 166 mph over the finish line.

We also went to down to Ocean Village, near Southampton, for a sprint which was won by Martin Groves in his Mallock. Ocean

Village was still being built at that time and the course, on a 'not yet public' road was a terrible rough and bumpy track – we were banging and crashing all over the place. I couldn't get on with it at all.

In between we had another couple of trips to Gurston, which left me lying second in the Gurston Down Top Six championship just behind John Meredith.

Then it was back to Shelsley Walsh and while I wasn't concentrating on the hill climb championship, I had registered for it and was rather pleased to take the final point that day behind some of the top drivers. While it would be another year before he took the first of his five British titles, David Grace took FTD ahead of co-driver Richard Brown and the man who would eventually take the 1992 title – sixteen years after he last won it – Roy Lane. Beating Peter Harper's Vision-BDA and Paul Gething's Anson-Rover in the run-off was an added advantage. I have to say that, thinking back, I didn't do myself any favours with the Rovercraft. One of my early recollections of the car was that it was very hard on the suspension and from the old Marsh Special days we tended to run very soft. The idea being that the wheels would follow the road surface more easily whereas if the suspension was hard they'd be pattering on top of it. So I put softer springs on the Rovercraft and in retrospect that was a bad thing to have done. In the current cars there is virtually no suspension.

Before returning to sprinting we took in the 25th anniversary of Gurston Down hill climb. Having taken BTD at the very first meeting I had to go along, but I didn't make the results this time, probably as a result of the car being developed for sprinting rather than hill climbing. But it's always nice to be at a venue when special anniversaries are being celebrated as the atmosphere is always so good.

Already it was September and time for Brighton again. This year we finished fourth in the run-off, just behind Roy Woodhouse in his ex-Ian Scheckter March 822 chassis that replaced the one written off at Weston, so we must have been making progress.

Also in September was New Brighton, which is across the Mersey from Liverpool on the Wallasey Peninsula. Again the long drive was worth the effort. Despite a very rough track with kerbstones to avoid and roundabouts to negotiate the wrong way, we finished sixth in the championship run-off which was won, with a new course record, by new champion Chris Hill.

What would turn out to be the last ever Weston-Super-Mare Speed Trials threw its usual challenges at us rain, sand and wind but we overcame these and finished fifth in the run-off behind John Gray, Roy Lane, Ken Ayers and Les Edmunds. I mentioned that Roy Woodhouse had fallen foul of the conditions in 1991, but this year he finished just behind me which would have been a relief, I'm sure.

The final event of 1992 was another blast round the airfield course at South Cerney, where Clive Harris snatched FTD from us on the very last run. The win would have been nice, but that was a good way to end a season in which I'd also finished second in the Gurston Down Top Six Challenge. John Meredith took a second consecutive title ahead of myself and Steve Jewell in his Chevron.

The 1993 season seemed to start rather early with Prescott on April 4. I suppose some of the dates depend upon Easter but these days, as I've got older, if the start of the season is early in April I'll let one or two events go by before I venture out. We managed to get ninth in the Avon/BMTR run-off at the Midland Championship Prescott, which was a good start to the year. Then a couple of weeks later came the first club event of the year at Gurston where we won the unlimited racing car class and only just missed out on FTD to Simon McBeath's Pilbeam-Hart MP54. Those McBeath brothers were really giving me a hard time – Simon's brother Andy was just a hundredth of a second behind me for third FTD!

Gurston was followed by Curborough (ninth in the run-off) and then an outing for the 4WD Marsh Special to Wiscombe. I can't quite remember why I took the Special but the sloping grass paddock was a little on the damp side and whereas many people had difficulty I just motored up it under power.

Another trip to Prescott with the Rovercraft in early May, but it was out of the results and into the bodyshop. Coming out of the Esses the boost came in with a bang, the tail went out and we hit the barrier on the inside, which rather rearranged things. Roy Lane did the repair work for me in double-quick time, which I appreciated as it meant we could go to Curborough in the middle of the month.

I only made twelfth in the Curborough run-off as the car wasn't handling quite right, although a test session at Goodwood got that sorted out. But the highlight of 1993 for many hill climbers must have been the inaugural Goodwood Festival of Speed. It was run more like an old fashioned hill climb, with drivers able to drive more than one car, though several people commented on my absence from the event. Quite simply I hadn't been invited to enter, but I was delighted that my sometime double driver, Gillian Goldsmith, took the Ladies' award in an Aston Martin DBR1.

Aintree in July was once again worth the long drive as we had our best sprint championship result to date with third in the run off, less than two seconds behind winner John Gray. Continual development on the car was paying off with a finish line speed down the old Railway Straight of over 180 mph.

However rain interfered with things the next day at Three Sisters. I couldn't use the twin turbos of the Rovercraft to best advantage due to lack of grip and we only managed sixth in the top twelve run-off.

If the highlight of 1993 for many had been the Festival of Speed, I think that for me it was the July meeting at Gurston. By this time the Rovercraft was developing around 600 bhp and we stopped the clocks in 29.90. This was the first time I'd managed a sub-30 at Gurston and I took FTD at the same time. It also left me tying for second place with Simon McBeath in the Gurston Top Six championship, Simon's brother Andy being in the lead, a couple of points clear. I'm sure that some of the improvements to the Rovercraft were due to data logging, telemetry and the consequent adjustments that could be made. Incidentally, on a somewhat different plane, for the rainy events I used to carry a little umbrella with me in the Rovercraft. I got the idea from Joy Rainey who wasn't able to get in or out of her car by herself so if it was raining she would put up her umbrella and sit there underneath it. The cockpit of the Rovercraft was quite roomy so I was able to wedge a fold-up umbrella down the side.

Colerne in August was another good result for me with 166 mph on the main straight and third place in the championship run-off. I think we were also the fastest in a straight line that day.

But now came an event that I think must rank as the worst I have ever been to. On September 11, Simon Law and I were driving the Rovercraft at Brighton Speed Trials – we always shared a drive there – when Simon had a fatal accident in the car.

I'd been witness to a number of fatalities during the course of my racing, indeed I was following Harry Schell at Silverstone when he hit the wall at the apex of Abbey and was killed. And yes, these things do stick in your mind, but in a different sort of way because back then you half expected things like that to happen. I don't think we were unfeeling in those earlier days, but we were very much in a racing driver's frame of mind and knew that accidents could happen. But Simon's accident was much more upsetting.

It really all started at the beginning of the week when we'd gone up to Enstone, an old airfield near Oxford, on the Monday or Tuesday to give the car a final run. Simon had a feeling we could take the record at Brighton and he wanted the car to be just right. We took it up the main runway, which is slightly uphill, and measured out our half mile using an odometer. Maybe it wasn't dead accurate, but we were pulling 170 mph at the end of that measured distance.

On the morning of Brighton the track was damp and we were not allowed to use slicks. Simon said he would go first and make sure everything was as he wanted it. Just after the finishing line, the car veered off to the left and into a building with stone steps running up alongside. Simon was taken to hospital by ambulance, but I think he was dead when he got there.

Originally the track had been one kilometre long and had been shortened to half a mile as the cars were reaching extremely high speeds. But even over the half-mile John Gray, who took his run just before Simon that day, was regularly running 180 mph at the end so speeds were getting higher again. Just after the finish of the half-mile course there was a bumpy section where you needed to sit with your elbows wedged against the cockpit sides. I remember going up the track in an open-sided ERA years before, when it was a kilometre, and being rather concerned that I might be bumped out of the car.

But on that fateful morning we knew that there had been an accident, although it was quite a long time before we knew that Simon had been killed. The Brighton and Hove Club organisers had to clear the track and then decided to shorten the course to a quarter-mile before the event could continue. Meanwhile Simon's brother Nick, along with Rovercraft telemetry man Liam Humberstone, had to go to the hospital and formally identify the body. It must have been a very harrowing day for them, too.

There were, inevitably, a number of people who thought they knew what had happened including one eye-witness who saw the back wing fall off, which is odd considering it was still attached to the car when it was recovered. There had to be an inquest, so the car was loaded onto a lorry and taken to the Police Headquarters in Brighton. We were allowed to look at the car and there were lots of questions asked, telemetry examined and so on. What I think happened was that Simon looked down at the instruments as he crossed the finish line, hit one of the bumps, reacted instinctively and grabbed the steering wheel, which put him off course. What we do know is that it was only two seconds from the car crossing the line until everything stopped and that he was recording around 170 mph.

Then came the funeral. I was asked to be one of the pallbearers and the whole tragedy was the end of a very happy relationship, one I remember with great fondness even to this day. Sadly, Rovercraft is no more either. Nick sold the business when the factory lease ran out. I think, also, that he had more interest in the engineering side of things rather than the engine development.

Liam Humberstone left Rovercraft and went to university at Preston, where he now teaches. I am still in touch with him and he very kindly helps me out with advice from time to time. Had the Rovercraft engine development continued we were looking for 700 bhp plus – as it was, we already had some 620 bhp.

Before we finally leave the Rovercraft, I must mention the two mementos I have of the car. From that awful day at Brighton I have one of the driveshafts which had been bent into an S-bend by the force of the impact. The other one I have is a bent con-rod. At one event at Weston-Super-Mare the car wasn't running properly and halfway down the course the engine backfired – the noise could be heard from the startline! Simon took the engine to pieces after the event and found the bent con-rod caused by the backfire. Some people might think it rather macabre to keep mementos like that, but they bring back such good memories of the happy times before Simon's accident that I don't like to part with them.

Following Brighton, motorsport, like life in general, carried on and even before I had left the Speed Trials people were offering me drives in their cars, or mentioning cars for sale. Early the following week David Render, a long-time supporter and sponsor of the British Sprint championship through his company Warecrete, rang up to ask what I was going to do about the championship. I had thought I might get out the old Marsh Special and do one or two events just for fun, but David suggested I bought his Toleman-DFL, which would be much more suitable as I was lying third in the championship at the time. The long and the short of it was that I sent David some money and collected the car from Ray Rowan's place on my way up to Aintree for the next championship round. Ray did all David's work for him and made sure the car was all ready and in tip-top condition for me. It was really well sorted for David and it suited me as well. I took to it very quickly.

Ray had obviously done a good job on the 3.9-litre TG191 because at that first event with the car I missed out on FTD by three tenths of a second and came second in the championship run off to 1993 champion Chris Hill. David Render finished seventh in his other Toleman, the 2.7-litre Hart powered car while Ray's SPA-Judd unfortunately failed to start in the run-off due to driveshaft problems. The Toleman was a very nice car to drive, much firmer than the Rovercraft as you could really feel it shaking you sometimes, but we were just two seconds away from the course record at Aintree, which was rather good considering I hadn't driven the car before.

After Aintree we went to Gurston and took FTD, but this time I missed the 30 second barrier by just two hundredths. However, the result was enough to earn me the Gurston Down Top Six Challenge title ahead of Andy McBeath and Simon Durling in his Pilbeam MP62, which was a great end to the season. And in the British Sprint series I came fourth overall behind Chris Hill, John Gray and Patrick Wood.

Back at Prescott for the start of the 1994 season, I didn't manage to qualify the Toleman. It was a good car on tracks that weren't quite so tight but at Prescott I found it a bit of a handful, especially in those early days when I was still learning how to drive it.

Conversely, the April Gurston meeting saw us back on FTD form with a 31.38 on a drying track. Gurston is one of my favourite venues these days. It's my local hill climb and has a good number of meetings each year, which means you can stay dialled into the hill a little bit. However on that day I did have a few starter motor problems. Originally the Toleman wasn't fitted with an on-board starter motor but had one of those arrangements where you insert a starter drive into the back of the gearbox and use a battery on a small trolley. But this detached starting didn't really suit my mode of operation (although I do have a separate starting battery with onboard starter motor on the Gould), so an on-board starter was cobbled up. It was never ideal and gave rather a lot of trouble, but fortunately it never affected the performance of the car.

A trip to the Isle of Man was always a trip down memory lane and Lhergy Frissel, part of the motorcycle TT course running out of Ramsey and over the Mountain section, was also the longest hill on the British circuit. Its 2.2 kilometres gave the Toleman some chance and we finished fifth in the British championship run-off, which was my best hill climb result since my return to motorsport. Mark Colton took a well deserved FTD in his Ray Rowan built Roman while David Grace in second and Patrick Wood in third were both driving Pilbeam-Cosworth V8s. Future British Hill Climb champion – and World Touring Car champion – Andy Priaulx brought his Pilbeam-Hart home fourth while the ever enthusiastic Bill Bristow scored his first ever RAC championship points at the wheel of his Vision-Hart sportscar.

The Isle of Man meeting actually began on the Thursday with an event on the extended five kilometre course. The significance of this was that it was the length that qualified for a European Championship hill. It was the inaugural event for this course and Graham Hickman took his F1 3.5 Jordan-DFR 193 up for FTD with an average speed of just under 100 mph and a finish line speed of 150 mph.

I was surprised that more people didn't take the opportunity to run on the Thursday as it was an extra run up the hill before the championship event. Being a road course, the track was wider than normal. But what I found slightly disconcerting was the surface, which had just been redone by spraying it with tar and then covering it in chippings. The sprayer hadn't been wide enough to cover even half the track, which was done in three stripes with an overlap on each and then the white lines plonked on top. The car definitely seemed to have a mind of its own; first you were sliding on the white lines and then a bit of overlap would come into play. After a bit of practice I found that either I'd got used to it or we got faster and seemed to glide over the irregularities. It didn't seem so bad, except for coming down the hill. I always use the return down the hill to learn a bit more of the geography of a venue but here it was quite dangerous. If you took one hand off the wheel the car would dart about all over the place.

In fact I was finding it quite difficult to learn Lhergy Frissel. In the end I drove the American Day Van I used as a support vehicle up and down the hill several times. However, when you got back in the racing car you couldn't see over the walls and I did catch myself out a couple of times.

I remember that Peter Harper gave me a bit of a scare one year at Lhergy Frissel. There was quite a long way to go after the finish before a convenient turning or gathering point and I was sent off down the hill only to meet Peter coming the other way. Somebody had heard that the last car was over the line and off we were sent, but of course Peter hadn't actually got to us by then.

Now I've not mentioned John Garnett before, but he was one of the sprint regulars. I don't quite know why I picked on John, but I often used to plague him with practical jokes. Once I tied a cucumber to his timing strut. Why? I'm not really sure except that I had one in the van and obviously thought he could do with one. Not that his culinary skills were up to much as he seemed to live off ready meals which he was just about able to put in the oven. So at one of the prize giving events in Kidderminster I presented him with a cook book. John wasn't at Lhergy Frissel and I thought it a shame that he should miss out on the local flavour, so I had a parcel of Manx kippers shipped to him. What he did with them I don't know, but he seemed to take everything in good part even if he did have to keep looking over his shoulder at events. One prank he didn't take in quite such good part was when I changed the name on the side of his car from John to Alf (Garnett), but generally he was fine. He even put up with me sticking a pair of deer horns onto his crash helmet and I have to admit that since he gave up sprinting, meetings haven't quite been the same.

After the two hill climbs on the Isle of Man we were also able to enter a British Championship sprint on the Sunday at Jurby Airfield. It was a fairly typical airfield track but I do remember, when we came round the last corner towards the turn-off for the paddock, impressing Championship Co-ordinator Paul Parker with a bit of opposite lock. I just kept the boot well in and did a lovely power slide. After all, there's no point getting older if you can't use your experience, is there! Roger Kilty took FTD at Jurby in his Pilbeam-Hart MP40 with the man who would take that year's championship title, Patrick Wood, ahead of Kilty and myself. Ken Ayers and Steve Jewell rounded off the British championship entry as with so far to travel, not many had bothered to make the trip.

We were still in the points at Gurston's May hill climb round, but this time a little lower down the order. Roy Lane had the top spot followed by David Grace, Mark Colton and Andy Priaulx. It wasn't until you got down to ninth that you found my name just behind local driver Chris Cannell, who fulfilled two ambitions that day in his ageing Ralt RT1 with 3.9-litre Rover V8 power. The first of these was a top ten placing, the second being to pass through the finish beam at 120 mph. It's always nice when someone manages achievements like this at a hill climb.

I also found time to fit in a sprint championship round at Colerne, finishing sixth behind Russ Ward's Chevron-Rover (this was Russ's first ever British run-off win), Patrick Wood, Roger Kilty, local man Dave Cutcliffe and Chris Hill. John Garnett also made the run-off in his Lola-DFR, but I can't remember if I got up to any mischief that day…

Then came New Brighton again and my first ever British Sprint victory. But it wasn't all plain sailing. The course, as I mentioned before, wasn't the smoothest in the series and the Toleman bottomed out and damaged the clutch slave cylinder, which was mounted very low down. I also had problems with a duff battery, but once all this was sorted out we did the business. Patrick Wood took FTD on one of his timed runs, but my first place in the run-off was good enough to put me into second place behind Patrick in the championship, sneaking ahead of Roger Kilty.

But the next Gurston was not one of my better meetings. It was wet, with water running across the lowest part of the course near the speed trap, just before Hollow Bend. I approached unabated, wedged my elbows tight in the cockpit and pressed on. But the car aquaplaned off to the left into a field full of straw waiting to be picked up. The Toleman ran down one of the lanes of straw, which the front wing scooped up and shot over my head so I couldn't see where I was going. I ended up with half a bale's worth wedged under the car and couldn't move.

A damaged nose was repaired in double quick time with assistance from any number of fellow competitors who very kindly helped, but we failed to spot the damaged suspension until later, by which time it was too late to do anything about it. I was understandably rather disappointed, but cheered up no end when I was approached by Ian Drowne, one of the motorcycle competitors, who asked if I would like to go up the hill on a demonstration run in the chair of his sidecar combination. Naturally I said yes and some leathers were quickly found. Ian ran only a smallish engine in his combination, but the surge off the start line was greater than I'd expected. During the run Ian kept looking down to see if I was still there or to check whether I was hanging out properly and we made it to the top quite nicely. I don't know what the time was, but even though it was only a demonstration run I feel sure the clocks were running. I couldn't have done too badly because Ian asked if I'd like another run, giving the impression that he would take it a little more seriously – which he did. Unfortunately he muffed a gear change between Karousel and Deer Leap (I think he caught his toe on the ground and got a box of neutrals) which spoilt the run, otherwise it would have been quite a serious attempt.

In fact this wasn't the first time I'd been in the chair of a sidecar combination. I was once invited to go for a ride round Pau when I was there with the Cooper. Now Pau is very similar to Monaco, but without the sea. There are some casino gardens to go through where there was actually a duck marshal, to keep the ducks on the pond and off the track. There were always bikes for the supporting races as the organisers at Pau couldn't afford a second lot of cars and one of the riders, a Mr Tickle, came and asked if I had a particular size of drill, as he wanted to drill out one of his carburettor jets. On returning it, he asked me if I fancied having a ride round with him to try it out. His usual passenger, his wife, was recovering from having slid off the chair earlier when a burst oil pipe had made things rather slippery. I said yes like a shot and became very preoccupied with putting myself in the right place at the right time. In fact I rather enjoyed it (though I didn't have a leather suit to wear) and so when Ian Drowne offered me the ride up Gurston I jumped at the chance.

Back to 1994 and to Aintree where a fifth place, despite an elusive a misfire, kept me in the runner-up position for the series despite all the usual suspects (Wood, Hill, Rowan and Garnett) being ahead of me. Now this misfire wasn't obvious to me at first. People were telling me that the engine didn't sound very good, but these Cosworth DFL engines have so much power (we're talking 500 bhp plus) and torque, that having eight cylinders you could lose one and still sound quite exciting. But as it turned out it was starting to go off song, which was why I was down in fifth place.

Then came another Gurston and, despite the off at Hollow at the previous meeting, another FTD. My first run was good enough to take the top spot, but never one to miss out on an opportunity I managed a sub-30 on the second timed runs to make sure of it. Always a most satisfying experience at Gurston.

A trip to Three Sisters for the sprint championship round at the end of July saw just two names ahead of me in the results. Local man John Garnett took FTD but he was only second in the run-off behind Roger Kilty, with myself in third, Clive Harris fourth and Chris Hill fifth. The championship was still far from over.

Then we went off to Shelsley Walsh for a round of the British hill climb championship, and the slight loss of power was enough to keep me down to ninth. I was a mere one hundredth of a second behind Russ Ward's Chevron-Rover but, as we all know, that one hundredth really counts. And this slight power loss came into play again at Gurston at the end of August where I missed out on a sub-30 by nine hundredths and ran second fastest, behind Chris Cannell.

By Aintree, Patrick Wood was acknowledged as British Sprint Champion, despite only finishing third in the run-off. Chris Hill led the way from John Garnett, while I was fourth. And with John ahead of me here and again at Three Sisters a couple of weeks later, he relegated me to a final fourth overall in the championship with Roger Kilty, who after a couple more years would go on to take back-to-back sprint titles before making a name for himself on the circuits in BOSS racing, having already sneaked through into second place. But that's the way things go and it was a fine first title for Patrick. Roy Lane, incidentally, finished eighth in the series having won it no less than ten years earlier. It says a lot for their enthusiasm for motor sport when you see that Roy was also third in the hill climb championship that year with Patrick fifth.

And at Gurston, my favourite hill, I finished sixth in the 1994 Top Six Challenge which was won for the first time, deservedly, by Chris Cannell. Not quite such a good result for me as the previous year, perhaps, but what better way to finish my first full season in the Toleman than with an FTD at South Cerney.

Looking back through my cuttings and results for 1995 I appear to have made a rather late start to motorsport that year, which may have had something to do with a little project I'd just started working on.

After Simon Law's fatal accident in the Rovercraft back in September 1993, I was left with an engine and a Hewland gearbox that had been repaired by Roy Lane. The question was what to do with them next. It seemed a terrible waste of all the development that had gone into the engine but I now had the Toleman, in which I was doing rather well, and didn't need another racing car. Having always drooled over Ray Christopher's GTD 40s, I decided to explore the possibility of using them in one of these. First I had words with Ray to see if GTD would be interested. As it turned out, they were more than keen to do a one-off special.

I borrowed a dummy engine that, together with my gearbox, went to GTD for them to build a chassis around. It was decided I would have a Mark 2 body as this was much higher with more room at the back and underneath, though I wasn't too sure where I was going to fit all the ancillary bits and pieces. Eventually the chassis, body and numerous boxes arrived and after about a year of burning midnight oil, I'd finally finished the car. There were oil pipes, oil coolers and intercoolers as well as twin turbos and all the extra parts for the dry sump to be considered. Sorting all this out became addictive; I would go out to 'just do' something on the car and find myself coming back in several hours later. Once I'd found space for the intercoolers, some very large diameter aluminium trunking had to be constructed and a suitable air filter found for both of them. Next an exhaust system was required, which I farmed out to a firm in the North Midlands to make from stainless steel. And of course we needed to install wiring (which I bought as a ready prepared loom) and instrument panels and so on. Eventually it was all finished and I had to take the car to the licensing authority at Portsmouth. They had to satisfy themselves that the car existed, that all the invoices I had for bits and pieces actually related to the parts that were in the car. Having done this I then had to get the car through its MOT, which is always a bit of a palaver. These days I end up sitting in the car to press the appropriate pedals and buttons, because generally the assistant can't get into the car. GTDs are a bit tight on space, especially if you're not used to hopping in and out of one. Since then I've made things a bit easier with a detachable steering wheel – though perhaps this is a sign of old age!

The car looks just the same as any other GTD 40, except that they normally use a Renault gearbox with a twin cable operated gear change which I found a bit weird and somewhat vague. It worked, but I used my Hewland gearbox for which I was able to devise a solid gear linkage.

I don't compete much in the GTD but I did take great delight in taking it to the 1995 Brighton Speed Trials and introducing it to everybody. The engine is too big to go to Brighton in a racing car, as big engined single seaters were banned from competing after Simon's accident. However, at the end of the standing quarter-mile the GTD was clocked at 139 mph, with one gear still to go. The only problem was that it was rather hard work driving it there. Out on the open road it's a delight to drive, but as soon as you start driving anywhere near traffic it becomes very tiresome because there's no synchromesh on the gearbox. So every time you stop at traffic lights you have to feed the gear lever in gently to engage the dogs, because I'm not one of these people who just shoves it in with a big clunk. Also it has a sintered clutch (not a soft, Ferodo-type lining but one with metal deposits on the plates) which tends to be either in or out. And just to make life more difficult the clutch is a triple plate, to be able to transfer all the torque and horsepower to a car considerably heavier than the single seater that the engine and gearbox were designed for.

I don't drive the GTD that much, but I did take it up to the Midlands for the family to see. It did 18 miles to the gallon, which is not too bad when you consider it's a 4.5 twin turbo. I have to admit to trying to drive it sensibly, as I didn't want to be picked up by the police. I have done a sprint at Goodwood in it, but it was a bit difficult from the noise aspect and since then I've added a bit more silencing. I've also taken the car to Thruxton when I was invited to take part in a Supersprint practice session. However they decided there might be some complaints about the noise if I took it round. It's not particularly noisy but the Hewland gearbox does make quite a racket.

But even if I didn't get out very early for the 1995 season, I did manage to go to the Isle of Man for the Lhergy Frissel round of the British Championship in mid-May. *Speedscene* editor Jerry Sturman thought the Toleman sounded rather flat and in fact the DFL was very slowly going off song, but I couldn't hear it because of the noise and we still managed fifth in the championship run-off behind Mark Colton, David Grace, Andy Priaulx and his father Graham.

At Ingliston in the middle of May we were only sixth after the first rounds. I may have tinkered with the engine a bit at lunchtime because there was a remarkable improvement on the second runs (*Speedscene* writer Robin Boucher said it suddenly sounded better) and we improved by over three seconds to finish third in the run-off behind Chris Hill and John Garnett. Ingliston was quite a tricky little course. It was on the site of an agricultural showground and the access road all the way round, which wound in and out of buildings, was in fact one of Scotland's premier race circuits.

Gurston Down's 150th meeting on May 28 was, appropriately enough, a round of the British Hill Climb championship. The event showed that the Toleman wasn't quite right with only eleventh place in the run-off. You can make all sorts of excuses on the day, it's only when you look back on things that you realise what was happening. In some events the engine problem didn't have quite the same effect on the results as it did at others. I was still under 30 seconds at Gurston (29.66), but Andy Priaulx lowered the outright course record to 27.14 in a battle with Mark Colton.

At Pembrey in June for a Sprint Championship round, we were third behind Hill and Garnett before another visit to New Brighton. The course was a bumpy as ever but the Wallasey & DMC organisers had installed a new chicane in an effort to try and slow the cars down along the seafront. This didn't make a huge difference to me and we took FTD that day in 52.04 seconds. John Fellows was second with John Garnett in third place, but I don't think Chris Hill was there that day. Obviously the engine was feeling up to the job as we established a new course record. Incidentally, a picture appeared in *Speedscene* after New Brighton showing me apparently taking orders for fish on my clipboard. I expect somebody heard about John Garnett's kippers from the Isle of Man as that was where we were due to go next.

The picture shows me wearing glasses, which were quite often bifocals. My near vision had started to deteriorate a little and I needed glasses for reading. When I went for an eye test I was told I was within the legal limits for driving, but I asked if they could sharpen things up a little for me. I could see things in the distance but it wasn't until I got a bit closer to things like motorway signs that I could honestly say I was reading them. At New Brighton I was wearing bifocals, the idea being that I could see the instruments with the bottom part and with the top half I was looking at the road. But the wretched things were more trouble than they were worth, bouncing up and down on my nose so much that I had to take them off and manage without them.

Another little story about spectacles is that when I started wearing them for reading I ended up with some half glasses so that I could still see distances over the top. On one of my trips to Austria I was having dinner with the Brenter family when I brought them out. Erich Brenter is a bit of a joker and made some comment about the glasses, which the whole family then wanted to try on. There was even more amusement when I told them I had half glasses because I couldn't afford full glasses.

But back to motorsport and we were off to Lhergy Frissel again. The five kilometre course on the Thursday was an event I liked to do if possible as it meant you got a bit more practice in driving over the shorter championship course. However, we don't seem to have done terribly well in the championship event even if we were recorded at over 100 mph, while still learning the hill. Andy Kittle and Peter Harper were also going well. In fact Peter eventually took FTD with an outright hill record for the 5 km course, making history with the first 100mph average speed from a standing start on a British hill climb.

The weather wasn't ideal on the Saturday of Gurston's June double-header, when John Forsyth took FTD. But it was dry and sunny on the Sunday and good conditions for the Toleman. Chris Cannell – who was starting to become something of a nuisance – had cured an earlier misfire and was doing his best to beat me. I held him off, if only by three hundredths of a second for FTD in 29.63 seconds.

After Aintree (where I finished third in the championship run-off) we went to Three Sisters. The *Speedscene* report included a picture of myself and John Garnett. I suspect that Jerry Sturman was getting a bit of mileage out of the kipper story as John was sitting in his car, which sported a sticker saying 'I'd rather be fishing'. I don't know who gave him that but on this occasion at least, it wasn't me.

This was a rather low period for sprinting and hill climbing as it was around this time that Mark Colton had his fatal accident at Craigantlet when he hit a telegraph pole. It was such a shame; he was rather a good driver and could have definitely have made an even bigger name for himself.

Mark's accident was on one of those dual event weekends where we sprinted at Kirkistown on the Friday and then hill climbed at Craigantlet on the Saturday. Driving the van and trailer through Belfast I remember seeing a lot of police and military activity in the distance. Closer inspection revealed it to be one of the Irish parades coming in our direction so I pulled over to let them pass and wound down the window to watch. While I was sitting there one of the marchers near the front came across to the van and shook hands with me. Fortunately everything passed off very peacefully and I was soon able to proceed.

Kirkistown was, in fact, a round of the British Sprint

Championship and is similar in some ways to Curborough, although much faster. Both are ex-military or airforce establishments with some of the buildings left – and both are (or were) a bit rough. I managed fourth place in the run-off at Kirkistown, so it was worth the trip even if John Garnett did take third.

The July Gurston meeting was good for me in that I took FTD in 29.97, which also helped my standing in the Gurston Top Ten Challenge. After the meeting I lay third, three points behind leader Andy McBeath and two behind John Forsyth with only one championship meeting left.

Back up to Liverpool for another sprint championship round at Aintree where I was third again, behind John Garnett (on winning form with FTD) and Chris Hill.

It was now two years after the V8 Rovercraft engine had last been to the Brighton Speed Trials, at the time of Simon Law's tragic accident. With the engine now installed in the GTD 40, Brighton 1995 saw the car's motorsport debut. Unfortunately I had forgotten to fit a timing strut, which shows that these things can happen to the most experienced people, but in true motorsport fashion this was soon rectified (Richard George coming to the rescue) and I was delighted with the car and its performance. With a 2-litre limit now imposed on single seaters, Mike Lee took the four-wheel FTD in his Lyncar-BDG (behind seven motorcycles…). Sadly I forget who came second, but third fastest car was Jim Tiller in the venerable 7.3 litre Allard with Racelogic traction control, and following Jim was the GTD 40. It was a great run, which I thoroughly enjoyed and I felt, in a way, it was a memorial to Simon. On the way we managed to just pip Justin Bell's Chrysler Viper (which may have been his Le Mans car) by 0.04 seconds and took the Dave Wilson Memorial Trophy for the fastest GTD.

Early October saw the final event in the Gurston championships and I am delighted to say that the car and I were both on top form and we took FTD. We must have been on top form to beat Chris Cannell in his Ralt Rover by a whole second. This put us in first place overall for the Top Ten Championship with Chris Cannell in second, Andy McBeath third while John Forsyth and Richard Fry tied in fourth.

One week later we were back at Three Sisters where Ray Rowan shared the car with me. I felt I was starting to struggle with it a little and had asked Ray if he could come along and make a few suggestions. I tied with Bill Bristow on 40.37, but took fourth place on aggregate. This was the last round of the British Sprint Championship in 1995 with Chris Hill taking his third title ahead of John Garnett and myself.

A week later, South Cerney was our final event of the season. It was rather a windy day and a number of us were red flagged because of the cones blowing about all over the course. Russ Ward in his Chevron-Rover provided some good competition and Mike Lee was there too, so I didn't have it all my own way. But in the end the Toleman took FTD with Russ in second and Mike third. One man who did make his mark that day was Russ's son Ashley who, on his maiden drive in the V8 powered F2 based car, took fourth – not bad for a twenty-two year old.

With the season over, the Toleman went to Ray's place in Walsall where we weighed it and found it to be rather on the heavy side. Much discussion ensued during which Ray told me he was selling the Judd engined Roman. It was decided it might be an idea if we did a deal whereby I took his car and he took mine in part exchange, once I'd had a test drive. Off we went to Three Sisters on rather a damp day where I found I wasn't able to drive the Roman to its fullest extent. I found it had a power surge at certain rpm, which I didn't get with the DFL because it was so flexible. The outcome of all this was that I decided to have the Roman but keep my 4-litre DFL engine, which Ray duly transferred for me.

Not much work happened in the garage over the winter of 1995 as I was in for repairs myself. I'd had a second heart attack on January 16 and a subsequent heart by-pass operation. So I didn't feel quite ready to take part in the early Gurston meetings but went along in a supervisory capacity, to help my son Peter who'd bought a Reynard-BDG from John Knapton.

By the end of May I was feeling more the ticket and, in typical Marsh fashion, was sprinting at Colerne and hill climbing at Gurston on the same weekend. Getting out in competition again after the by-pass was a psychological milestone, but I have to say that Colerne was slightly more successful as we came fourth in the sprint championship run-off. Obviously I was getting back into the swing of things.

Next came Pembrey when both Peter and I went down for a sprint and were pictured together in *Speedscene* where the Roman was described as 'somewhat demanding'. It was certainly different from the Toleman as Ray liked his cars very firm on the road. Once I got used to it, this stood me in good stead for the more modern cars like the Gould, which have a similar characteristic. The Roman was set up for hill climbing and so needed a bit of adjustment before it could become a sprint specialist. One slightly unusual thing about the car is that when I bought it, the front wing had been tried on the circuits. Whereas cars now have high noses with supports going downwards to take the wing, on the Roman it was the other way round. There was a strut on the nose with the wing mounted quite high. The whole thing was stuck up on this sort of pylon affair and I had rather a frightening moment with it at Aintree when the wing suddenly started to vibrate alarmingly. My theory is that it was because the aerodynamics were causing more downforce on one side. Eventually I went to a Gould front wing and didn't seem to have any more problems with it. But even with the car being 'demanding' at Pembrey we still managed to finish ahead of John Garnett, which would have been quite satisfying.

After Pembrey came the Aintree/Three Sisters double header where John managed to reverse the Pembrey placing, getting ahead of me on both days. At Three Sisters we were separated by Dave Cutliffe, who became an absolute nuisance! He had a little Van Diemen with home developed aerodynamics and was a very good driver. He was able to drive this thing flat out whereas we were treating the twisty course with a little bit of respect.

At MIRA, Dave and John were both ahead of me in the run-off. By this time, John had his 3.5 Lola-Judd/Merlin T90/50 to play with rather than the 3.5 Reynard-DFV/Gardner 89D he'd shared with Carl Amos at the beginning of the season.

In fact the pair were ahead of me again when we went to Croft. But I did have some sort of excuse this time as it was my first visit there and it poured with rain. Funnily enough I had never competed at the Darlington race circuit in the early days and on this visit the weather didn't help and neither did the tarmac.

Part of the circuit had been resurfaced with a different type of tarmac. On the old surface there was water everywhere with huge plumes of spray thrown up by the cars, but on the new stuff it was just damp. It must have had some excellent draining properties because there was good grip too. Combine this with learning a new circuit and what was, to me, a rather new car as well and you can see why I only ran sixth in the run off.

Around this time the whole Marsh family was competing in motorsport. There was Peter sprinting and hill climbing his Reynard and now my eldest son, Simon, had acquired a Mallock from Tony Brown, which he too was sprinting. On top of that Paul, the youngest, had bought a trials car, which was how I'd made my own debut in motorsport. Peter and Simon are still competing today, but after several years in trials Paul sold the car when it started spending more time in the garage than it did competing. This was partly because it had a hybrid engine that started giving problems. He found he was spending a fortune, only for the repairs or modifications to let him down again. The frustrations of that and the fact he was getting involved in home improvements made him decide to sell the car. But, having given it a try and enjoyed it he could always go back to it when circumstances improved.

I mentioned earlier that I'd taken the GTD to a Supersprint practice at Thruxton. The event was towards the end of the 1996 season and while the GTD hadn't been allowed to play I'd also taken the Roman along and took fourth place in that behind Chris Hill, John Garnett and Carl Amos. Chris sportingly lent me some spare hose when I discovered a pinhole leak in the car's water system – it's nice that sprinting and hill climbing still have such a friendly spirit.

When we arrived at Thruxton we were taken round the circuit in Chief Instructor Bill Coombs' car by way of an introduction to the circuit. I remember there were three of us in the back of this car, which was just as well because it needed three of us to hold us all in place. I'm still not sure how the tyres didn't come off the wheels, but fortunately they didn't.

This was also the first time I'd come across Truck Racing

and that was an incredible sight. I was fascinated by it and went to have a good look at some of the devices fitted to the trucks. I also took the GTD 40 to a sprint at Goodwood where, once again, it was something of a family affair with both Simon and Peter competing in the Mallock and the Reynard.

A couple of events at Gurston were followed by a British Sprint championship round at Curborough, another wet event, then the Aintree and Three Sisters sprint championship rounds again. A series of finishes around the middle of the championship run-offs meant an overall seventh place in the championship at the end of the season. On the whole I was quite pleased with this result, bearing in mind I'd missed the beginning of the season while recovering from my heart by-pass operation and had a new car to learn.

David Render was out competing at those latter sprints, on one occasion finishing sixth in a run-off to my seventh. David had been very good to me earlier that year, after my operation. He had a similar one not that long before and as well as coming to see me in hospital, afterwards he used to ring up to see how I was and to tell me what to look out for. After he'd sold me the Toleman he'd bought himself a 2.8 Pilbeam-Hart MP43 sportscar and was going quite nicely in it. I drove it for him once at Brighton when he had a slight hiccup after his heart operation. This was discovered when he went back for his 'MOT' to renew his HGV licence. For this they put him on a treadmill. Halfway through they stopped him and said that something wasn't quite right. Apparently one of his three by-passes wasn't there. Either it hadn't taken properly or it might have been absorbed, but unfortunately he couldn't drive competitively after that.

In some ways it was rather nice driving David's sports car at Brighton and in others it wasn't. He came along to supervise and was telling me how to drive the car, which conflicted slightly with how I felt I ought to drive it. I hadn't driven a sports car competitively for some time, plus the Pilbeam had a 2.8 Hart engine and I'd never driven a Hart before, but I do remember that it had the most delightful gearbox. David had taken FTD with the car the previous year and was rather keen that I should do the same, but I just wasn't able to match his times. If I had done we would most certainly have won.

After Brighton the car went back to Ray Rowan and I think

he had a drive in it too. The general opinion was that the engine had lost some of its sparkle and had started to go off-song. The car was subsequently passed on to Mike Sidgwick and later Rhys Howells, who ran a twin turbo Rover V8 in it but who unfortunately lost his life in the car, in a testing accident at Llandow.

David and I still find ourselves on the phone to one another every now and then. Recently he started grumbling at me that I shouldn't be driving a big racing car any more. Why didn't I do what he was doing? He's become an E-Type enthusiast and goes on 'gentlemen's rallies', the sort where you have a continental motoring holiday, calling in at a race circuit and having a drive round before going on to either the next one or to the Chateau that you are staying in. One day I might, but at the moment I tell him I'm not quite ready for it yet. However, I was very pleased to tell him that I was starting to listen to his advice and was getting a lighter, less powerful car, one more suited to an elderly gentleman! When I told him what it was (my new Gould V6) he told me I was still doing too much and that I should get an E-Type and join him. At least we can have a good laugh together.

My delayed start to motorsport in 1996 meant I lost my Gurston Top Ten Challenge crown, albeit to a most worthy winner, Simon Durling. Having done only a couple of rounds I finished joint ninth, level with Bill Morris and Sue Hayes.

Then, towards the end of the season I suffered another slight setback – I broke my arm. *Speedscene* reported that I had fallen out of a tree while pruning branches but that wasn't quite correct. I didn't exactly fall out of the tree, but I did make a rather unscheduled exit from a ladder.

One of our oak trees had a dead branch and being slightly tidy-minded in certain respects, this branch offended me. It had to come off. It was about twelve feet up, so I propped my ladder up the tree and started the chainsaw. Now this branch was quite long with several smaller branches on the end of it. After I'd sawn through most of it, it broke off and dropped to the ground. As it went down, the smaller branches at the end caused it to twist in my direction, sending both me and the ladder flying. I dropped like a stone and immediately knew I had done myself a mischief. There was a tremendous bruise on my left arm where the branch hit it, and it was all a bit complicated because I was lying half in, half out of a ditch alongside the hedgerow. The man who was with me ran for help and one of the gardeners brought a car to take me to Queen Alexander's Hospital in Havant, where the arm was duly x-rayed and pronounced broken. Unfortunately I didn't break it in a very convenient place so they didn't plaster it, just gave me a sling and told me to be careful.

So there I was, with my arm in a sling, missing motorsport events and very well aware that the start of the shooting season was almost upon us. In the end I had to learn to shoot with one arm which, after two or three shoots, worked out quite well. If anything I was shooting slightly better than before, or at least taking shots that other people seemed impressed by. There was also speculation about my shooting with a gun in each arm when the broken one had mended!

I was still having a weekly massage for my back and chest muscles to help with my posture following the heart operation, so when I turned up with my arm in a sling they thought they'd better try and do something about that too. It did seem to take rather a long time to get better and in retrospect I should have had it pinned. Perhaps that would had stopped it stiffening up, which it still does. Peter and his wife had an automatic Daimler at the time and kindly loaned it to me so I could get about. One shoot captain in the Midlands was rather surprised to see me semi-disabled when I climbed out!

Chapter Ten

Having already mentioned shooting, this might be an appropriate place to have a break from motorsport and talk about my life-long interest in shooting.

It started when I was a boy, when two of my holiday interests were accompanying the head keeper and the forester. I don't remember being specifically taught to shoot, but I had the inevitable air-gun when I was at prep school and father used to take me round the farm buildings to shoot sparrows – or at least shoot at them.

I used to take the gun on holiday to Angelsey and pot at seagulls on the chimney pots - I'd go 'plop!', the seagull would fly away and the pellet would bounce back off the brickwork. But from there I progressed to a double barreled .410, quite a serious little gun which did the rounds of the young people in the family, and was allowed on some of the family shoots.

After the war, when things began to get back to normal, father was able to spend a little more time at home rather than rushing off to meetings with the Ministry of Food or whoever and we were able to spend a little more time together. About this time I progressed to a 16 bore, which is a little bit smaller than a 12 bore.

I was taken to quite a number of interesting places on the shooting field and in particular was introduced to wildfowling. For this, you stand out in great big waders on a terribly cold and windy day, or in the early morning before it's light, and wait for ducks and geese. The geese fly between their night-time quarters on inland water and the sea, where they spend the daytime. Inevitably, I caught what's known as Goose Fever. To see 150 or so geese flying in a big V formation, knowing that they're probably coming to the field where you're standing in the hedgerow, is a magical, unbelievable sight and sound.

There was, of course, shooting up on Anglesey where father had rented land for wildfowling. He got so keen on it that he bought the adjacent farm when it came up for sale. It had little pools down in a boggy hollow, with lots of reeds. We used to go down there a good half-hour before it got light and cross ditches using wooden planks to get in position. As the morning light came up the ducks would

Toleman at Gooseneck on the Isle of Man TT course

GTD with twin turbo engine from the Rovercraft

With son Peter and his Reynard at Pembrey in South Wales

The Gould GR37 DFR at Gurston's Karousel

Gould GR55

With Liza in the paddock at Gurston

Fantastic line-up of hill climb champions at Shelsley, 1997

British Sprinters at Thruxton, mid 1990's

The current equipment (Gould GR55 V6) at Ashes, Gurston Down

Now let me see

The Top 10 champion finishers in 2005 with their ladies

A special award presented at the January 2006 British Championship dinner

At Soal Farm with some of the equipment

With Malcolm Dellingpole in a Dellow at Shelsley on a demonstration run

Liza and I at our wedding

come in for a drink of water before flying out to sea to sleep for the day. They came back in the evening to feed on pasture land or wind-flattened corn. We used to shoot duck in the morning before breakfast and on the way back to the house, stop off at a phone box (no mobile phones in those days!) and ring the housekeeper to say we were on our way, so that she could start to fry the eggs. We'd have breakfast, a quick change round, then go back to the marshes and walk up in line with a couple of keepers. We'd have a whole host of different prey; duck off the dykes, the odd hare or pheasant and maybe some snipe. Then we'd go off to the local pub for our lunch, which would often be quite late, and if there was still time we might have another walk round. After all this we might go off again for the evening flight. But a couple of days of tramping round in our heavy thigh boots proved fairly hard going.

Father had a shooting arrangement with the Marquis of Anglesey, whose land bordered Father's, whereby they shared a couple of keepers. Indeed the Marquis once came to a morning flight. I remember this was after I'd graduated to a 12 bore, because he'd run out of cartridges and wanted to borrow some of mine!

I also went down to the River Severn, to shoot with father and my uncle Ron. It was near to Peter Scott's place at Slimbridge; father had a link with the well-known ornithologist through the Dudley Zoo.

For a youngster they were memorable days. I once went with father to Essex and stayed in a little pub there with the other members of a shoot syndicate. It was just after petrol rationing had been lifted and we drove there in Father's eight-litre Bentley. We needed to fill up to get home and went to the local blacksmith, who had a pump. 'Fill it up', said father. The blacksmith was used to putting in, say, two gallons so after about five he came up to the window. 'Carry on,' said father, 'fill it up'. When the blacksmith got to about 18 gallons he started looking underneath the car to see if it was coming out anywhere.

On the Norfolk Broads we went wildfowling with a man called Jimmy Wentworth-Day who wrote articles about shooting and country matters for *Country Life* and *The Field*. We went to Norfolk several times. I remember meeting Lord de Lisle, but another visit was a complete washout; we ended up in Yarmouth eating bloaters.

At some stage, too, father had a couple of geese that we'd shot stuffed and mounted on boards, which he used as decoys

I became really keen on wild fowling and on my twenty-first birthday, Grandfather Ceney gave me a pair of 12 bores which I still have to this day. These had been specially built for the gunsmith's sons who, unfortunately, did not return from the war.

I carried on doing little bits of shooting here and there, mainly on family shoots on the farms up at Kinver. There was some sort of syndicate arrangement; uncle Ron was in it, a cousin of father's, Peter Marsh, used to come quite regularly and there was uncle Fred as well. He was in the cloth trade in Birmingham, a dry old stick who always made me think of partridges. In addition there was Uncle Bert, who owned the Midland Gun Company. I was fascinated to watch him at lunchtime. At the end of the meal he'd discreetly take his teeth out, give them a little polish under the table and then slide them back in again.

Once I'd discovered motorsport, shooting took a little bit of a back seat. All the family shoots were on a Saturday and, of course, there were now trials to go to.

After moving to Hampshire I didn't take part in many organised shoots. Until, during one of his brief phone calls, father asked if I'd like to go up to Kinver for a day's shooting. This re-awoke my interest. But soon after father became unwell and found that organising the shooting parties was getting quite stressful. It was rather like organising a dinner party when you have a plan in mind, then try to match up the guests so that they all get on. So on shoot days I started to take on the role of what is now known as Shoot Captain. He's the one who gets everybody in the right place at the right time, liaises with the keeper and so on.

In the mid to late seventies Father became even more ill. He'd been complaining about a pain in his leg, in which was discovered a blockage that seriously restricted blood flow. He had an operation to convert a vein to an artery and was out of action for a month or two, which was when I started doing a bit more of the planning for him. He wouldn't let the operation get in the way of his enjoyment though. The woodsman had a four-wheel-drive Subaru pick-up, in the back of which he mounted a typists chair. With the aid of a straw bale or two, father used to climb in, sit in the chair and still enjoy his shooting. He tied some shock cord from the arms of his chair to the cab of the pick-up to stop him spinning round when he pulled the trigger! Father didn't have much time for illness.

Father's shoot, as I call it, was in the Midlands and was looked after by old Mr Beaumont. Father employed Mr Beaumont as a woodsman or forester and he became the Head Keeper. He's still alive today - he's ninety something now. But father had also bought some property near Stow on the Wold and two or three times a year father and several friends, along with Mr Beaumont, would have a walk round this Cotswolds shoot with their guns. They used to do quite well, but it was completely un-organised, what you'd call rough shooting. Father had an old employee there, Eric, who looked after the general maintenance, kept the hedges about right and put down a bit of corn for the wild pheasants. But after a year or so, Father had a stroke. He became a semi-invalid and wasn't able to shoot there any more.

Now that I'd come back into shooting a bit more I used to go to the Cotswolds shoot and suddenly found myself taking over the rough shooting there as well as organising the Kinver shoots. These weren't as satisfying for me for various reasons whereas the Cotswolds were much closer and Father had always planned that farm as a shoot for the future. He'd planted a lot of woodlands, which were now starting to grow. Richard Fry and a few other racing and hill climbing friends used to come with my boys, Simon, Peter and Paul and my nephew Richard Hollingworth, who incidentally drives a Westfield.

After a while I became aware that we were shooting too many birds. I told father that we ought to be putting a few down especially for shooting and not relying totally on the wild population. We organised a release pen for a couple of hundred birds and it all grew from there.

Father had also thought about the future of this property in different ways. He acquired another farm which was let to a syndicate, and not long before he died he acquired the adjacent farm to Swell Wold, which was the main property. That made a block of about 1000 acres, which is quite a useful size for a shoot. When father died, he left the properties in trust for his four grandsons. We shot there for a year or so after father had gone, but it was a long way to go just for a picnic or a walk round with a gun. Those were, really, the only interest the boys had in it and they decided to sell it. The year before it was sold they let the shooting to a syndicate, but it took some time for them to actually get their money when they sold it. This was due to EU subsidies. It was rather complicated, but the family company had an arrangement whereby it rented the farm from the boys' trust company and farmed it in partnership with a local farmer. This was to enable the family company to claim VAT etc., but it meant that the farming arrangement had to continue for one or possibly two years, because of changing EU regulations.

The trust company is still going and some of the farm cottages were kept within its ownership so that the boys would have a bit of income from their rental.

So for shooting we're now just left with Soal Farm. It's something that has built up very slowly. It started after I retired from active farming when my tenant farmer asked if he and a couple of friends could walk round with some guns. They shot, I think, about six pheasants. Then we got a bit more serious and started feeding the birds. In these last few years we've been rearing pheasants and putting them down.

We're limited by the physical size of the farm, which is only 120 acres and means that the pheasants only have to flap their wings a few times to be over the boundary. Fortunately my neighbour runs a big commercial shoot so we borrow a few birds from him. He can't grumble too much because I'm putting my own birds down and, of course, some wander off to him – it's just that his proportion of wanderers is bigger than ours!

We have six shoots for the guns each year and a seventh for the beaters, which is usually quite a fun occasion. There are one or two beaters who don't actually shoot and the boys join them to beat. In fact Richard Fry, who of course does shoot, has acted as a beater as well. The first year or two they didn't tend to shoot very much even though they enjoyed their day. After that they were quite pleased if one or two of my boys shot with them rather than beating for them and this helped them to increase the bag.

We usually have about eighteen or twenty people gathered

and about eight guns standing, with the rest acting as beaters. Though sometimes we chop and change a bit. We don't tend to start until 10 o'clock, as there are one or two farm workers who have work to do beforehand, and we go on until mid-afternoon when the light goes. Sometimes we've shot as many as fifty-five pheasants in a day, which is good considering we only put down 250 birds. One season we actually shot sixty-odd percent of what we put down, which is a very good percentage.

Our good results are to some extent due to my neighbour and his shoot and there's a story about him. As I mentioned, he runs a commercial shoot and rears a lot of extra birds (both pheasants and partridges) which he sells as youngsters. He was renting a field from my tenant in which to rear these young birds when he had an accident while transferring the birds in plastic crates. The whole lot fell off the truck and there were partridges everywhere, roosting on the house roof ridge at night, in the garden, all over the place. But we didn't shoot as many as you might think because they gang up on you. These are French partridge, bigger than English partridge and with red legs. They have a leader, who calls to them, and it's nothing to see thirty or forty birds in a gang (or covey as it's officially known). They tend to take off in this gang and you can only shoot two, or if you're lucky, three from each group.

This happened a year or so ago, but we still have partridges that come to sleep on the roof – sometimes they get very cheeky and come to feed with the chickens. They don't breed well in the wild though. Having never had a mother to teach them what to do, they tend to make rather bad mothers themselves. I watched a hen going through the garden with some chicks; she wasn't looking after them. A good mother will keep clucking away, calling them to order and letting them know where she is, but this one wasn't doing any of that. We've have hawks and other birds of prey about too, and they're only too keen to take advantage of any meal that's going.

I do enjoy running the shoot here. I enjoy the shooting itself of course, although I'm also very happy if it's a nice day and everyone else is enjoying themselves even though I'm not in the thick of it. I particularly enjoyed teaching my second wife, Liza, (who I met in April 2000 and married in January 2001) to shoot. I get a lot of pleasure from watching her enjoy the sport and now she shoots very well indeed. We always go to the BRDC clay pigeon shoot at West Wycombe. It was originally BRDC v BARC, but now it's just club members and visitors. There are two sets of prizes and it's usually the visitors that win the major ones.

Knowing that we have the winter shooting season gets me out and about throughout the year. I'll take the dog for a walk through the woods, stand there and look at the trees and decide which ones to fell come the spring. I think this constant management helps keep the woodland in better order, as well as giving us wood to burn on the fires a year later.

I do most of the cutting and leave it to my woodsman cum keeper to load the trailer and do the log splitting, but I enjoy getting out and working in the woods, deciding which way it would be best to take a tree out to do the least damage to the trees around it, which way it's weight will take it and so on. I learnt to use an axe and chainsaw in my school holidays, under the auspices of my father's woodsman, and it's very satisfying to know I can still tell to within a foot or so where the top of a tree will finish up when its felled. I remember watching old Mr Beaumont deal with a roadside oak with a chainsaw. It was a really big tree and by the time he got towards the end of the cut it was late in the afternoon. Then it went 'plonk!' and just stood there, right next to the road. You couldn't climb it to put a rope on it and pull it over, it would have been far too dangerous. I forget exactly what they did do with it in the end, but it was quite late before they'd finished.

Before ending this shooting chapter I should add that we do our utmost to make sure that the whole bag is used. The guns take some birds home with them and so do the beaters. Any left over are shared round for friends to enjoy. It would be a terrible waste otherwise and I couldn't have that. It's like fishing, you must use your catch or you should put it back.

Chapter Eleven

The 1997 season dawned, as most of them seem to these days, only too soon after Christmas when to my mind the weather hasn't warmed up quite enough. The Roman wasn't ready for the start of the season. We had been fitting Motec engine management equipment and there were a few delays while the engine mapping was set up on the test bed. So I took the four-wheel-drive Marsh Special to Gurston in April and again to Prescott in early May. Unfortunately at Prescott I biffed the barrier at Orchard, which involved a bit of work at home afterwards.

The problem I found with the Special was that I had to learn to drive it all over again. It wasn't quite as I remembered it from the old days. I tend to get a bit enthusiastic at the start line and put rather a lot of revs on the clock – well, relatively speaking as the maximum is only six and a half thousand – and with the front wheels spinning it's difficult to get directional stability straight away. Once, at Shelsley, I nearly joined the commentator in his hut and at Goodwood for the Festival of Speed we were rather twitchy off the line. At Prescott, however, it was a case of driver error. I forgot to change my mental computer programme from the Roman to the Marsh Special, zoomed round Orchard, the back end let go and I couldn't hold it. We spun across the course and clouted the barrier on the outside. I nearly got away with it, but not quite. The weather was rather on the damp side so that may have been a contributory factor, but I can't really blame it on that.

After Prescott I had neither the Toleman nor the Marsh Special to play with. My son Peter took pity on me and kindly allowed me to share his 2-litre Reynard BDG at Gurston. It was quite useful for Peter as I rather liked driving his car and was doing faster times than he was, which gave him a yardstick to aim for. He knew the car should go round Hollow Bend faster and when I proved it would, it gave him the confidence to give it a try – although I'm not sure whether he actually enjoyed being beaten by his father.

Then we come to the British Hill Climb Championship's Golden Jubilee celebration at Shelsley Walsh, where the MAC decided it would be nice to gather as many past hill climb champions together as possible. We had a group photo taken with seventeen of us and it was good to see everyone together. On top of that we had a jolly good day of motorsport too.

At last the Roman was ready and we went to Gurston's double header in June for a try-out, ending up fifth fastest overall after a bit of a battle with Andy Fraser's Tipadel Gould-DFR.

The Aintree/Three Sisters weekend of sprinting was another enjoyable outing at the end of June with Mark Harrison sneaking ahead of me into sixth place in the run off by just four hundredths of a second on the Saturday. He was again ahead of me on Sunday but this time had a bit more of a lead.

1997 saw the Gurston July meeting coincide with my birthday and what better way to celebrate than by taking FTD. Andy Fraser gave me a good run for my money in the Gould, which may have spurred me on to greater efforts and a new personal best of 29.29. It was amusing, in a way, because another Gould driver, Richard Fry, had been working on me saying that I really needed a Gould myself. Almost won over, I had rung David Gould and said he'd better come to Gurston with his order book. At the end of the meeting David came up to me in the paddock saying that he felt a bit daft for saying it, but that I didn't really need one! I placed an order anyway, for a new Gould GR37, because apart from the GTD, which didn't really count because it was basically a kit car, I hadn't had a new racing car since the sixties. I also thought that if I had the very latest equipment it might last me out and be something that was worth passing on.

After Gurston we had a bit of a break and then took the Roman across to Ireland for some sprinting in mid-August before going back to Gurston on the August Bank Holiday weekend, prior to Colerne's British sprint round on the Monday. I finished twelfth in the Gurston run-off so I wasn't in the points, although it was good to qualify. But at Colerne I managed to improve on this and finished fifth, beating Colerne specialist Dave Cutcliffe, in his very rapid Van Diemen Twincam, by a hundredth. Nothing spectacular, but a good weekend of motorsport nevertheless.

September saw more sprinting, this time at Aintree, but it was rather a disappointing meeting as I had a clutch problem and it wasn't something I could sort out on the day. It meant removing the whole of the back of the car, which is not easy on the Toleman as it's quite tricky to line everything back up again. It's not something you can do on trolley jacks, you really need chassis stands.

September also saw the annual pilgrimage to the Brighton Speed Trials. This was the year I drove David Render's Pilbeam-Hart MP43. Jerseyman Peter Le Druillenec just pipped me by taking FTD in the 6.4-litre Miller Exocet Chevrolet. This was a remarkable car, based on a Chevron B54 sportsracer tub with an engine built by American drag racing specialist Ron Shaver. The all-aluminium V8 produced 650 bhp and drove through a Hewland DG300 gearbox.

Then in October we went to Three Sisters where David Cutcliffe took revenge and beat me to fourth place by exactly the same margin – a hundredth of a second – as I had beaten him at Colerne. We also went to Curborough, which I always quite enjoy, where I finished fourth behind young Mark Harrison after a good battle.

And so the 1997 season drew to a close. I'd finished seventh in both the British Sprint Championship and the Gates of Brockenhurst Gurston Down Top Ten Challenge – all in all a very satisfactory year's motorsport.

The 1998 season started, as usual, with Gurston Down in mid-April and the debut of my new Gould Ralt-DFR, the GR37S. The car's co-constructor, David Gould's son Sean, came along to lend a hand at the meeting which was also Kelvin Jouhar's first competitive outing in the ex-Roger Moran/Tim Thompson Pilbeam-Vauxhall MP62. I just pipped Kelvin by three tenths of a second. However, Chris Cannell managed to beat both us both to take FTD in his Pilbeam-DFL, the car that Andy Priaulx had taken to the 1995 British hill climb title, but it was a very good start to the season with a new car.

Knowing that I had both launch control and traction control on the Gould, people flocked to watch me leave the line at Gurston. I did quite an impressive start in the wet and on returning to the paddock there were comments such as: 'that's wonderful,' and: 'it really is marvellous'. 'It would be,' I said, 'if I'd got it switched on!' which rather took the wind out of their sails.

It was about this time that I lost my long time friend, Peter Blankstone, who sadly died in South Africa from heart-related problems. I had known Peter and his wife Margaret for many years. They came boating with me on more than one occasion and also became interested in flying. Both Peter and Margaret flew. Peter would fly out and Margaret would fly back and they landed on the airstrip at Soal Farm several times. But my main motor sporting association with Peter was that he had a Brabham Quattro with the Marsh four-wheel-drive transmission system.

When I was building the system I made three sets up. One was for me, one for Ray Terry who put it into an older sports car and one for Peter. I drove the Brabham, a BT18 with 4.5 Oldsmobile engine, at Bouley Bay one year. Peter and Margaret felt they weren't getting the best out of it and asked if I like to drive it, to perhaps give them a few tips. I was pleased to do this and was able to give them the odd pointer, as the Brabham did require a slightly different technique on occasions. On the whole it was a very nice little car.

Peter was a great competitor and a true motor sport enthusiast, he was also chairman of the Midland Automobile Club and sat on the RACMSA Speed Events Committee.

In mid-May came a couple of sprint championship rounds with the first at Donington Park. I had a few gear selection problems with the new car, which was the first GR37 with a sequential gearbox, and only managed tenth place in the championship run off, which was rather disappointing. Mind you, it was my first visit to Donington and I have to admit that I didn't learn it particularly well. It's a superb circuit, but very fast and I didn't want to push my luck too far and go off. We were also playing around with the launch control at that meeting. The people who built the system came along and I don't think they really proved that it was much of an advantage. One of the things about launch control, as opposed to traction control, that I wasn't happy with was that it allows you to sit on the starting line with your foot flat on the throttle and the engine running on about two cylinders. You can hear that the poor old engine doesn't like it and it doesn't exactly give you confidence to let in the clutch. I got them to raise the revs a little to try and improve the situation but in the end I gave up on the thing and never used it.

Traction control, on the other hand, was quite useful. I set it to become operative at about 25 mph because you need wheelspin off the startline to get the car moving. I can only sense that it's working but I'm told that, particularly in the wet, onlookers can hear it. I find that with a bigger engined car it does give you more confidence, again particularly in the wet, to put your foot to the floor. It doesn't seem to be mentioned as much as it used to be, but an awful lot of people are running it these days.

The Club that ran the first ever meeting at the revived Donington Park circuit, Nottingham Sports Car Club, were celebrating their 50th anniversary at the meeting which had a record British sprint entry of 240. Sky TV were there filming several pit lane interviews. After they did mine they went on to John Garnett. Poor John was very embarrassed by the whole thing and wished they would just go on to the next person. Eventually they came back to me and did quite a long interview about my career.

After the May National at Gurston, where I finished a satisfying seventh in the championship run-offs, we went to Pembrey for a double header of sprint championship rounds. The Saturday saw John Garnett take FTD followed by the Eyles brothers, Tony and Rodney, in their Ralt-Hart. I finished fourth on this wet day in Wales. Sunday saw Carl Amos take his first ever win followed by John Garnett, Dave Cutcliffe and myself, again fourth. The Eyles brothers only managed fifth and seventh this time but it was an amazing weekend for Tony as Saturday's event was only his second ever sprint event.

I like going to Pembrey, they're lovely people, but somehow, events there never seem to run smoothly. It's a shame because people start to get a bit irritated, which spoils things rather. For example, during the day a car crossed the finish line and promptly spun off, but the marshal on the spot was so busy watching the car go off that he forgot to red flag the next car. All was well on that occasion, but people remember things like that.

This seems to have been a time of 'fourthitis' for me because at Aintree in mid June I again came fourth in the run off. Incredibly, there was a tie for FTD with the champion, Roger Kilty and John Garnett both on 35.46, the aggregate advantage going to Roger Kilty by just five hundredths!

My fourthitis disappeared the very next day though. After

we'd moved up the road to Three Sisters I only managed seventh in the run off. Tony Eyles was again in good form as he finished fourth this time, while John Fellows and I battled it out for sixth. On this occasion John's Roman-Judd produced the goods relegating the Gould but Roger Kilty, now well on his way to a second successive British sprint title, took his third win of the season in the Pilbeam-DFR.

A week later we went to Curborough, a course that I could never seem to get the hang of. It used to frustrate me no end and at this meeting I only managed ninth in the first run-off, although that might have had something to do with the gear selection problems I encountered. The second run-off was better – I tied for fifth with Tony Eyles. At one Curborough meeting I tagged onto Roy Lane while he was walking the course and asked him to tell me how he drove it. He whispered in my ear a couple of times and I got on much better after that.

The gear selection problems dogged me for quite a bit of that season, bent selector forks at the root of the problem. I don't know why because I'm not particularly heavy-handed. It may have been a design fault, or a weakness but David and Sean did a few modifications. John Jones, a farmer in the West Midlands, ran the ex-works Pilbeam-Vauxhall which also used a sequential gearbox and didn't seem to have any problems, however but his was 2-litre, four cylinder engine, not a 3.5 V8 like mine.

July saw a fifth place at Knockhill, a tenth at MIRA and an eighth at Lydden Hill, all in British sprint rounds. It's a shame that Knockhill is so far away because it's a circuit I really rather like. Sometimes they run a two lap sprint at there and that makes it even more interesting, as the first corner, Duffus Dip, becomes completely different on the second lap. In some ways Lydden is a bit like Knockhill with both up and downhill sections. In fact this Lydden meeting was my first time at the Kent circuit, where I found that I didn't seem to learn new courses as quickly as I used to.

Then in early August we went over to Northern Ireland to Kirkistown, or as Jerry Sturman called it in *Speedscene*, 'Kiltystown', after yet another FTD from Roger Kilty. The event was over a lap and threequarters of this very fast circuit. Roger's winning time was 99.79

seconds as opposed to my third placed 105.12, three seconds behind Carl Amos.

On my first trip to Kirkistown I went all the way up the M6 to Heysham and over on a ferry trip to Belfast, but that involved a lot of driving. The second year I went I decided to catch the high speed ferry from Holyhead, leaving just a short drive up through Southern Ireland. Having got off the boat in Dublin I saw a signpost that said 'Motorway' and thought I'd give that a try. It was all of two miles long. 'How very Irish', I thought! Then, of course, I had to cross over the border into Northern Ireland where the army was very much in evidence. One little town I went through I was rather distracted by a platoon of soldiers suddenly appearing from a side road.

Two days after Kirkistown, we were at Nutts Corner for the final event of Ulster Speed Weekend and fifth place in the championship run-off behind Steve Liptrott's 2-litre Ralt-Cosworth RH430. With the long journey over to Ireland it made the weekend rather tiring, especially as in between Kirkistown and Nutts Corner there was a British hill climb round at Craigantlet on the Saturday. But it was a very enjoyable few days and well worth the effort.

Mid August saw the British hill climb championship back at Shelsley Walsh where I finished eighth in the run-off, just behind Richard Fry in his Gould. However, this wasn't the highlight of my weekend by any means.

For many years I've wandered round the motorcycle paddock whenever the National Hillclimb Association are running their bikes at the same meeting. I'm particularly fascinated by the trikes, many of which are obviously home built. I'd had already passengered for Ian Drowne on his sidecar outfit and was looking at Bill Chaplin's trike when he said 'I bet you'd like to have a ride on that'. I agreed that I wouldn't mind in the slightest! Wheels were put in motion and I was invited to do a demonstration run in the lunch break. I would need a passenger of course. But my long-time friend and former double driver, Gillian Goldsmith, was there. Gillian is such a good sport and always good for a laugh and as soon as she got wind of what was going on she said 'I'm coming with you'.

Borrowing leathers was no problem, but motorcycle boots are never easy for me and I found I couldn't change down very easily.

Using the ball of the foot, changing up was no problem, but getting the toe of the boot under the pedal to change down was more of a challenge. I was fortunate in that the Suzuki GSXR engine was very flexible and would pull from very low revs.

At the start there's usually some sort of arrangement between driver and passenger whereby one communicates to the other before the clutch is let go. I did a couple of quick, standing starts on the spin-up area, just to get the feel of things, and when the green light came on the plan was that Gillian would give me a tap on the shoulder to say she was ready to go. Well, I forgot I had a passenger. The green light came on and I went. Fortunately she was able to grab something and come with me or it might have been rather embarrassing. She entered into the spirit of the whole thing with great enthusiasm. Jerry Sturman described the run in *Speedscene* and included a 'fashion note', which said: 'Tony wore appropriately sombre period black leathers while an energetic Gillian turned out in a rather more opulent, multicoloured set borrowed from the enthusiastic NHCA fraternity!'

I can't thank Bill Chaplin enough for the opportunity to drive his trike (with which he went on to become the overall Motorcycle Hillclimb Champion in 1998, partnered by Livvy Klimpke) and enable Gillian and myself to experience Shelsley Walsh in this quite different way.

There were, of course, the usual July and August meetings at Gurston Down while the season wore towards its close with a fifth in the run-off at Ty Croes, a third at Aintree and a ninth at Three Sisters. In my defence there, I have to tell you that it was raining at Three Sisters which did rather favour those with smaller engined cars.

So at the end of a fairly busy year, my 1998 record for the Farndon Engineering RAC British Sprint Championship and Gates of Brockenhurst Gurston Down Top Ten Challenge read sixth and eighth respectively.

As usual, Gurston Down was the venue for my first event of the new season, 1999, where Sean Gould was sharing the car with me at the traditional April double-header. Unfortunately, I snapped a gearbox input shaft on the Saturday. Sean took the car back to Newbury overnight to replace it and had a puncture on the trailer during the return trip for his pains, but managed to get the car back to Gurston in time for Sunday's meeting. Simon Durling took both FTD awards in his Pilbeam-DFL, but on Sunday I was right behind him with Chris Cannell's similar, ex-Priaulx car hot on my heels. Very close behind Chris was Andrew Fraser in the Tipadel Gould-DFR. It was about this time that Andrew started to become something of a nuisance to me!

Curborough was another event with a problem or two in the fuel pump department. I'd had problems with this the previous year at Colerne, when I'd discovered the cockpit knee deep in fuel. I removed the seat and the tank inspection plate between the seat and engine compartment, to discover that the fuel pump casting had broken. It was an electro-mechanical pump. The mechanical part was driven by a flexible drive from one of the camshafts. You need fuel pressure to start a fuel injected engine, so the pump was also driven by what I think was a windscreen wiper motor, which could be turned off once the engine has started provided you keep the revs up. At Colerne the casting had cracked somewhere between the motor and the fuel pump and was pumping fuel out, so that was the end of that day. However at Curborough the crack was in a different place, so I managed to limp round and finish tenth in the run-off.

Another trip to Gurston meant another double drive with Sean Gould, who put in a great run. There was the usual battle between Chris Cannell, myself, Richard Fry and Karl Davison which was won this time by Chris.

In fact in 1999 I didn't do an awful lot other than Gurston. The next meeting I remember was when David Grace clinched the British Hill Climb Championship at Gurston on the August Bank Holiday weekend. He did have one or two problems at the meeting with his gearbox. Sportingly, one of the two people helping him fix it was Roger Moran's mechanic, Dave Wilson. I think Roger was lying a close second in the championship at the time, which just goes to show how much everyone helps out when there is a problem. I think hill climbing has always had this reputation and I hope it always does.

At the end of the season Sean Gould made the long drive up to Three Sisters with me to share the car again. In fact he put in an extremely quick time and took the class win, which was great. I managed to hold onto second but John Fellows in the Roman was doing his best to take it off me. Although I didn't do as many sprint championship rounds that year, it was good to take third place in the run-off.

The 2000 season doesn't seem to have started quite as early as others have. One good reason for this was that in April, I was busy meeting my future wife Liza in Manila.

I could almost blame my son Peter for my marriage to Liza! He had brought a party of colleagues out sailing one day, among whom was this lovely Filipino lady, and said 'That's what you could do with Dad, a Filipino wife'.

Having corresponded for quite a while and progressed to weekly telephone calls, the idea was that Liza would come over here for six months to see me, the house, the countryside and a bit of motorsport, then we could decide if things were going any further. This didn't happen as the authorities wouldn't give her a visa, telling her to apply again in six months. When she applied again I decided to fly out and support her application, which was successful this time, and also visit her family. Only one member of the family knew about me but as soon as they saw us they realized that something a little more serious was going on. I sat down at the kitchen table with Liza's five brothers, one of whom spoke quite reasonable English although the others could understand the language to a greater or lesser degree. At the end of this 'interview', once they were sure I was on the level and not after Liza's money, I was given approval, there were handshakes all round and Liza came back to England with me.

But by the end of May I was back in the swing of motorsport. By this time there were two run-offs to count for points at British championship meetings and I got into both of them at Gurston Down. OK, I was out of the points in the first one and only scored one point in the second but I felt that wasn't bad against the likes of Graeme Wight Jr, David Grace, Simon Durling, Roger Moran and Roy Lane. These were among the top names in British hill climbing in 2000 and I wasn't getting quite as much driving time as I would have liked, with the ongoing sequential gear change problems. In fact they sidelined both myself and Sean Gould at the July Gurston club event, which was fortunate for local driver Karl Davison. After I was able to lend him parts to sort out a suspension problem on his own GR37, he went on to take FTD.

Fortunately at Colerne the gearbox behaved itself well enough for me to take fifth in the British sprint run-off, and the Gurston championship finals event in September was another good day for me even though I ran over a pheasant at Hollow Bend. I spotted the bird casually walking down the edge of the track towards me and hit it with the back wheel. The marshals flagged me down on my return run, insisting that I took my 'trophy' back to the paddock, but I'm afraid it was rather mangled! On the results front I finished third overall that day behind Roger Moran, who took FTD on a guest drive in Karl Davison's Gould with Karl himself second overall.

After a run-off fourth at Three Sisters, the car was put to bed for the winter. But despite having not attended many events in 2000, it was rather nice to finish in the top ten (joint tenth place with Richard Jones, on an outing in Richard Fry's Gould) in the Gurston Challenge. Incidentally Tony Wiltshire, who finished ninth in his self developed Ralt-Rover K RT30, is now doing rather well in the British Sprint Championship aboard a Peugeot powered RT34.

I was rather busy in the early months of 2001 as Liza and I were married at Petersfield Registry Office on January 20th. Much later, on October 8th 2003, the marriage was blessed in the Philippines, in Tagum City. All the three boys get on well with Liza, even if they were a little surprised when I'd told them, around Christmas 2000, that we were getting married so soon.

Getting married to Liza didn't really have any effect on my motorsport as she took to helping me at meetings like the proverbial duck to water. Although she doesn't have any intention of competing, she did take her MG TF to the Gurston Hillclimb Drivers School and thoroughly enjoyed herself.

But back in 2001, a lot of early season meetings were cancelled or postponed when Foot and Mouth disease hit the country. I think this made people realise just how dependent 'grass roots' motorsport is on the farming community for its continuation.

We were all extremely grateful when we were allowed back out to play and one early event was a sprint round at Aintree. Although Liza did take to motorsport, she did have one or two initial worries at that first Aintree meeting when I lost a wheel, which she didn't think was a very good idea at all! I'd had the car up on jacks with the wheels off the previous week. When I put them back on, I only did them up finger tight and was distracted before tightening them all up. So there I was, rushing away from the startline at about 90 mph, when suddenly the nearside front wheel parted company with the rest of the car and I sat there watching it bowling off into the scenery. Fortunately these modern racing cars are so stiff on the suspension they're quite happy to run on three wheels. But the marshals came running, found the wheel (and amazingly the wheel nut too), just lifted the car up and put the wheel back on for me to carry on round the track.

It could have turned out much worse if the wheel had come off halfway round Country Corner, the first left-hander, but the day turned out quite well as I finished fourth in the championship run-off behind Tony Eyles, Rodney Eyles and Peter Griffiths.

Pembrey's double header proved rather a mixed weekend for me. I finished fifth on the Saturday, which was fine, but then suffered clutch failure and wasn't able to take part on Sunday. Well, I might have got one run in the morning, but thought it would be better to come back home and start doing something about the clutch.

Gurston's June meetings were, as usual, most enjoyable and then it was off to Shelsley Walsh with the Marsh Special for the Midland Automobile Club's Centenary meeting. This was a superb event with an excellent display of cars and many old friends and acquaintances to meet.

Back at our local hill, BARC Southwest Centre was celebrating its 200th meeting at Gurston Down. You may have guessed that Gurston is a rather special place for me after not only advising on the layout of the hill but taking FTD at the very first meeting in 1967. Fittingly, the event coincided with British Championship rounds and Graeme Wight Jr took FTD and won one of them, while the other went to Tim Mason, which at that point left Graeme just three points ahead of Tim in the championship.

Once again, we went straight from Gurston to Colerne and the British sprint round where, according to Jerry Sturman in

Speedscene, I '… indulged in a spin first time round.' Near the end of the course there's a right-hand hairpin and just as you hit the brakes for this the track's rather bumpy. I arrived there all at sixes and sevens, got caught out, rotated and proceeded on my way. I still managed eighth in the run off, just behind engine builder Phil Price in his 3.3 Reynard-DFZ/Connaught.

With the April meeting having been postponed due to Foot and Mouth restrictions, mid-September 2001, the traditional end-of-season Gurston event, was raised to double-header status. BARC SW is very fortunate in their relationship with the Hitchings Brothers Partnership, who own Gurston Down. Some venue landlords are not nearly as accommodating about date changes. But even though I do like Gurston I have to admit to being elsewhere on the Saturday of the double-header weekend. This was as a result of an invitation to the Goodwood Revival meeting.

I had been invited to be on the 'Dream Grid' for the opening of the Goodwood Revival meeting and this was made up of cars and drivers from the appropriate time. I was to drive a Cooper-Climax Bobtail sports racing car. We were led round the circuit for a few laps by a pace car, which kept pulling ahead of us, forcing us to catch up. I have to admit to enjoying several corners...

The opening ceremony was very moving, with a blessing by Canon Lionel Webber who explained that God was not in heaven as normal that day, he was at Goodwood! Lady March then sang an anthem and a military band performed before the flying displays started. These were something else again. Goodwood was just as I remembered it and to be able to meet some of the competitors from my early days in motorsport was wonderful.

Straight after Goodwood we were off to Gurston for another excellent day's motorsport and a good battle between the top runners. Karl Davison took FTD on both days, with Simon McBeath guest driving Karl's Gould-Judd on the Sunday. Simon did very well to finish fourth overall behind myself and Phil Cooke, second and third overall respectively. This was the final event of the Gurston Top Ten Challenge which Karl won for the second year in a row, with myself second and Phil third. Coincidentally, exactly the same order in which we finished Sunday's event.

Despite a late start to the 2001 season, we managed to fit in quite a few events and finish- ninth overall in the British sprint series. Not bad, perhaps, for someone who had celebrated his seventieth birthday that year.

Tailpiece

I hope you have enjoyed reading the tales about some of my adventures and outings as much as I have enjoyed telling them and my thanks to Barbara Daniel for her invaluable advice on publishing a book, to Jerry Sturman for checking and editing everything, to Howard Stockley for proofreading, to Simon Taylor for his kind words in the Foreword and, finally, to Gwyneth Wright for helping me get my experiences down on paper and for keeping me on track with everything. I am sorry if, in telling my story, there are people who's names I have missed out or forgotten. I have never been very good at names and had I known when I was twenty or thirty that I should be writing down my experiences I would have paid more attention at the time.

I also hope you get as much enjoyment from your involvement in motorsport as I do from mine. My involvement didn't finish in 2001, that merely seemed as good a place as any to finish recording things, being the fiftieth anniversary of my discovery of motorsport and the year of my seventieth birthday. I look forward to competing, supported by Liza, at venues around the country with my Gould GR55 in 2007 and shall continue to do so as long as my health permits and my enjoyment of motorsport continues – no E Type Jaguar for me just yet!

My sons are not competing much at present, mainly due to family and work commitments but I hope they will return to motorsport when they can. They are, however, still enjoying their ski bobbing; Peter was twelfth in the Combination event in the World Championships and third in the B Nations event in 2006 while Simon was Senior Mens Champion in 2005 and second in the same championship in 2006.

During my time in motorsport I have seen many changes in car design, technology, safety and so on but I still maintain that learning car control at grass roots level motorsport is one of the best groundings you can have for better driving on the road or in competition. It can also be great value for money and a great deal of fun, and I am grateful to fellow competitors at all levels across the years for the camaraderie that has made motorsport so worthwhile.

watch which lines, and so on the top drivers take. While I have not been involved personally with much marshalling I should like to take this opportunity of saying thank you to everyone who does – it is you who make motorsport, at all levels, possible all over the world.

Tony Marsh
Soal Farm
2006

Appendix One
Competition Cars Driven by Tony Marsh

Car	Engine	Owner	Comment
Dellow Mk I	1.2 Ford E93A s/v	AEM	
Dellow Mk II	1.2 Ford E93A s/v	AEM	
Dellow Mk V	1.2 Ford E93A s/v	AEM	
TMS 1 & 2	1.2 Ford E93A s/v	AEM	Built by AEM, based on Dellow
Cooper Mk 4	1.3 JAP twin	AEM	Ex-Peter Collins
Cooper Mk 5	0.5 Norton	Henry Taylor	
Cooper Mk 8	1.1 JAP twin 0.5 Norton 0.5 JAP	AEM	
Cooper Mk 6	1.1 JAP s/c	Bertie Bradnack	
Cooper Bobtail T39	1.1 Climax FWA	AEM	
Cooper Monaco T57	2.0 Climax FPF	AEM	
Cooper T33	3.4 Jaguar	Bertie Bradnack	1955 Goodwood 9 hr race
Cooper T43	1.5 Climax FPF	AEM	1957 (1 yr only)
F2 Cooper T45	1.5 Climax FPF	AEM	1958
Cooper T51	2.7 Maserati	Fred Tuck	1961 May Silverstone
Cooper T52 FJ	1.0 BMC A-Series	MRP	1961 July Silverstone
BRM P57	1.5 BRM V8	AEM	Returned to BRM
BRM P48	1.5 Climax FPF 2.5 BRM P25	AEM	BRM an alternative engine for hill climbs only
Maserati 250F	2.5 Maserati	BRM	Bought by BRM for brake testing

Car	Engine	Owner	Comment
Aston Martin DB3S	3.0 Aston Martin	Aston Martin	Testing at Silverstone
Lotus Mk 18	1.5 Climax FPF	AEM	
Lotus Formula Junir	1.1 Ford 105E	Ted Robbins	1961 May Silverstone
Lotus Elite	1.2 Climax FWE	Team Elite	Le Mans, Nurburgring and Goodwood endurance races
Lotus Mk 11	1.5 Climax FWB	Max Trimble	
Lotus Mk 12	1.1 Climax FPF	AEM	Renamed Motus
Connaught sports	1.5 Lea Francis	Peter Bell/ George Boyle	Crystal Palace
Reliant Scimitar	2.6 Ford 6-cyl	Reliant Car Co	
Simca Saloon	1.5 Simca	Peter Bell/ George Boyle	Column change!
Haggis Imp Saloon	1.0 Hillman Imp	Bob le Sueur	1966 Wiscombe
Johnny Walker F4	0.25 Triumph	Johnny Walker	1966 Prescott demonstration
ERA R11B	2.0 ERA/Riley	Peter Bell	
Ferrari Tip 625	2.5 Ferrari	Ian Sievewright	1962 Shelsley
Marsh Special	1.5 s/c Climax FPF 2.0 Climax FPF 4.2 Buick V8	AEM	
Marsh Special 4WD	4.2 Buick V8	AEM	1967 hill climb championship winning car
Marsh BRM	2.5 BRM P25	AEM	Destroyed at Rest-and-be-Thankful
Marsh Special 4WD	3.9 Rover V8	AEM	Re-acquired from Graham Galliers

Car	Engine	Owner	Comment
Rovercraft	4.5 twin turbo Rover V8	AEM	Dismantled after Brighton Speed Trials
Toleman TG191	3.9 Cosworth DFL V8	AEM	Ex-David Render
Roman	3.9 Cosworth DFL V8	AEM	Ex-Ray Rowan
Gould GR37S	3.5 Cosworth DFR V8	AEM	Sold to Martin Groves
Gould GR55	2.5 Cosworth/ Opel V6	AEM	Current competition car
GTD 40	4.5 twin turbo Rover V8	AEM	Engine from Rovercraft

Appendix 2
Hill climb and sprint courses at which Tony Marsh has competed

NLU = no longer in use as a motor sport venue
ST = Speed Trial

Hillclimb	Location
Barbon	3 miles north of Kirby Lonsdale, Cumbria
Blandford Camp	2 miles east of Blandford Forum, Dorset (NLU)
Bouley Bay	On north east coast of Jersey
Brunton	8 miles south east of Marlborough, Wiltshire (NLU)
Castle	1 mile south of Lostwithiel, Cornwall
Craigantlet	On north east outskirts of Belfast
Doune	8 miles north east of Stirling, Stirlingshire
Dyrham Park	6 miles north of Bath, Wiltshire (NLU)
Firle (Bo Peep Hill)	10 miles east of Brighton, East Sussex (NLU)
Goodwood (Festival of Speed)	2 miles north east of Chichester, West Sussex
Great Auclum	5 miles south east of Reading, Berkshire (NLU)
Gurston Down	1 mile west of Broadchalke, Wiltshire
Harewood	8 miles north east of Leeds, N Yorkshire
Les Val des Terres	Main road south out of St Peter Port, Guernsey
Lhergy Frissel	TT course south out of Ramsey, Isle of Man
Longleat	5 miles west of Warminster, Wiltshire
Loton Park	9 miles west of Shrewsbury, Shropshire
Lydstep	3 miles south west of Tenby, Pembrokeshire (NLU)
Prescott	4 miles north of Cheltenham, Gloucestershire
Rotherfield Park	4 miles south of Alton, Hampshire (NLU)
Shelsley Walsh	9 miles north west of Worcester, Worcestershire
Westbrook Hay	2 miles west of Hemel Hempstead, Herts (NLU)
Wiscombe Park	5 miles south of Honiton, Devon

Sprint Course	Location
Aintree	North Liverpool, within Grand National race course
Blackpool	Blackpool seafront, Lancashire (NLU)
Blandford Camp	2 miles east of Blandford Forum, Dorset (NLU)
Brighton (ST)	Madeira Drive, Brighton, East Sussex
Chateau Impney	1 mile east of Droitwich, Worcestershire (NLU)
Colerne	6 miles north east of Bath, Wiltshire
Croft	5 miles south of Darlington, North Yorkshire
Curborough	3 miles north east of Lichfield, Staffordshire
Debden	3 miles south of Saffron Walden, Essex
Donington Park	7 miles south east of Derby, Derbyshire
Goodwood	2 miles north east of Chichester, West Sussex
Gosport	Lee-on-Solent Airfield, Hampshire (NLU)
Jurby	7 miles north west of Ramsey, Isle of Man
Kirkistown	14 miles south east of Newtownards, N Ireland
Knockhill	5 miles north west of Dunfermline, Fifeshire
Long Marston (ST)	4 miles south of Stratford-upon-Avon, Warwicks (NLU)
Lydden Hill	9 miles south east of Canterbury, Kent
MIRA	3 miles north of Nuneaton, Warwickshire
North Weald	3 miles north east of Epping, Essex
Nutts Corner	8 miles west of Belfast, Northern Ireland (NLU)
Ocean Village	Southampton (NLU)
Pembrey	6 miles west of Llanelli, Carmarthenshire
Rhydymwyn	14 miles west of Chester, Flintshire (NLU)
Southsea (ST)	Southsea, Hampshire (NLU)
Stapleford	5 miles west of Brentwood, Essex, (NLU)
Staverton	3 miles west of Cheltenhan, Gloucestershire (NLU)
Three Sisters	1 mile north of Ashton-in-Makerfield, Lancashire
Thruxton	5 miles west of Andover, Hampshire
Ty Croes	8 miles south west of Holyhead, Anglesey
Wellesbourne	5 miles west of Stratford-upon-Avon, Warwickshire (NLU)
Weston-Super-Mare (ST)	Weston-Super-Mare seafront, Somerset

Appendix Three
Race Circuits at which Tony Marsh has Competed

NLU = no longer in use as a motor sport venue

In the UK

Aintree	North Liverpool, within Grand National race course
Boreham	2 miles north east of Chelmsford, Essex, later Ford Motorsport Centre (NLU)
Brands Hatch	6 miles south east of Swanley, Kent
Castle Combe	5 miles north west of Chippenham, Wiltshire
Charterhall	12 miles south west of Berwick-upon-Tweed, Borders (NLU)
Crystal Palace	5 miles north east of Croydon, South London (NLU)
Ibsley	3 miles north of Ringwood, Hampshire (NLU)
Mallory Park	5 miles north east of Hinkley, Leicestershire
Oulton Park	3 miles north east of Tarporley, Cheshire
Silverstone	4 miles south of Towcester, Northamptonshire
Snetterton	9 miles north east of Thetford, Norfolk

Overseas

Avus Germany	Road circuit with banked section on outskirts of Berlin (NLU)
Brussels Belgium	Road circuit in Heysel, Brussels (NLU)
Chimay Belgium	Road circuit in southern part of Hainaut province (NLU)
Clermont Ferrand France	Road circuit in Auvergne region
Innsbruck Austria	Road circuit near Munich, in the Inn Valley, Tyrol (NLU)
Le Mans France	Road circuit in the Sarthe region, south west of Paris
Modena Italy	In the Po valley, near Bologna in the Emilia-Romagna region
Montlhery France	Road and banked circuit, between Paris (south) and Orleans
Nurburgring Germany	Purpose built race circuit at Nurburg, in the Eifel mountains near the Belgian border
Pau France	Road circuit in the Pyrenees Atlantique region, near SW border
Solitude Germany	Road circuit near Stuttgart (NLU)
Spa-Francorchamps Belgium	Road circuit near Francorchamps, in the Ardennes region
Zeltweg Austria	Airfield Circuit near Knittelfeld (NLU)

Index of Personalities